Golden Codgers

There all the golden codgers lay . . .

W. B. YEATS

RICHARD ELLMANN

Golden Codgers

BIOGRAPHICAL SPECULATIONS

1973
Oxford University Press
NEW YORK AND LONDON

To my dear son Stephen

Contents

	Preface	ix
	Acknowledgements	xi
1	Literary Biography	1
2	Dorothea's Husbands	17
3	Overtures to *Salome*	39
4	The Critic as Artist as Wilde	60
5	Corydon and Ménalque	81
6	Discovering Symbolism	101
7	Two Faces of Edward	113
8	A Postal Inquiry	132
9	'He Do the Police in Different Voices'	155
	Notes	171
	Index	185

Preface

A secret or at least a tacit life underlies the one we are thought to live. We are silent about it either because we do not know it, or, knowing it, find it dull, or because, for reasons of fondness or embarrassment, we are tender on its account. One of the pleasures of writing novels and poems is that this sub-surface life can be drawn upon and transformed without incurring the responsibilities of autobiography or history, yet with happier obligations imposed by an art form.

Because the urge to divulge is almost as strong as that to withhold, writers generally allow some access to their unspoken histories. But visiting hours are short; parts of the grounds are cordoned off. Biographers are obliged to move in a gingerly and often circuitous fashion. In their endeavour to recover from oblivion distinctive elements of writers' lives, they attend as closely to careless words and acts as to premeditated ones. Some chapters in this book begin from first drafts or dwell upon weak spots repaired by later revisions, on the theory that here the inner life impinges most frankly; some find in the completed work even more conclusive evidence of repetitive theme, clusters of imagery, or compulsions to transform certain kinds of material. In other chapters the obscure self is pursued into letters and journals, where the limited audience for which these were intended leads to special degrees of candour or restraint. Friendship and love may usefully be studied because the reflection of one person in another's eyes offers its small intimations. And, language being our art as well as our signalling device, favourite words or phrases may have an inward besides an outward story to tell.

Although the emphasis in this book is on a series of individual writers, I have tried to show something of their interplay with people about them. Two chapters deal explicitly with the pressure of contemporary ideas as a force in private determination. Writers press upon each other, and may learn rather than originate aims, themes, and assumptions.

Ultimately what the biographer seeks to elicit is less the events of a writer's life than the 'mysterious armature', as Mallarmé called it, which binds the creative work. But writers' lives have their mysterious armature as well. Affection for one leads to interest in the other, the two sentiments tend to join, and the results of affection and interest often illuminate both the fiery clay and the wrought jar.

I wish to thank Maurice Saillet for his benevolence and acuteness in aiding me to discriminate the relations of Wilde and Gide. Gordon S. Haight kindly gave me some necessary information about George Eliot. Catharine Carver helped and encouraged me. All the chapters bear the impress of Mary Ellmann.

RICHARD ELLMANN

New College, Oxford
16 *January* 1973

Acknowledgements

A number of the chapters in this book have appeared elsewhere, for
the most part in somewhat different form. For permission to in-
corporate previously published material, I wish to thank the Dele-
gates of the Clarendon Press, who published 'Literary Biography',
my inaugural lecture at Oxford in 1971; the *Times Literary Supplement* for 'Dorothea's Husbands' (1973); the Comparative Literature
Association and *Tri-Quarterly* for 'Overtures to *Salome*', first published in the *Yearbook of Comparative and General Literature*, No.
17 (1968); Random House and W. H. Allen & Co. Ltd. for 'The
Critic as Artist as Wilde', my introduction to *The Artist as Critic:
Critical Writings of Oscar Wilde* (1969); the University of London for
'Corydon and Ménalque', a John Coffin Memorial Lecture delivered
at University College in 1971; E. P. Dutton & Co. for 'Discovering
Symbolism', which draws a few sentences from my introduction to
a reissue of Symons's *The Symbolist Movement in Literature* (1958); the
English Institute and Columbia University Press for 'Two Faces of
Edward', from a volume I edited, *Edwardians and Late Victorians*
(English Institute Essays, 1959), published in 1960; Faber and Faber
Ltd. and The Viking Press for 'A Postal Inquiry', the introduction to
my edition of *Letters of James Joyce*, vols. II and III (1966); the *New
York Review of Books* for 'He Do the Police in Different Voices'
(1972). Passages from the original drafts of T. S. Eliot's *The Waste
Land* (1972) are quoted by permission of Mrs. Valerie Eliot, copy-
right owner, Faber and Faber Ltd., and Harcourt Brace Jovanovich.

R.E.

Golden Codgers

1 Literary Biography

A historical survey of literary biography, or a survey of the abundant recent examples, is not my purpose here. What seems feasible is to illustrate, rather, problems that particularly beset biographers at the present time. The relation of the literary biographer to his subject has perhaps never been easy, and as posthumous biographical scrutiny has grown more intense, a premonitory shiver has been felt by many creative writers. Every great man has his disciples, says Oscar Wilde, and it is usually Judas who writes the biography. Joyce describes the biographer, not much more winningly, as the biografiend. No one has any trouble understanding why T. S. Eliot and George Orwell both stipulated that no biography be written of them, at least with any help from their widows. The biographer is necessarily intrusive, a trespasser even when authorized. For while he is neither inimical nor in his judgements Rhadamanthine—and goodwill seems to be a prerequisite—he introduces an alien point of view, necessarily different from that mixture of self-recrimination and self-justification which the great writer, like lesser men and women, has made the subject of his lifelong conversation with himself.

Yet some correction of self-portraiture is warranted because the sense of ourselves which we have in isolation is to a large extent fabricated, an ennoblement or a debasement. Alone we can be braver and handsomer than others see us, and think of those perfect ripostes which somehow just failed—when we were at the party—to come to our lips. And alone, too, we can be more monstrous than we really are. Autobiography is essentially solitary, though there are examples, such as the first volume of V. S. Pritchett's autobiography, of almost total self-effacement in this form. But biography is essentially social. For the biographer, who himself represents the outside world, the social self is the real self, the self only comes to exist when juxtaposed with other people. The solitary self is a pressure upon the social self, or a repercussion of it, but it has no independent life. No doubt Robinson Crusoe would disagree, but the overstatement may encourage us. Besides, Defoe, not Crusoe, wrote the book.

How intimately can we know the self of another person? When we read Boswell we are surprised in that decorous author to find that Boswell believes he is rendering Johnson's private life. He quotes Dr. Johnson's remark that a man's domestic privacies should be investigated because prudence and virtue may appear more conspicuously there than in incidents of vulgar greatness. But we are now only too well aware that the domestic life may yield examples of attributes other than prudence and virtue. Recent biographical conjectures about Dr. Johnson himself offer such intimations. We can now see that Boswell dealt with a *social* privacy, the interrelation of one man with another in civilized appointed meetings. There are deeper levels of privacy, where propriety gives way to impropriety, where, if Katharine Balderston is right, Mrs. Thrale at Dr. Johnson's earnest request whips his naked back, or if Professor Balderston is wrong, other unseemly acts take place which we assume even if we can't document.

Boswell tells us nothing of these. Partly, of course, because he didn't share our estimation of the importance these further kinds of intimacy might possess. Today we want to see our great men at their worst as well as their best; we ask of biographers the same candour that our novelists have taught us to accept from them. Napoleon warned of the danger of trusting one's valet, but Napoleon was anxious to protect his grandeur. One reveals character to an office clerk as well as to a chairman of the board, through digestion as well as cerebration. To dwell, as a biographer today would dwell, upon the influence of Lichfield on Dr. Johnson, would not be Boswellian; to deal with Johnson's relations with his parents as something central, rather than as something to be got over to reach the adult Johnson—the finished product—without too great delay, would also seem to Boswell gratuitous. More than anything else we want in modern biography to see the character forming, its peculiarities taking shape—but Boswell prefers to give it to us already formed. No doubt it was hard for Boswell to conceive of Dr. Johnson as a small boy in short trousers, at least until that short-trousered small boy began to translate Virgil and Homer. It is hard for us too. And primarily Boswell wants to reveal Johnson's *force* of character, while today we should ask him to disclose to us the inner compulsions, the schizoid elements—such is our modern vocabulary—which lay behind that force. A Boswell alive today would have difficulty in representing so amusingly Johnson's scorn for Scotsmen; he would feel the need to tell us the origins of this xenophobia, and much of the comedy would evaporate before cumbersome explanation. We should want to know more about Johnson's early indifference to religion, which began at the age of nine, he told Boswell, on account of his weak eyes—a curious explanation (was the prayer book badly printed?)—and continued until as a student at Oxford he happened upon William Law's *Serious Call to a Holy Life* and became religious again. This is the panoply of the mind, not its basic workings.

The greatness of Boswell's biography, the sense it imparts of a man utterly recognizable and distinct, demonstrates that other methods of biography are not necessarily better; but none the less we feel compelled today to explore carefully aspects of the

mind and of behaviour that he would have regarded as not
worthy to record and not suitable to publish. We can claim to
be more intimate, but even our intimacy shows occasional
restraints, little islands of guardedness in a blunt ocean. We
have savoured the emotional convolutions of Lytton Strachey's
love life with Carrington and their friends, but the precise
anatomical convolutions remain shrouded by the last rags of
biographical decorum. One characteristic of Ernest Jones's biography of Freud is that even Jones, an analyst writing about an
analyst, stops short at certain points and says, 'But we must
leave this matter to the psychoanalysts.' This is appealing from
Philip Drunk to Philip Sober; one has the sense of descending
into a cave only to be told that the real cave is further down,
and unfortunately closed to the public. The battle to use Freudian techniques has been won; but victory has not been conclusive, because while techniques are needed, these remain, as
Jones saw, difficult to convert for lay purposes. As we push back
into the mind of a writer, we are apt to lose sight of his conscious
direction, of all that gives shape to what might otherwise be his
run-of-the-mill phobias or obsessions and distinguishes his grand
paranoia from our own squirmy one. It is relevant, though
already suspiciously pat, to point out the existence of an Oedipal
situation in childhood, but in the works of a writer's maturity
this is usually so overlaid with more recent and impinging
intricacies that we run the danger of being too simple about the
complexes. We may reduce all achievement to a web of causa-
tion until we cannot see the Ego for the Id.

And yet the pursuit of the finished man in the child is irresistible for us, and Freud offers more help than other psychologists.
In Jean-Paul Sartre's three biographies, of Baudelaire, Genet,
and Flaubert, he attempts to unite Freudian with existential
psychology. Towards Baudelaire he adopts a highly critical
attitude; he describes how the poet's mother rejected him, and
how as a direct consequence he set himself to be different from
her and her companions, to achieve uniqueness as a form of

vengeance. In this pursuit he abolished his natural self and all immediacy of response, he became a dandy, but beyond dandyism, he ceased to be a person, he became a 'freedom-thing'. (Here Marx too plays a part.) This analysis reduces Baudelaire to his weaknesses; it centres on the origins of maladjustment and leaves him overwhelmed by them. The poems of Baudelaire carry a different implication, that he was a man who was successfully unhealthy. The success is hard for Sartre to clarify or even to admit.

His book on Genet is more sympathetic and better suited to its subject; the castigation which he is so quick to administer to Baudelaire he avoids for Genet, because Genet accepted his identity and lived it. Sartre has an unexpected description of the way this identity was established. When Genet was ten, he says, the following incident occurred:

The child was playing in the kitchen. Suddenly he became aware of his solitude and was seized with anxiety, as usual. So he 'absented' himself. Once again, he plunged into a kind of ecstasy. There is now no one in the room. An abandoned consciousness is reflecting utensils. A drawer is opening; a little hand moves forward.

Caught in the act. Someone has entered and is watching him. Beneath this gaze the child comes to himself. He who was **not** yet anyone suddenly becomes Jean Genet. He feels that he is blinding, deafening; he is a beacon, an alarm that keeps ringing. *Who* is Jean Genet? In a moment the whole village will know. . . . The child alone is in ignorance. In a state of fear and shame he continues his signal of distress. Suddenly

. . . a dizzying word
From the depths of the world abolishes the beautiful order . . .[1]

A voice declares publicly: 'You're a thief.' The child is ten years old. That was how it happened, in that or some other way. In all

---

[1] . . . un mot vertigineux
Venu du fond du monde abolit le bel ordre
(Genet, *Poèmes,* 56.)

probability, there were offenses and then punishment, solemn oaths and relapses. It does not matter. The important thing is that Genet lived and has not stopped reliving this period of his life as if it had lasted only an instant.

So for Genet thiefhood became, with a sort of triumph, his identity, his essence, willed and loved by him. (Baudelaire, on the contrary, decided to be somebody else.) Sartre's theory of Genet's development requires this primal episode, and he boldly reconstructs from later manifestations what must have been the causative moment. I find this brave and attractive: it moves biography towards both science and fiction simultaneously. On the other hand, certain weaknesses in Sartre's interpretation have begun to show up since 1952, when this daring book was published. Sartre conceives of Genet as so riveted to this childhood memory, in which a child dies and a hoodlum rises up in his place, that he conceives of himself as a *dead man*. In this character Genet is outside history, and above all outside politics, Sartre said. But subsequently Genet, perhaps in part to defy his biographer, has participated in politics as if he were still alive. In fact, at one demo in Paris, Genet and Sartre, one dead, one alive, were observed taking part in the same housing protest. That is why it's always better to wait until the subject of your biography is dead, literally rather than figuratively, since it reduces the possibility of authoritative refutation.

Sartre's biographies have shrunk in time-span and swelled in size, as if, once the relations of society and the plural selves within the individual have been set spinning, more and more complicities require expression. The pocket-size *Baudelaire* gave way to a corpulent *Saint Genet* which has now been succeeded by the three-volume *L'Idiot de la famille, Gustave Flaubert de 1821 à 1857*. Sartre's method in all three proceeds, as his fictions proceed, by elaborate schematizing, based upon choice and potential freedom in a world of class struggle. He bullies his subjects quite as much as he portrays them. His relentless plumbing of the mind discovers a chamber of horrors, with distorting mirrors, instruments of self-torture and self-abuse, abasements, refuges, secret panels, terrible voices that scream to Flaubert, 'You are an idiot', as to Genet, 'You are a thief'. It seems clear that Sartre has invented a new form—the Gothic biography. One of its chief terrors is length. But his adventurous conception, that it is really possible to map out every aspect of the mind and to verbalize processes largely inarticulate, makes most other lives of writers seem superficial. Sartre's excesses are the kind that more muted biographers will happily batten on.

The sense that there may be in the life of a literary man, or of other men, a moment in which everything is thrown into question and everything decided, has attracted not only existentialist Freudians but also a Freudian revisionist such as Erik Erikson. His *Young Man Luther* (1962), though concerned with a subject not primarily literary, has had an effect on a number of recent biographies, notably one on John Keats. Erikson's contention is that psychoanalysis must take into consideration not only inner drives but also the social and intellectual pressures of the age. He announces in his book, 'It cannot escape those familiar with psychoanalytic theory that the Renaissance is the ego revolution *par excellence*.' I think we could say that it has not escaped those unfamiliar with psychoanalytic theory either. Biographers have always felt a duty to the external as well as the internal world, but for a Freudian to do so takes on the air of discovery.

Erikson's inspection of Luther does deal somewhat with his surroundings, but mostly it follows a predictable pattern, in finding that the young man, revolting against his irascible father, transferred to God his father's characteristics and so invented the savage God of Lutheranism. But as Roland Bainton, a non-Freudian biographer of Luther, has pointed out, Luther did not invent this savage God, who had already been invented by the medieval schoolmen. That they should all have had irascible fathers and been determined by filial revolt is less than likely. The difficulty with psychohistory is that instead of representing history as an influence upon the individual, it makes history a kind of Greek chorus confirming what is already assumed to be there.

In establishing what psychoanalytic events take place, Erikson has something of the same arrogance as Sartre, though in a patriarchal guise. Wanting to find in Luther an exemplification of the *identity crisis*—that marvellous phrase of his—he begins his book with an account of the fit which Luther is alleged to have suffered in the monastery at Erfurt during his early or middle twenties. 'He suddenly fell to the ground. . . . [Erikson says] "raved" like one possessed, and roared with the voice of a bull: *"Ich bin's nit! Ich bin's nit!"* or *"Non sum! Non sum!"*. The German version is best translated with "It isn't me!", the Latin one with ,"I am *not*!".'

The difficulty with this account is that it was promulgated three years after Luther's death by three contemporaries, 'none of them a later follower of his', as Erikson puts it, a slightly disingenuous way of referring to three men who were Luther's enemies. It may not have happened. Erikson knows this and concludes,

If some of it is legend, so be it: the making of legend is as much part of the scholarly rewriting of history as it is part of the original facts used in the work of scholars. We are thus obliged to accept half-legend as half-history, provided only that a reported episode does not contradict other well-established facts; persists in having a ring of truth; and yields a meaning consistent with psychological theory.

The notion that legend-making has need of professional assistance from scholars, or that they must take on the obligation of rewriting history as well as writing it, makes for some uneasiness. The criteria of admitting rumours are certainly loose; in Luther's case, so little is known of his early life that almost any reported episode could fall in with established facts; as for the ring of truth, that is something possessed by all fictions; and consistency with psychological theory is not difficult to achieve when events are constantly seen as transformations of other events. Sartre says, if it didn't happen this way, it happened in some way like it; Erikson says, if it didn't happen, it as good as happened. But he seems, in comparison with Sartre, cavalier in not admitting when he is being speculative, when historical.

For Erikson the identity crisis is one of seven crises, and this number improves upon Freud, who had only three. No doubt it's helpful to extend the crisis period beyond anal, oral, and genital stages, into later life. But the application of this model to any life is extremely flexible. Erikson indicates that Luther's fourth crisis, of identity, was delayed by several years, so his fifth and sixth crises, which he calls intimacy and generativity, were pushed together—and it wasn't until the last, his integrity crisis, that Luther got back on schedule. I suppose any biographer knows that his subject's life, like all lives, moves between moments of relative calm and relative tension. But the division into seven, even if Shakespeare used it too, is magical and arbitrary. Ultimately Erikson's work is not so much biography as delineation of therapeutic possibility. At the end of his book on Luther, as of his more recent book on Gandhi, Erikson concludes that each of his subjects might have been helped by therapy.

All in all, our modern views of inner economics suggest that Luther's fixation on these [anal] matters absorbed energy which otherwise would have helped the old Luther to reaffirm with continued creativity the ideological gains of his youth; and if this energy had been available to him, he might have played a more constructive role in the mastery of the passions, as well of the compulsions, which he had evoked in others.

There is no doubt that posthumous therapy would help a good many of the dead, but one would have to be sure that Luther's fixation on anality was not, as Bainton insists, common speech in the sixteenth century. Psychohistorians will have to take account of changing fashions in expression, of the possible banality of anality in Luther's time.

In literary biography one of the more conspicuous attempts to apply Freud's discoveries has been Leon Edel's biography of Henry James. Edel began his book twenty-odd years ago, apparently convinced of the value of Freudian techniques. In the first volume he ends a chapter about Henry James's supposed decision, on the basis of his father's and mother's marital relationship, to avoid marriage as a 'deterrent to a full life' with these remarks:

> In a list of names he set down in his notebook when he was fifty, Henry James included that of 'Ledward' and then, as was often his custom, he improvised several variants, apparently as they came into his mind: 'Ledward-Bedward-Dedward-Deadward.' This appeared to be a casual rhyming of led-bed-dead. It was, in effect, a highly condensed statement springing from Henry's mind of the theme of 'De Grey,' 'Longstaff,' *The Sacred Fount* or that story of Merimée's he had liked so much in his youth, 'La Vénus d'Ille.' To be led to the marriage bed was to be dead.
> Henry James accordingly chose the path of safety. He remained celibate.

Of course we all long for *aperçus* and are eager to find slips of the tongue as good as those that Freud interprets so persuasively in *The Psychopathology of Everyday Life*. The difficulty here is that we're not dealing with slips or associations, but with rhymes—as one means of the verbal artist's choosing names. Would it not be possible to say that James, searching for a name like Ledward, tried various possibilities as anyone might do whether his parents were happy together or not? That he tried them in alphabetical order—there is no rhyme with A, so he tried B and Bedward; there is no rhyme for C, with D there is Dedward—then he experimented with spelling Dedward in the alternative way. But Edel is determined to use this as a clinching point, so he rejects the conscious explanation, which I admit is bathetically obvious, in favour of a challenging unconscious one. Even if it be granted that unconscious associations are dominant here, there is no reason for assuming that James is

speaking about the marriage bed; it could be the death bed—
to be led to the death bed is to be dead. We could as easily prove
by this evidence that James had a death wish (if the death wish
were not now in analytic disrepute) as that he had a marriage
phobia.

In later volumes Edel sometimes adopts Freudian techniques,
sometimes not. That some of James's chills and fevers should
be pronounced psychosomatic, and others be just chills and
fevers, is probably inevitable, posthumous diagnosis by biographers being as hazardous as diagnosis by doctors when the
patient is alive. But in the penultimate volume Edel seems almost
ready to give up Freud, as when he describes the turmoil in
Henry James's mind: 'Two forces contended within: his intellect
and his emotions. . . . Rational form and mind were thus inter-
posed against the chaos of feeling.' This is the psychology not
of Freud but of Alexander Pope. Apparently aware that his
readers may be getting confused, Edel in the preface to this
volume explains his biographical method in these terms:

The physical habits of the creative personality, his 'sex life' or his
bowel movements, belong to the 'functioning' being and do not
reliably distinguish him from his fellow-humans. What is characteristic is emotional life and the way in which the emotions dictate—
other elements and mysterious forces aiding—the exercises of the
demonstrative and symbol-making imagination.

This is certainly lofty, but isn't it peculiar to say, in this generation, that the emotional life has nothing to do with sex life or
bowel movements? 'All the rest', says Edel sweepingly, 'is
gossip and anecdotage', but there must be a connection between
the artistic imagination and the everyday gestures of living and
of speaking, which gossip and anecdotage often—as Boswell
demonstrated—supremely preserve.

What seems to me a more persuasive example of the use of
psychology, and especially post-Freudian, can be found in
George Painter's biography of Proust. He tells us that during a

visit to Auteuil, when Proust was nine, the boy walked with his family in the near-by Bois de Boulogne:

On the way back he was seized by a fit of suffocation, and seemed on the point of dying before the eyes of his terrified father. His life-long disease of asthma had begun. Medically speaking, his malady was involuntary and genuine; but asthma, we are told, is often closely linked to unconscious conflicts and desires, and for Proust it was to be, though a dread master, a faithful servant. In his attacks of asthma the same causes were at work as in his childhood fits of hysterical weeping; his unconscious mind was asking for his father's pity and his mother's love; and his breathlessness reproduced, perhaps, the moment of suffocation which comes equally from tears or from sexual pleasure. He sinned through his lungs, and in the end his lungs were to kill him. Other great writers, Flaubert and Dostoevsky, suffered from epilepsy, which stood in an inseparable and partly causal relation to their art. Asthma was Proust's epilepsy. In early years, it was the mark of his difference from others, his appeal for love, his refuge from duties which were foreign to his still un-conscious purpose; and in later life it helped him to withdraw from the world and to produce a work 'de si longue haleine.' Meanwhile, however, he was only a little boy choking and writhing in the scented air under the green leaves, in the deadly garden of spring.

What is clever, almost too clever, about this passage is that it uses psychological interpretation half-literally, half-figura-tively. 'Asthma, we are told,' says Painter (who like Edel and the rest of us is chary of referring to the psychoanalysts by whom we have been told), 'is often linked to unconscious conflicts and desires.' It is also partly hereditary, or at least the predisposition to it is, but for the moment this etiology is irrelevant to Painter's purpose and he ignores it. He hazards a conjecture that the boy's breathlessness reproduces the moment of suffocation which comes equally from tears or from sexual pleasure. This is daring and fine, though I think it channels asthma rather narrowly into the two tendencies which Painter knows were in Proust's life anyway. And two tendencies, in fact, rather prominent in most men's lives. The reference to Flaubert's and Dostoevsky's epilepsy seems to sanction this interpretation, though the disease worked quite differently in those two authors; and when Painter tells us that asthma was Proust's epilepsy, we may become confused and wonder whether epilepsy was Dostoevsky's asthma, why Proust was not an epileptic, or Flaubert not an asthmatic, if these diseases are really so closely akin. Painter wisely doesn't insist too hard at this point and more factually reminds us that asthma was a refuge from duties for Proust in childhood, and later a help to his withdrawal from the world to produce his great work. Then Painter boldly suggests that the work itself was a long breath, not a gasping or short one, and here the Freudian theory of art as sublimation is drawn upon. The French phrase, *de si longue haleine,* which is metaphorical, becomes almost literal—Proust breathes in his work because he cannot breathe anywhere else. Then in the final sentence, a Proustian one, Painter recalls us to the little boy in the Bois, but again implies the whole course of Proust's work as he leaves him, at the end of the chapter, 'choking and writhing . . . in the deadly garden of spring'. Not only is spring a dangerous time for asthmatics, but Painter is suggesting the idealized view Proust took of his childhood as an Eden-like garden, into which Painter inserts the serpent; and further still, he is implying the mixture of evil and beauty in Proust's books. The paragraph neatly balances the acceptance of a psychological interpretation of asthma as metaphor, and its acceptance as medical fact. If we ever find that asthma is purely hereditary or chemical and has nothing to do with father and mother except that they transmit it, this passage will not be invalidated. It is the biographer manipulating psychological theory, not allowing psychological theory to manipulate him.

In Boswell's life of Johnson there is a passage in an early section where Boswell has to consider a very similar problem, that of Johnson's hypochondria. Here is the way Boswell deals with it:

The 'morbid melancholy,' which was lurking in his constitution, and to which we may ascribe those particularities, and that aversion to regular life, which at a very early period, marked his character, gathered such strength in his twentieth year, as to afflict him in a dreadful manner. While he was at Lichfield, in the college vacation of the year 1729,[1] he felt himself overwhelmed with an horrible hypochondria, with perpetual irritation, fretfulness, and impatience; and with a dejection, gloom, and despair, which made existence slavery. From this dismal malady he never afterwards was perfectly relieved; and all his labours, and all his enjoyments, were but temporary interruptions of its baleful influence. How wonderful, how unsearchable are the ways of God! Johnson, who was blest with all the powers of genius and understanding in a degree far above the ordinary state of human nature, was at the same time visited ₁with a disorder so afflictive, that they who know it by dire experience, will not envy his exalted endowments. That it was, in some degree, occasioned by a defect in his nervous system, that inexplicable part of our frame, appears highly probable. He told Mr. Paradise that he was sometimes so languid and inefficient, that he could not distinguish the hour upon the town clock. . . .

But let not little men triumph upon knowing that Johnson was an HYPOCHONDRIACK, was subject to what the learned, philosophical, and pious Dr. Cheyne has so well treated under the title of 'The English Malady.' Though he suffered severely from it, he was not therefore degraded. The powers of his great mind might be troubled, and their full exercise suspended at times; but the mind itself was ever entire. . . . Amidst the oppression and distraction of a disease which very few have felt in its full extent, but many have experienced in slighter degree, Johnson, in his writings, and in his conversation, never failed to display all the varieties of intellectual excellence.

Boswell is on the defensive, and he makes an excellent pleader. He is resolved to treat Johnson's malady as a proper one for a great man, a malady that has its own grandeur about it. Hence the sudden invocation of God's ways as wonderful and unsearchable, hence the insistence that only a few men have experienced

[1] Here the modern biographer would leap to conclude that Johnson had only to return to his parents for a vacation to become mentally deranged.

the disease in its total destructiveness. It is for Boswell a mysterious disease, either sent by God inscrutably, or else centred by evil chance in the inexplicable nervous system, a theory we would perhaps call somatopsychic. But above all, Boswell walls off the disease from Johnson's achievements, and the achievements become greater because they are brought into being over this obstacle. Painter, as a modern biographer of a modern writer, who after all made the disease part of his subject-matter, is readier to depict asthma in Proust without excuse; he wishes to work out Proust's strength through his weakness. For Boswell Johnson is not culpable, is not weak, and his strength has nothing to do with his disease. We are willing today to admit that weaknesses are conducive to the development of genius, rather than hindrances upon it. In fact, we are probably too willing—we make talent and sickness synonymous—in a culture of humiliation we look for the same sensations in history; Strachey was crude but in this sense portentous. Our model for the artist is not Chaucer but Kafka: that scrawny, furtive face, which might belong to one of his own animal characters, seems the only appropriate physiognomy for genius.

The form of biography, then, is countenancing experiments comparable to those of the novel and poem. It cannot be so mobile as those forms because it is associated with history, and must retain a chronological pattern, though not necessarily a simple one. Even Sartre, after largely shrugging off chronology in Baudelaire's life, has observed a chronological pattern in treating of Genet and Flaubert. Of course there must be a pattern of explanation and theme and symbol as well, but I think some idea of the space between birth and death as processive, either an exfoliation or a sharpening definition, will have to persist. Biographies will continue to be archival, but the best ones will offer speculations, conjectures, hypotheses. The attempt to connect disparate elements, to describe the movements within the mind as if they were movements within the atom, to label the most elusive particles, will become more venturesome.

Psychological emphases are bound to change. Theories which once seemed to make everything clear will be brought into question. For example, most present-day biographers are attracted to the theory of compensation, which Edmund Wilson calls 'the wound and the bow'. Samuel Beckett explains it by saying that 'the kick that the physical Murphy received, the mental Murphy gave. It was the same kick, but corrected as to direction.' This theory does not appear to be wrong, but it does appear to be less right than it used to, and more in need of being supplemented by other theories. Some biographers will probably follow Sartre in concentrating with great intentness on inner decisions, others may follow Painter's example in making the artistic work in large measure an absorption of outward circumstances. The influence of linguistics will be felt in an attempt to discover a writer's fundamental rhythm, as Leo Spitzer did with Diderot's tumescent-detumescent prose. I should anticipate that the biographer may wish to approach his subject at different levels, perhaps in the manner of William Faulkner's novel *The Sound and the Fury*, though presumably omitting the chapter which Faulkner assigns to an idiot.

Whatever the method, it can give only incomplete satisfaction. That three biographies of Keats have recently appeared warns us that biographical possibilities cannot be exhausted; we cannot know completely the intricacies with which any mind negotiates with its surroundings to produce literature. The controlled seething out of which great works come is not likely to yield all its secrets. Yet at moments, in glimpses, biographers seem to be close to it, and the effort to come close, to make out of apparently haphazard circumstances a plotted circle, to know another person who has lived as well as we know a character in fiction, and better than we know ourselves, is not frivolous. It may even be, for reader as for writer, an essential part of experience.

cowardice of the European Kurtz, and that the confrontatio[n]
with Marlow, captain of English ships and master of Engli[sh]
prose, bearer of an indisputably English name, was symbolic[ally]
rehabilitative. To commit suicide is to yield to the m[...]
jungle, to write is to colonize with the efficiency so high[ly re-]
garded by Marlow. Kurtz and Marlow meet in the 'h[eart of]
darkness' as in the recesses of Conrad's mind: one dies, t[he other]
contrives to be reborn. Conrad did not let this them[e...]
return to it in *Lord Jim* and other works must have be[en...]
ing and stanching of the old wound.

This preliminary example may embolden an[...]
two characters, and their possible prototypes, i[...]
George Eliot, contrary to T. S. Eliot, made n[o...]
impersonality of the artist. She confided that [...]
fiction, *Scenes of Clerical Life,* drew upon fam[...]
[a]nd many characters from her other books[...]
prototypes in her experience, often with [...]
models then, probably habitually.
[...]e George Eliot herself, Dorothea [...]
[...], it is Mr. Casaubon who has[...]
He is a pedant of such Sahar[a...]
[...e]ntify him has not often [...]
[...]ndidates, the one most [...]
[...]oln College, Oxford [...]
[...] marriage with a [...]
[...]ith George Eli[...]
[...]r (of the si[x...]
[...]his   [...]sly borr[...]
[...]had[...]
[...]pencer   [...]mblan[...]
[...]o ever   w[...]
[...]arded.
[...]er proto-
[...]elist Mrs.
[...]d George

2 Dorothea's Husbands

A novelist, intent on his art, swallows into it other people along with himself. The living originals of fictional characters are elusive because they have been obliged by the writer to answer purposes not their own. It is as if they were evicted from a universe of free will into a deterministic one. The peril of confusing universes is one to which we have been alerted by fastidious critics and structuralists alike. Yet many novelists are themselves liable to this lapse, and fondly imagine that they have created characters out of people they have known. To follow them a little way is at worst devoted, and at best profitable, since the mode of translating characters from the one universe to the other must be close to basic movements of the mind, and so of critical as well as biographical consequence.

It may be easier to approach George Eliot by way of a writer more patently obsessive. In *Heart of Darkness*, Conrad made avowed use of his own trip to the Congo a dozen years before. Much of the narrative turns out to have an immediate parallel in his experience: Conrad did go to Brussels for his interview, did ship up the Congo River on a steamboat, did rescue a sick agent named Klein who died on the trip back. Yet the story has a quite different feel from the *Congo Diary* and from his letters of the time. And there is an important discrepancy: Klein was no Kurtz, no symbol of spiritual degradation. If anything, he

was nondescript. It would seem that the motive powe
story must have come from some other region than th

This area may be guessed at with the help of
pointed out in Jocelyn Baines's life of Conrad. The
dence of Conrad's uncle, Thaddeus Bobrowski,
Conrad, at the age of nineteen, did not—as he alv
wards—fight a duel and suffer a bullet wound. '
instead was that he gambled away at Monte Ca
his uncle had sent him, and then in self-dis
This attempted suicide was probably the ce
rad's life. In the light of it, the qualities
prides himself in *Heart of Darkness*—his
patience, his coolness under pressure—w
of those displayed by the young Conrad
he inflicted this wound, Conrad must
scar—as a sign and symbol of a p
abandon himself. To call his villair
was to memorialize this phase of
Joseph Conrad but still Konrad
to be shortened to Korz.

When recovered from his v
and sailed on an English coas'
afterwards he had determine
weakness. He decided to pr
but as an Englishman. In
examinations which con
tive capacity. If 1875 v
was the year of his vir
as first mate, he beca'
Writing was a wa'
declares, 'mine i'
Marlow, whose
practised a con'

It would s
attempt was

letters. These letters have not survived. But aside from the
flexibility of style and mind so notable in Pattison, so lacking in
Casaubon, it is now clear, from a letter of George Eliot published
in the *Times Literary Supplement* on 12 February 1971 by Professor Gordon S. Haight, that as early as 1846 she was already
diverting her friends by concocting the terms of a pedant's
proposal of marriage. Casaubon's letter balances precariously
on the questions of whether he is seeking a wife or someone to
read to him, and of whether he is actuated by love or myopia;
the proposal of 'Professor Bücherwurm', which George Eliot
pretends to relay to Charles Bray, similarly hinges on the ambiguity of the Professor's securing as his bride someone to translate
his books from German. In 1846 George Eliot did not know
Pattison, and evidently she had no need to know him in order to
evolve Casaubon's letter.

To consider other possible models for Casaubon is to turn up
many of George Eliot's acquaintances. Pedantry was not a scarce
commodity among them. Ideally the culprit should combine
arid learning with sexual insufficiency. This felicitous blend is
unexpectedly hard to find. No doubt the laws of Middlemarch,
rather than those of experience, demanded that Casaubon's
mind symbolize his body, and his body his mind. If George
Eliot drew details from models, she used more than one. Fo
example, and Beatrice Webb saw enough resemblance to re
to him as Casaubon. George Eliot knew Spencer well, and
have been perplexed for a time at his failure to marry any
herself included. But if his nubility was in doubt for he
ability was not; it is only a later age that wishes Spenc
been Casaubon enough to finish fewer books. Besides, s
came to regard George Eliot as the greatest woman w
lived, an accolade she would not have so meagrely re
For the author of the 'Key to all Mythologies', a clo
type is Dr. R. H. Brabant. It was he whom the nov
Eliza Lynn Linton, well acquainted with both him a

Eliot, identified positively as Casaubon. Brabant had similar
difficulty in bringing a book to fruition. According to Mrs,
Linton, he 'never got farther than the introductory chapter of a
book which he intended to be epoch-making, and the final
destroyer of superstition and theological dogma'. Under the
influence of the German rationalists, Brabant presumably intended to eliminate from all religions that supernatural element
which they had eliminated from Christianity. It seems unlikely
that he used the word 'key', an inappropriate one for his
enterprise. Although Gordon S. Haight, George Eliot's astute and
scrupulous biographer, accepts Brabant as the model, there are
several obstacles to close identification with him as with Pattison.
Brabant's loins were not nearly so exhausted: he did not manifest sexual indifference. He was married, he had a daughter and
a son; at the age of sixty-two he squired George Eliot about in a
manner which she found happily equivocal in intention, and
which his blind wife acutely resented.

Moreover he was a physician, and evidently a good one; his
book was a sideline, a token of intellectual community. He had
a gift for companionship, and was friends with Coleridge,
Moore, Landor, and others. He also had friends in Germany,
notably Strauss and Paulus, and it was he who some years later
introduced George Eliot, translator of *Das Leben Jesu*, to
Strauss, its author. Apparently he could converse more easily
in German than she could, and in this respect too he is
unlike Casaubon, whose ignorance of German is scored heavily
against him. Mrs. Linton describes Brabant as 'well got up and
well preserved', while Casaubon is prematurely withered. He
was also a man of many interests, in the theatre, art, and science,
as references in George Eliot's correspondence and John
Chapman's diaries confirm. Most of all, he was a man of
enthusiasm, generously tendered to the work of others rather
than his own.

George Eliot did feel a brief spell of veneration for Brabant,
as Dorothea did for Casaubon, but with more semblance of

justification. Whatever Brabant's defects as an idol, he was in the same cultural movement as she was. If he dithered, it was not over 'Cush and Mizraim' like Mr. Casaubon, but over what George Eliot also considered the most pressing spiritual problems of the time. She followed his lead with Strauss, she borrowed his copy of Spinoza. If he was dull, he was dull in the swim. So expert a novelist would not have forgotten him—she may have derived from him not only hints for Casaubon but some for Mr. Brooke, a friend of Wordsworth and everyone else. But she was after other game than the Polonius who benignly called her, as his second daughter, 'Deutera'—an improvement on Mary Ann.

Pattison, Spencer, and Brabant hang upon Casaubon's coattails, but their intellectual interests are far afield. Comparative mythology such as Casaubon's had got off to a heady start in the eighteenth century with Jacob Bryant's *A New System: or, An Analysis of Ancient Mythology*. Mr. Haight has pointed out that George Eliot made use of Bryant's theory of 'Chus and Mizraim', Cush (so respelt by Bryant) being represented as the father of all the Scythian nations, and Mizraim as father of the Egyptians. There are further connections that can be offered: Bryant's theory of the Phoenicians (as sons of Esau) (VI, 226–39), of the ancient priests called the Cabiri (III, 341–61), and of Dagon the fish god, whom he identified both with Noah and with the Indian god Vishnu (III, 134–6; IV, 140–1; V, 236),[1] are all behind Mr. Casaubon's researches. It was as if George Eliot had Bryant ready in case she was suspected of deriding a living comparative mythologist, and she could keep him more easily in reserve because his work was evidently a familiar subject for joking between her and her friend Sara Hennell. Her concocted Professor Bücherwurm had offered the notion that Christianity was merely a late development of Buddhism, which was like making Vishnu a prior version of Noah, and Sara Hennell, in reply to her friend's comic letter

[1] References are to the third edition (1807), in six volumes.

about Bücherwurm's marriage proposal, quoted Bryant's favourite Egyptian source, Berosus. Yet George Eliot did have a comparative mythologist of her own day, whom she knew well, to fuse with Bryant. This was Robert William Mackay, the author of *The Progress of the Intellect as Exemplified in the Religious Development of the Greeks and Hebrews*, published by George Eliot's friend John Chapman in 1850, and at his request and Mackay's reviewed by her in her first article for the *Westminster Review*.

That Mackay was connected with Casaubon was proposed, as Mr. Haight recognizes, by Frances Power Cobbe in her 1894 *Life* of herself (II, 110–11): 'Mr. Mackay was somewhat of an invalid and a nervous man, much absorbed in his studies. I have heard it said that he was the original of George Eliot's *Mr. Casaubon*. At all events Mrs. Lewes had met him, and taken a strong prejudice against him.' Miss Cobbe is mistaken about George Eliot's feelings towards Mackay, which were always friendly. Perhaps on this account, Mr. Haight dismisses the identification with him as hearsay. But it is not difficult to establish that Mackay contributed a small portion to *Middlemarch*. His book, unlike Brabant's unfinished one, was a revival of comparative mythology. He was more learned even than Bryant, with a dozen footnotes to the latter's one; George Eliot noted his 'industry in research', a virtue constantly claimed by Casaubon. If his search for vegetation gods is difficult to summarize, it is because, as George Eliot complained in her review, much of it seemed mere 'extracts from his commonplace book', rather than results of 'digested study'. It was such a book as Dorothea might have compiled after Casaubon's death. Some of it was manifestly absurd, but George Eliot took a benign view of his objective, which she summarized in this way:

It is Mr. Mackay's faith that divine revelation is not contained exclusively or pre-eminently in the facts and inspirations of any one age or nation, but is co-extensive with the history of human development. . . . The master key to this revelation, is the recognition of the presence of undeviating law in the material and moral world—of that invariability of sequence which is acknowledged to be the basis of physical science, but which is still perversely ignored in our social organisation, our ethics and our religion.

Here at last is the word 'key', which Mackay himself had not used. It is his kind of locksmith that George Eliot has in mind in Casaubon's Key to all Mythologies.

There are further ties. 'Poor Mr. Casaubon himself was lost . . . in an agitated dimness about the Cabeiri' (chapter 20), and poor Mr. Mackay had followed Bryant to the extent of designating as 'Orphic or Cabiric' the primitive period of mythology (I, 276). (She noted in her article that this was an older view, but refrained from tracing it to Bryant.) If Mr. Casaubon, in dictating to Dorothea, announces, 'I omit the second excursus on Crete' (chapter 48), it is perhaps because Mr. Mackay had devoted a whole chapter to Crete and its god, 'Minos-Zeus' (II, 310–22), and Mr. Casaubon may well have felt that this first excursus was enough. If Ladislaw could say of Mr. Casaubon (chapter 22), 'He is not an Orientalist, you know. He does not profess to have more than second-hand knowledge there,' it was because Mr. Mackay had conceded in his preface (I, viii), 'In quoting from Oriental sources the writer is under the disadvantage of ignorance of the languages; but he has taken pains to get the best possible aids.'

Mackay may have had marital designs upon George Eliot; he soon shifted them to another affective object. The resultant marriage obviously interested her. After it he appeared 'rather worse than otherwise', she reported. Following his return from a wedding trip to Weymouth, she asked him how he and his wife had liked it: 'Not at all, not at all,' he replied, 'but it was not the fault of the place.' The barrenness of Rome for the honeymooning Casaubons is at least glimpsed here.

Mackay served to update Bryant and to fill in details of Casaubon which other friends could not supply. As ultimate model for the character, he, like Brabant, is disqualified by his positive qualities. What remains to be found is the source of energy which produces both Casaubon's intensity, and the intensity of contempt, mixed with sporadic pity, which his being arouses in author and characters alike in *Middlemarch*. Mr. Haight, sensible of George Eliot's unusual venom, attributes it to her temporary infatuation with Brabant and later disillusionment with him, but so much feeling after twenty-five years of subsequent friendship, and three years after Brabant's death, seems disproportionate. Brabant was at worst one of her own follies.

Her own follies: putting these Casaubons *manqués* aside, we come to George Eliot herself. F. W. H. Myers related in the *Century Magazine* for November 1881, that when asked where she had found Casaubon, 'with a humorous solemnity, which was quite in earnest, nevertheless, she pointed to her own heart.' This remark deserves to be considered. She meant by it exactly what Flaubert had meant when he said, '*Madame Bovary, c'est moi.*' Flaubert too had his Brabants and Mackays, and secured a few useful details from actual events and persons, but in his writing he had other things to think about. What must be sought is not a Casaubon, but casaubonism, and this George Eliot found, as Flaubert found *le bovarysme,* in herself. Casaubonism is the entombing of the senses in the mind's cellarage. As a young woman George Eliot was liable to this iniquity, and all her life she was capable of what Myers calls 'almost morbid accesses of self-reproach'.

Casaubon is the only character in George Eliot's work up to this time to have a sexual problem, in the sense of being aberrant. What the problem may be is not easy to say definitely. Whether his marriage is consummated or not is left obscure. Living when she did, George Eliot had reason to be delicate and reticent about such a matter, but her vagueness had literary as well as Victorian causes. Impotence is a disaster, not a vice; if Casaubon cannot consummate his marriage, he is to that extent as pathetic as Ruskin. Too much sympathy would be out of order. George

Eliot's fictional universe never allows her men and women to shirk moral responsibility, and Casaubon is no exception. She said that the idea of Casaubon and Dorothea had been in her mind from the time she began to write fiction, and one reason for her long delay in taking up the theme may have been the difficulty of handling Casaubon's sexual insufficiency. She finally solved the difficulty by blending impotence or near-impotence with a choice of chilliness over warmth, in which his culpability would be clear.

This can be traced in terms of one of those recurrent images which George Eliot used with minute attentiveness. At the centre of Casaubon's situation is the seed. As an image it is evoked three times. One is at dinner at Mr. Brooke's house before Dorothea's engagement. In defence of her not going out to ride, Mr. Casaubon says with sudden fervour, 'We must keep the germinating grain away from the light' (chapter 2). The association of darkness and seed is here fixed, with the residual implication that Mr. Casaubon's grain may not be of the germinating kind. Then in chapter 48 his Key to all Mythologies is unexpectedly rephrased as 'the seed of all tradition'. His inability to construct a key, or make a seed, might seem beyond his control. But his blameableness is established in a passage in chapter 42, to which Barbara Hardy has called attention. Mr. Casaubon's difficulties are here explicitly voluntary, not involuntary; as Dorothea is about to take his arm, he keeps it rigid;

There was something horrible to Dorothea in the sensation which this unresponsive hardness inflicted on her. That is a strong word but not too strong. It is in these acts called trivialities that the seeds of joy are for ever wasted, until men and women look round with haggard faces at the devastation their own waste has made, and say, the earth bears no harvest of sweetness—calling their denial knowledge.

Mr. Casaubon chooses self-isolation like choosing self-abuse. The image of Onan is invoked to symbolize his spirit, which in turn is reflected in his physical denial.

This passage, while bold, is not quite unique in George Eliot's writings: it has one counterpart, a personal statement, in a letter she wrote in late adolescence (16 March 1839) to her old teacher Miss Lewis. The letter is startling because in it the future novelist repudiates novels, on the grounds of their effect upon her fantasy life. In this burst of candour she declares:

. . . I venture to believe that the same causes which exist in my own breast to render novels and romances pernicious have their counterpart in that of every fellow-creature.

I am I confess not an impartial member of a jury in this case for I owe the culprits a grudge for injuries inflicted on myself. I shall carry to my grave the mental diseases with which they have contaminated me. When I was quite a little child I could not be satisfied with the things around me; I was constantly living in a world of my own creation, and was quite contented to have no companions that I might be left to my own musings and imagine scenes in which I was chief actress. Conceive what a character novels would give to these Utopias.

Not absence of feeling, but deflection of it, appears to be the charge she is levelling against herself. Mr. Haight in his biography advises against taking these statements seriously, although in his edition of the *Letters* he notes that J. W. Cross, in *George Eliot's Life*, omitted the sentence that contains 'contaminated', 'diseases', and 'to my grave'. Evidently Cross took them seriously. To use these weighty words lightly is not in character for George Eliot. If they have any serious meaning at all, then she is declaring that she has been contaminated by novels which have aroused in her erotic fantasies, as opposed to the merely megalomaniac ones of childhood. In *Felix Holt* Mrs. Transome reads French novels and so takes a lover. But George Eliot in adolescence found no such requital. Insofar as Casaubon was an expression of her own 'almost morbid accesses of self-reproach' —made vivid by her early evangelicalism—it would seem that his sexual inadequacy was a version of her struggles with adolescent sexuality, and that these struggles stirred in her sensation

which remained painful even in memory.[1] The images of darkness which make up Casaubon's mental landscape would then
be wincing recollections of 'the mental diseases' which she had
predicted she would 'carry to my grave'. Casaubon's sexual
insufficiency was an emblem for fruitless fantasies, of which she
too felt victim. It was probably in this sense that he drew his
strength and intensity from her nature.

The severity with which Casaubon is treated, aside from
occasional remissions, would then derive from her need to
exorcise this part of her experience. For a woman who prided
herself on her plenitude of heart, these early short-circuits of
sensual emotion were painful to think on. No wonder that she
makes Casaubon die of fatty degeneration of the heart. He is the
repository of her inferior qualities, as Dorothea of her superior
ones. She instilled her callow misimaginings, suitably shifted in
clef, into old Casaubon, and her ripe affirmations into young
Dorothea.

The place of Dorothea's second husband, Will Ladislaw, in
this drama of George Eliot's mind is not immediately apparent.
To a considerable extent Will had to be made congruent with
Dorothea, even to the point of sharing or paralleling her traits.
Like her, he has a somewhat undirected aspiration to achieve
good and useful works, and he has a slight maliciousness to
balance her mild vanity. In some ways he too radiates out from
George Eliot, even in his person. His rippled nose and strong

---

[1] In a letter written to Miss Lewis a year later, she uses the word 'sin' to describe
her oppressive fantasies:
With respect to my own state of soul of which I have said nothing for some
time, I fear that my sins or rather one particular manifestation of them, have
forsaken me instead of my forsaking and abhorring them. I feel that a sight of
one being whom I have not beheld except passingly since the interview I last
described to you would *probably* upset *all*; but as it is, the image now seldom
arises in consequence of entire occupation and, I trust in some degree, desire
and prayer to be free from rebelling against Him whose I am by right, whose I
would be by adoption. I endeavoured to pray for the beloved object to whom I
have alluded, I must still a little while say *beloved*, last night and felt soothingly
melted in thinking that if mine be really prayers my acquaintance with him has
probably caused the *first* to be offered up specially in his behalf. But all this I
ought not to have permitted to slip from my pen.   (*Letters*, I, 46–7.)

jaw are an idealization of his creator's features, and are allowed to make him handsome though she felt they made her ugly. In his indictment of Casaubon's mythological researches, he follows closely, as Thomas Pinney has noted, George Eliot's review of Mackay and particularly of her strictures on Mackay's predecessors:

The introduction of a truly philosophic spirit into the study of mythology—an introduction for which we are chiefly indebted to the Germans—is a great step in advance of the superficial Lucian-like tone of ridicule adopted by many authors of the eighteenth century, or the orthodox prepossessions of writers such as Bryant, who saw in the Greek legends simply misrepresentations of the authentic history given in the book of Genesis.

Ladislaw says to Dorothea, 'Do you not see that it is no use now to be crawling a little way after men of the last century—men like Bryant—and correcting their mistakes?—living in a lumber-room and furbishing up broken-legged theories about Chus and Mizraim?' Yet if she modelled Ladislaw a little upon herself, she needed and found another model as well. The choice troubled her. She said that the ending of her novel might disappoint, and perhaps the main reason was that, aside from marrying Ladislaw to Dorothea (like Blake fusing Los with Enitharmon), she could not make him inevitable in the Middlemarch terrain.

Prototype hunters have left Ladislaw alone, on the assumption that George Eliot was too happily fixed in her life with Lewes to have anyone else in mind. Her commitment to Lewes was as much beyond suspicion as it was outside law. If she could not take his last name legally, she took both his last and first names extra-legally. When Harriet Beecher Stowe asked if the Casaubon marriage bore any resemblance to her own, George Eliot replied, 'Impossible to conceive any creature less like Mr. Casaubon than my warm, enthusiastic husband, who cares much more for my doing than for his own, and is a miracle of freedom from all author's jealousy and all suspicion. I fear that the Casaubon-tints are not quite foreign to my own mental complexion. At any rate I am very sorry for him.' (She echoes here her comment as author in *Middlemarch* (chapter 29), 'For my part I am very sorry for him.') Lewes was in fact one of the more engaging minds of his time, willing to tackle scientific, philosophical, and literary subjects, and with a gift of sympathy which George Eliot found indispensable to her existence as well as to her writing. If Thomas and Jane Carlyle could not refrain from calling him 'the ape', or Douglas Jerrold from calling him 'the ugliest man in London', he was not the less likeable; and George Eliot was more indulgent of his ugliness than of her own. He himself sometimes joked about playing Casaubon to his wife's Dorothea, but he had more in common with Ladislaw. He too spent some time as a young man in Germany and knew the language fairly well. He did not have 'a Jew pawnbroker' for his grandfather, an imputation made about Ladislaw, but he had Jewish associations and several times played Shylock on the stage. He had a versatility that smacked of dilettantism, so that he dissected dragonflies one moment and Comtism the next. But like Ladislaw, his variety did not prevent intensity. 'Our sense of duty', says George Eliot in chapter 46, 'must often wait for some work which shall take the place of dilettantism. . . .'

George Eliot was jealous of her husband as well as notably fond of him. Mrs. Linton quotes her as saying, 'I should not think of allowing George to stay away a night from me.' Yet sporadic deflections of erotic feeling are not inconsistent with marital content or vigilance. In her case a superabundance of amorous sentiment, beyond any immediate object, is suggested by the effusively affectionate correspondence she lavished upon women friends even though, as she had to make clear to Edith Simcox, it was men who interested her. The search for Casaubon begins with others and ends with George Eliot; the search for Ladislaw spreads out from her to her husband and beyond. In this character her critical powers, which enabled her to recognize limitations in Dorothea as in heroes outside of fiction such as

Luther and Bunyan,[1] are largely suspended. He occupies a special position in her work, because he is the first character of either sex in her novels to be irresistibly handsome and at the same time good. Early reviewers remarked upon him as constituting a new departure in George Eliot's novels. In *Adam Bede* Hetty is beautiful, but is punished for being so; she is not so good as she looks. The same is true of Tito in *Romola*. Only Ladislaw is treated with utter indulgence, even to being encouraged to toss back his curls on numerous occasions, as if George Eliot feared she had not made him fetching enough. It seems possible that she had herself been suddenly captivated by the image of a handsome young man.

The first important meeting of Dorothea and Ladislaw takes place in Rome, and since George Eliot had been to Rome just three and a half months before she began *Middlemarch*, her sojourn may be scrutinized a little. This was the second visit that she and Lewes had paid to that city, and it did not work out as well as the first. On the way there he had suffered from sciatica, and once arrived he was not in the mood to enjoy Rome. He wrote in his journal, 'I have had enough of it and want to be at home and at work again.' Mr. Casaubon had similar thoughts. But George Eliot did not share her husband's impatience. 'Here we had many days of unbroken sunshine . . .' was her summary. It was now she had the meeting which was to prove so momentous in her life, with John Walter Cross, then twenty-nine.

This meeting had long been in prospect. She had met Cross's

---

[1] I should imagine that neither Luther nor John Bunyan, for example, would have satisfied the modern demand for an ideal hero. . . . The real heroes, of God's making, are quite different: they have their natural heritage of love and conscience which they drew in with their mother's milk; they know one or two of those deep spiritual truths which are only to be won by long wrestling with their own sins and their own sorrows; they have earned faith and strength so far as they have done genuine work; but the rest is dry barren theory, blank prejudice, vague hearsay . . . their very deeds of self-sacrifice are sometimes only the rebound of a passionate egoism.

(*Scenes of Clerical Life,* chapter x of *Janet's Repentance*.)

mother two years before, thanks to Herbert Spencer, who boasted in later life that he had brought George Eliot into touch with both her husbands. At that time Mrs. Cross's other children were in England, but John was in the United States, carrying on the American side of the family's banking business. He must have been a frequent topic of discussion between the Crosses and Leweses.

On an April day in 1869 George Eliot was walking with Lewes in her beloved Pamfili Doria gardens, when she met by accident Mrs. Cross's oldest daughter and her husband, who like the Casaubons took their wedding trip to Rome. Further meetings were arranged, and when, some days later, Mrs. Cross, her son John, and another daughter arrived, they were invited on 18 April to visit the Leweses in their rooms at the Hotel Minerva—the same hotel they had stayed at on their first Roman visit in 1860. John Walter Cross shared the veneration of all members of his family for George Eliot's writings, and must have testified to that. Thanks to him, one bit of the ensuing conversation has survived: 'And I remember, many years ago, at the time of our first acquaintance, how deeply it pained her when, in reply to a direct question, I was obliged to admit that, with all my admiration for her books, I found them, on the whole, profoundly sad.' Her pain carried over into *Middlemarch*. This conversation is closely paralleled in chapter 22 when Ladis-law admonishes Dorothea, 'Would you turn all the youth of the world into a tragic chorus, wailing and moralising over misery?' She replies, as George Eliot must have replied to Cross, 'I am not a sad, melancholy creature', but he is not so easily put down, and eight chapters later has written her a letter which 'was a lively continuation of his remonstrance with her fanatical sympathy and her want of sturdy neutral delight in things as they were—an outpouring of his young vivacity. . . .'

Cross, nothing if not vivacious, had just returned from the United States, and must have been asked about his travels there. His work had been in New York, where he had invested heavily in the railroads, but, as a magazine article he wrote later confirms, he had also been to California. Something of what he said must have put George Eliot in mind of the penultimate project which she attributes to Ladislaw (before his ultimate one of marrying Dorothea), that of promoting a settlement in the 'Far West'. Cross was in fact excited about what he repeatedly called in print the 'New World'; he praised it because it 'rests on the basis of industrialism as opposed to militarism'. He thought his fellow-countrymen wrong to criticize it, and wrote later, 'One thing is certain, namely, that since all gain of *real* wealth in America *must* be of advantage to England it will surely be the first sign of impending decadence if the business men of this country, instead of putting their shoulders to the wheel to carry their chariot over all obstruction, content themselves with cherishing a vindictive feeling to rivals. . . .' This kind of imagery, natural to Cross,[1] is twitted a little in Ladislaw's projected painting of 'Tamburlaine Driving the Conquered Kings in His Chariot', intended as he says to symbolize 'the tremendous course of the world's physical history lashing on the harnessed dynasties', and to include 'migrations of races and clearings of forests—and America and the steam engine'. Cross's westward travels, the steam engine which drove the trains that carried him, the extension of the railroads to the furthest points of the New World (as he remarked in an article devoted to them), the sympathy for American energy, all found a way into George Eliot's book.

He must have delighted her. The contrast of Ladislaw's youth and Casaubon's age, of the passionate unscholarliness of the first and the uneasy ferreting of the second, would then be an idealized registration of the effect on George Eliot of her meeting with Cross. By implication it promised Dorothea in fiction something better than widow's weeds and good works after

[1] For example, in his *The Rake's Progress in Finance* (1905), 127–8, he writes that 'the serious question is how to steer warily, for we have already pointed the nose of our ship towards State Socialism and it may be difficult now to alter the course.'

Casaubon's death, and so brought the whole of *Middlemarch* into focus. It can only have been a secret tribute to Cross, and one he would have appreciated, that among the misty details of Ladislaw's upbringing one fact stands out clear and is mentioned twice—he went to Rugby. So did Cross.[1]

Momentarily even the beloved Lewes must have appeared to disadvantage beside this taller, handsomer, sharper-sighted, younger banker. Cross was to prove his devotion steadily from this time on, and to be rewarded for it by having conferred upon him the titlè of 'nephew'. In *Middlemarch* Ladislaw, though actually Casaubon's second cousin, is often taken for his nephew. Cross was regularly and affectionately spoken of as Nephew Johnny, and in the letter George Eliot wrote to him after Lewes's death, in which she asked him to call, she addressed him as 'Dearest N.' Not that she considered for a moment infidelity to her husband; for every reason she was bound to him for life. But she was not averse to making renunciation of another cherished object a part of her bond to Lewes. As she remarks of Mary Garth's loyalty to Fred in *Middlemarch*, 'we can set a watch on our affections and our constancy as we can other treasures.' Certainly as a solution to her problems of ending *Middlemarch*, John Walter Cross had much to offer. She banked this banker in her fictional account.

The friendship of the Leweses with Cross grew deeper over the years. After Lewes's death George Eliot would not receive Cross for a time, but indicated she would do so eventually, perhaps before she received anyone else. And so it was. On the day he was asked to call, her old friend Herbert Spencer was turned away. Since Cross's mother and one of his sisters had died soon after Lewes, he and George Eliot could share each other's grief. As consolation in the next months, they read Dante's *Inferno* and *Purgatorio* together. There was no need to read the *Paradiso*, for the parallel with Beatrice required no en-

---

[1] Cross entered Rugby in April 1835, at the age of fifteen. N. C. Kittermaster, the present librarian of the school, informs me that he remained for two years.

forcement. Cross felt Dantean about George Eliot; she was 'my ideal', 'the best', and to marry her was his 'high calling'. George Eliot did not reprove this exalted feeling; in a letter to Mrs. Burne-Jones of 5 May 1880, she wrote: 'he sees his only longed-for happiness in dedicating his life to me.'

Ladislaw objects to Casaubon's ignorance of the Germans on comparative mythology, but George Eliot is at pains to indicate that he himself has little more than vague acquaintance with these arcane books. No erudition is allowed Ladislaw, only a general interest in art, poetry, and politics. His reformist political views are close to those of Cross, who espoused a non-revolutionary amelioration of inequity as a liberal goal.[1] A strong hint of George Eliot's sense of Cross as a Ladislaw figure comes in a patronizing (if also matronizing) letter she wrote him on 16 October 1879: 'Best loved and loving one . . . Thou dost not know anything of verbs in Hiphil and Hophal or the history of metaphysics or the position of Kepler in science, but thou knowest best things of another sort, such as belong to the manly heart—secrets of lovingness and rectitude. O I am flattering. Consider what thou wast a little time ago in pantaloons and back hair.' (Back hair was one of Ladislaw's attributes.) By this time Cross was thirty-nine and a settled man in City banking, but he still stood for her as the embodiment of youth, almost of boyhood, with an ignorance that surpassed knowledge. No doubt these feelings had grown in George Eliot over the ten years of their friendship, but the jingled Hebrew of 'Hiphil and Hophal' suggests that from the beginning he had stood as the polar opposite of 'Cush and Mizraim'. He was also the opposite of her husband, and of most of her old friends, in knowing nothing—as she indelicately underlines—of works in ancient languages, in metaphysics, or in science. Marrying Dorothea to

---

[1] Cross praises Dante for having seen the danger of the 'ever-increasing inequality in the distribution of wealth', and after himself opposing 'the crude spirit which would risk reducing order to chaos by violent methods', he endorses 'the spirit which is at work modifying and enlarging our ideal of possession from an individual to a social basis.'   (*Impressions of Dante* . . . , 92.)

Ladislaw had been George Eliot's only adulterous act. Artistically it proved to be a sin. Marrying Cross as Lewes's widow legalized the fantasy. In the same way her own reconciliation with her brother Isaac validated the reconciliation of brother and sister which she had fictionally imagined, in *The Mill on the Floss*.

Now, when they married, there was a strange reversal of roles, with a sixty-year-old Dorothea marrying a forty-one-year-old Ladislaw, a disparity almost as great as that between Casaubon and his bride. Cross's own sentiments could only have been intricate, since he was her nephew, son, pupil, and reader, as well as husband. The sense of being a once independently orbited fragment drawn back now into the parent body must have been immensely disturbing. Perhaps more than sexual awkwardness or disparity of age or health was involved in Cross's pitching himself into the Grand Canal at Venice during their wedding trip. It was a solution which George Eliot had never allowed Dorothea to contemplate. Fished out, and restored to the same bedroom, he gave no further trouble.

A final witness is Eliza Lynn Linton. She had known George Eliot as a young provincial, holding her hands and arms like a kangaroo. She had been invited to call just after the decision to live with Lewes, and she met her later on too. Mrs. Linton was jealous of George Eliot's literary pre-eminence, but she acknowledged it. She also wrote a long essay on George Eliot's works, and had this to say about the second marriage of Dorothea in *Middlemarch*:

And to think that to her first mistake she adds that second of marrying Will Ladislaw—the utter snob that he is! Where were George Eliot's perceptions? Or was it that in Ladislaw she had a model near at hand, whom she saw through coloured glasses, which also shed their rosy light on her reproduction, as that his copy was to her as idealized as the original, and she as ignorant of the effect produced on the clear-sighted?

In another place Mrs. Linton makes clear that she entirely dis-

approved of the marriage to Cross, as reducing the first
marriage to a house of cards, and it is clearly Cross she has here
in mind. She is unkind, but she does suggest the fictional complications for George Eliot of modelling Ladislaw on Cross, a
man distinguished more for youthful ardour and amorphous-
ness than anything else. (His skill in investment was hard to
idealize.) But George Eliot chose well in making him her husband, for he was impeccably discreet in his *Life* of her, and
during the more than forty years that he outlived her.

Cross did not allow his photograph to be taken, and in
general he effaced himself. But he was not devoid of ambition,
and he published two books. The first and more important had
the ragbag title, *Impressions of Dante and of the New World with
a Few Words on Bimetallism* (1893). His Dante essays provide a
contrast to the worldly report on American railroads, and
indicate that like Ladislaw he loved poetry. The preface perhaps
gives a sense of his goodhearted and unassuming but garrulous
temperament:

'Don't shoot the organist; he's doing his level best.' This ancient
American story of a notice prominently affixed in a church in the
Wild West, as a gentle appeal to the congregation, expresses the
mildly deprecatory attitude that I desire to assume to my readers—
if I have any—or rather the attitude that I hope they will assume to
me. 'Don't shoot the essayist; he's doing his level best.' I confess that
it is difficult to find a naked excuse for republishing old magazine
articles, and in my own case I cannot plead that any host of admiring
friends has put pressure on me to collect mine. I take it that the real
reason for the republication is always the same—a desire on the part
of the writer to leave some print of his footsteps, however shallow,
on the sands of time.   (pp. v–vi.)

This is johnnycrossism, abashed yet candid, the reverse of
Casaubon's closed room which no key could unlock. After a
lifetime with intellectuals, George Eliot chose a simpler love
for herself as she had had Dorothea do after Casaubon's death.
The Key to all Mythologies was not so hard to find. Her deci-

sion may have been sentimental, but it established the veri-
similitude of Dorothea's act.

The two husbands of Dorothea have different functions in
Middlemarch. The one is all labyrinth and darkness, the other all
candour and light. George Eliot was dissatisfied with the book's
ending, but she committed herself to Ladislaw in a way hard for
most readers to follow. Part of the reason lies in the very different histories of the characters in her internal dialectic. To berate
Casaubon, and to bury him, was to overcome in transformed
state the narcissistic sensuality of her adolescence. Old feelings
of self-reproach could be renewed, and the character, once
stirred by this motive power, could be furnished out with
details adroitly selected from people she had known either per-
sonally or through their writings. The result was a triumph, a
new creature. In Ladislaw, a fantasy of middle age, indulged
because innocuous, the character is deprived of her usual controls. She allows herself to idealize him, his only imperfection
being what is also his chief perfection—youth. He remains a
surrogate sun, lacking in energy and heat, no fiction but a fig-
ment executed in pastel colours. She had had much time to
reflect on the implications of Casaubon; but, if these speculations are valid, the new image of Ladislaw took her unawares,
as a result of the luxuriantly fantasied encounter in Rome with
her young admirer and future husband.

3 Overtures to 'Salome'

Salome, after having danced before the imaginations of European painters and sculptors for a thousand years, in the nineteenth century turned her beguilements to literature. Heine, Flaubert, Mallarmé, Huysmans, Laforgue, and Wilde became her suitors. Jaded by exaltations of nature and of humanism, they inspected with something like relief a Biblical image of the *un*natural. Mario Praz, bluff, and sceptical of Salome's allurements, seeks to limit them by arguing that she became the type of no more than the *femme fatale*. By type he means, he says, something 'like a neuralgic area. Some chronic ailment has created a zone of weakened resistance, and whenever an analogous phenomenon makes itself felt it immediately confines itself to this predisposed area, until the process becomes a matter of mechanical monotony.' But like most medical metaphors, this one doesn't apply easily to the arts, where repetition of subject is not a certain contra-indication to achievement. Most of these writers were conspicuous for their originality, and if they embraced so familiar a character from Biblical history, it was to accomplish effects they intended to make distinctive. As there are many Iseults, many Marys, so there were many Salomes, without monotony.

The fact that Wilde's *Salome* is a play, and a completed one, distinguishes it from other versions and helps to make it more original than Professor Praz would have us believe. Mallarmé was not merely flattering when he congratulated Wilde on the 'definitive evocation' of Salome,[1] or when he took care to avoid seeming to copy Wilde when he returned to work on his own *Hérodiade*.[2] Wilde's simple sentences and repeated words may indeed owe something to Maeterlinck or even (as a contemporary critic suggested) to Ollendorff—the Berlitz of that age—but they have become so habitual in modern drama as to seem anticipatory rather than derivative. The extreme concentration upon a single episode which is like an image, with a synchronized moon changing colour from pale to blood-red in keeping with the action, and an atmosphere of frenzy framed in exotic chill, confirms Yeats's oblique indication that he had learned as much from Wilde as from the Noh drama for his dance plays.[3] A torpid tetrarch (three Herods telescoped into

[1] '. . . cette jeune princesse que définitivement vous évoquâtes.' (Unpublished letter, Mallarmé to Wilde, March 1893.)

[2] 'J'ai laissé le nom d'Hérodiade pour bien la différencier de la Salome je dirai moderne . . .' (Draft of a preface to *Hérodiade*, in Stéphane Mallarmé, *Les Noces d'Hérodiade* (Paris, 1959), 51.)

[3] Yeats attended a performance of Wilde's *Salome* in May 1905, and found it 'empty, sluggish, and pretentious'. As he wrote on 30 May in an unpublished letter to John Quinn, 'The audience was curiously reverential, and as I came away I said to somebody, "Nothing kept us quiet but the pious memory of the sainted author."' But in 1935, in the preface to *A Full Moon in March*, he allowed that

The dance with the severed head suggests the central idea in Wilde's *Salome*. Wilde took it from Heine, who has somewhere described Salome in Hell throwing into the air the head of John the Baptist. Heine may have found it in some Jewish religious legend, for it is part of the old ritual of the year: the mother goddess and the slain god. In the first edition of *The Secret Rose* there is a story based on some old Gaelic legend. A man swears to sing a woman's praise; his head is cut off and the head sings. In attempting to put this story into a dance play I found that I had gone close to Salome's dance in Wilde's play. But in his play the dance is before the head is cut off.

Yeats's insistence on a Celtic basis for his plot is perhaps related to his insistence on a Japanese Noh origin for his dramatic form. It seems likely that Wilde's play, which he must have heard about or read when it was first published in 1893, four years before *The Secret Rose*, contributed ideas which Yeats later preferred to attribute to more arcane sources. The extremely stylized and concentrated treatment of a Biblical theme probably affected also Yeats's plays *Calvary* and *The Resurrection*.

one) lusting yet inert, a prophet clamouring from a well below
the floorboards, are more congenial figures now that Beckett
has accustomed us to paralysis, senile drivelling, voices from
ashcans, and general thwart.

Mario Praz, quick to deny Wilde any novelty, insists that the
play's culminating moment, when Salome kisses the severed
head of Iokanaan, is borrowed from Heine's *Atta Troll*. But in
Heine's version kissing the head is a punishment after Herodias's death, not a *divertissement* before it, and the tone of carica-
ture is quite unlike that of perverted horror which Wilde
evokes. If some source has to be found—and it always has—I
offer tentatively a dramatic poem called *Salome* published in
Cambridge, Massachusetts, in 1862, by a young Harvard
graduate named J. C. Heywood,[1] and subsequently republished
during the 1880s in London in the form of a trilogy. I have to
admit that in Heywood as in Heine, it is Herodias, not Salome,
who kisses the head, but at least she does so while still alive, and
in a sufficiently grisly way. Wilde knew one part of Heywood's
trilogy—he reviewed it in 1888, three years before writing his
own play—and he may well have glanced at the other parts.
Still, he isn't really dependent on Heywood either, since he
exchanges mother for daughter and, unlike Heywood, makes
this monstrous kissing the play's climax.[2]

To read Heywood or other writers about Salome is to come
to a greater admiration for Wilde's ingenuity. The general
problem that I want to inquire into is what the play probably
meant to Wilde and how he came to write it. Villainous women
were not his usual subject, and even if they had been, there were
others besides Salome he could have chosen. The reservoir of
villainous women is always brimming. The choice of Salome

---

[1] This edition was anonymous.

[2] According to E. Gomez Carrillo, a young Guatemalan writer who saw
much of Wilde during the composition of the play, other details changed
considerably in the planning, but the climax was always the same. (E. Gomez
Carrillo, *En Plena Bohemia*, in his collected works (Madrid, n.d. [1919?]), xvi,
190ff.)

would seem to inhere in her special relationship to John the Baptist and Herod. Sources offer little help in understanding this, and we have to turn to what might be called praeter-sources, elements which so pervaded Wilde's imaginative life as to become presences. Such a presence Amadis was for Don Quixote, or Virgil for Dante. In pursuing these I will offer no *explication de texte*, but what may well appear a divagation, though I hope to define a clandestine relevance. It includes, at any rate, those fugitive associations, often subliminal, which swarm beneath the fixed surface of the work, and which are as pertinent as is that surface to any study of the author's mind.

It will be necessary, therefore, to retrace certain of Wilde's close relationships. If Rilke is right in finding a few moments in a writer's life to be initiatory, then such an initiatory experience took place when Wilde left Ireland for England. He later said that the two turning-points in his life occurred 'when my father sent me to Oxford, and when society sent me to prison.' Wilde matriculated at Magdalen College, Oxford, on 11 October 1874, just before he was twenty. The two men he had most wanted to know at that time, he said, were Ruskin and Pater, both, conveniently enough, installed at the same place. He managed to meet Ruskin within a month, and though he didn't meet Pater so quickly, during his first three months at Oxford he made the acquaintance of Pater's *Studies in the History of the Renaissance*, which he soon called his 'golden book', and subsequently referred to in a portentous phrase as 'that book which has had such a strange influence over my life.'[1]

Three weeks after Wilde arrived, Ruskin gave a series of lectures on Florentine painting. During one of them he proposed to his students that, instead of developing their bodies in pointless games, in learning 'to leap and to row, to hit a ball with a bat,' they join him in improving the countryside. He proposed to turn a swampy lane near Ferry Hinccksey into a flower-

---

[1] At the Lord Queensberry trial Wilde spoke of Pater as 'the only critic of the century whose opinion I set high. . . .'

bordered country road. Such muscular effort would be ethical rather than narcissistic, medieval rather than classical.[1] Although Oscar Wilde found rising at dawn more difficult than most men, he overcame his languor for Ruskin's sake. He would later brag comically that he had had the distinction of being allowed to fill 'Mr. Ruskin's especial wheelbarrow' and even of being instructed by the master himself in the mysteries of wheeling such an object from place to place. At the end of term Ruskin was off to Venice, and Wilde could again lie late abed, comfortable in the thought that, as he said, 'there was a long mound of earth across that swamp which a lively imagination might fancy was a road.' The merely external signs of this noble enterprise soon sank from sight, but Wilde remembered it with affectionate respect, and his later insistence on functionalism in decoration and in women's dress, and on socialism based upon self-fulfilment in groups, was in the Ferry Hincksey tradition.

The road proved also to be the road to Ruskin. Wilde met his exalted foreman often during the ensuing years. In 1888, sending him a book, he summed up his feelings in this effusive tribute:

The dearest memories of my Oxford days are my walks and talks with you, and from you I learned nothing but what was good. How else could it be? There is in you something of prophet, of priest, and of poet, and to you the gods gave eloquence such as they have given to none other, so that your message might come to us with the fire of passion, and the marvel of music, making the deaf to hear, and the blind to see.

That (like this prose) the prophet had weaknesses, made him if anything more prophet-like. Wilde was as aware of Ruskin's weaknesses as of his virtues. His letter of 28 November 1879, by which time he had taken his Oxford degree, mentions that he

---

[1] Pater, on the other hand, much preferred the activities of what he called in italics the palaestra.

and Ruskin were going that night to see Henry Irving play
Shylock, following which he himself was going on to the
Millais ball. 'How odd it is,' Wilde remarks. The oddity lay not
only in attending this particular play with the author of *The
Stones of Venice*, but in proceeding afterwards to a ball which
celebrated the marriage of John Everett Millais's daughter. Mrs.
Millais had for six years been Mrs. Ruskin, and for three of
those years Millais had been Ruskin's friend and protégé. The
details of Ruskin's marriage and annulment were no doubt as
well known at that time in Oxford by word of mouth as they
have since become to us by dint of a dozen books. It was the
fact that Ruskin and the Millaises did not speak to each other
that obliged Wilde to leave Ruskin with Irving and proceed to
the ball alone.

To call the Ruskin ambiance merely odd was Oxonian
politeness. As soon as Ruskin had married, he explained to his
wife that children would interfere with his work and impede
necessary scholarly travel. Consummation might therefore
wisely be deferred until later on, perhaps in six years' time
when Effie would be twenty-five. Few can claim an equal
dedication to learning. In the meantime Effie need have no fear
about the possible sinfulness of their restraint, since many early
Christians lived in married celibacy all their lives. Effie tried to
accommodate herself to this pedantic view, and Ruskin in turn
was glad to oblige her on a lesser matter: that they go to live
in Venice, since he was already planning to write a book about
that city.

In Venice, while Ruskin sketched, Effie survived her boredom
by going about with one or another of their friends. Ruskin
encouraged her, perhaps (as she afterwards implied) too much.
If he accompanied her to dances and masqued balls, he often left
early without her, having arranged that some gentleman friend
escort her home. If she returned at 1.30 in the morning, he duly
notified his parents in England, at the same time adding that he
was completely at rest about her fidelity. Yet her obvious plea-

sure in pleasure, her flirtatiousness, her impatience with his studies, her delight in frivolity and late hours, struck Ruskin sometimes—however much he repudiated the outward thought —as forms of misconduct and disloyalty. He said as much later. That Effie wasn't sexually unfaithful to him didn't of course prevent Ruskin, any more than it prevented Othello before him, from considering her so, or from transposing her mental dissonance into larger, vaguer forms of betrayal.

The Stones of Venice will always stand primarily as a work of art criticism. But criticism, as Wilde said, is the only civilized form of autobiography, and it is as a fragment—a large fragment—of Ruskin's autobiography that the book claims an added interest. In novels and poems we take for granted that some personal elements will be reflected, but in works of non-fiction we are more reluctant, and prefer to postulate an upper air of abstraction in which the dispassionate mind contemplates and orders materials that already have form and substance. Yet even the most impersonal of writers, Thucydides, writing about the fortunes of another city, shaped his events, as Cornford suggests, by preconceptions absorbed from Greek tragedy. Ruskin made no pretence of Thucydidean impersonality, and the influence of his reading of the Bible is manifest rather than latent. But some problems of his own life also were projected on to the Venetian scene. Rather than diminishing the book's value, they merge with its talent and add to its intensity.

It may be easier to be convinced that *The Stones of Venice* is in part autobiographical if we remember Ruskin's candid admission that *Sesame and Lilies,* a book he wrote a few years later, was a reflection of one particular experience. His preface expressly states that the section in it called 'Lilies' was generated by his love for Rose La Touche. This love impelled him to idealize women, he says, even though 'the chances of later life gave me opportunities of watching women in states of degradation and vindictiveness which opened to me the gloomiest secrets of Greek and Syrian tragedy. I have seen them betray their household charities to lust, their pledged love to devotion; I have seen mothers dutiful to their children, as Medea; and children dutiful to their parents, as the daughter of Herodias. . . .' His love for Rose La Touche also covertly leads him to quarrel in the book with pietism because Rose was that way inclined. *The Stones of Venice* dwells less obviously, but with the same insistence, on the virtues and defects of the feminine character. As Ruskin remarks in *Sesame and Lilies*, 'it has chanced to me, untowardly in some respects, fortunately in others (*because it enables me to read history more clearly*),[1] to see the utmost evil that is in women. . . .' To Ruskin Venice is always *she* (to Mary McCarthy, invariably *it*), and the gender is not merely a form of speech but an image to be enforced in detail.

Accordingly Ruskin distinguishes two stages, with medieval Venice as virgin and Renaissance Venice as whore. The moment of transition is, apparently, the moment of copulation, and the moment of copulation is therefore (as in a familiar view of the Garden of Eden) the fall. When Ruskin describes the fallen state, he attributes to the city the very taste for masqued balls and merriment which he had ostentatiously tolerated in his wife. 'She became in after times', he declares, 'the revel of the earth, the masque of Italy: and *therefore* is she now desolate, but her glorious robe of gold and purple was given her when first she rose a vestal from the sea, not when she became drunk with the wine of her fornication.' At the end of the first volume he again asserts, 'It was when she wore the ephod of the priest, not the motley of the masquer, that the fire fell upon her from heaven. . . .' After that fire came another which changed the virgin city to its contrary:

Now Venice, as she was once the most religious, was in her fall the most corrupt, of European states; and as she was in her strength the centre of the pure currents of Christian architecture, so she is in her decline the source of the Renaissance. It was the originality and splendour of the Palaces of Vicenza and Venice which gave this

[1] My italics.

school its eminence in the eyes of Europe; and the dying city, magnificent in her dissipation, and graceful in her follies, obtained wider worship in her decrepitude than in her youth, and sank from the midst of her admirers into her grave.

Ruskin cannot bring himself to sketch out 'the steps of her final ruin. That ancient curse was upon her, the curse of the cities of the plain, "pride, fulness of bread, and abundance of idleness." By the inner burning of her own passions, as fatal as the fiery reign of Gomorrah, she was consumed from her place among the nations, and her ashes are choking the channels of the dead salt sea.' Just how passions should burn except inwardly may not be clear, especially since we can't suppose that Ruskin favoured the translation of sensual thought into sensual action, but pride, gluttony, and sloth secure a more sinister confederate in the unnameable sin of lust, whose self-generated fire is contrasted with that fire which had earlier fallen on the city from heaven.

Ruskin's stridency shows how much he had this problem at heart. In fact, consummation and defilement were irrevocably united for him, in his life as in his criticism. The Renaissance (a new term then but already favourable in its connotations) was for him not a rebirth but a relapse. (In *De Profundis* Wilde accepted this view.) Ruskin's revulsion extended from coupling to begetting to having been begot. He had more trouble than most people in allowing that he was himself the product of his parents' intercourse. A small indication is to be found in an epitaph which he wrote for his mother (who already had an epitaph) long after her death, consecrating a memorial well, as he writes, 'in memory of a maid's life as pure, and a mother's love as ceaseless. . . .'[1] In Ruskin's mind his mother had immaculately passed from maid to mother without ever becoming a wife.

---

[1] Ruskin's earlier dedicatory tablet had been taken down because the well became polluted. It specified that the name 'Margaret's Well' be given, but did not otherwise mention his mother, though the donor's name was given as

This singular epitaph may illuminate a point never adequately explained, why Ruskin dated the fall of Venice not only to an exact year, but to a specific day, 8 May 1418. His own explanation is that this was the death day of the aged Venetian military leader Carlo Zeno, and he makes his usual citation of Pierre Daru's *Histoire de la République de Venise* as his authority. But Daru doesn't give Zeno's death such consequence. Ruskin might more easily, and more consistently with his own views, have taken the year 1423, when the old Doge Tommaso Mocenigo died and the new Doge, Foscari, began his less glorious rule. He is alone among writers on Venice in attaching this significance to Zeno's death day, and in view of his known penchant for numerology the date invites attention. If Ruskin had been born exactly four hundred years after this date, in 1818, rather than in 1819, the choice might seem related to his theatrical self-laceration, as if to regret he had ever been born. But his terrors were for intercourse and conception rather than for birth. I venture to propose that the date so carefully selected was, putatively, four hundred years to the day before his own conception—that act so impossible for him to meditate on with equanimity. That the moment of Venice's fall should be reiterated in the moment of his own begetting and be followed by his birth into an England only too ready (as he announces on the first page of his book) to fall—like a semi-detached Venice—anchored firmly the relationships Ruskin wished to dwell upon. In his parents' fall, as in that of our first parents, he saw the determination of an age's character and of his own.

'John Ruskin Esq., M.A., LL.D.' The new inscription, never installed, was to read in full:

'This Spring
In memory of a maid's life as pure
And a mother's love as ceaseless,
Dedicate to a spirit in peace
Is called by Croydon people,
Margaret's Well,
Matris animae, Joannes Ruskin
1880'

Margaret Ruskin's marriage had made her a mother, while Effie Ruskin's 'dissolute' behaviour in Venice had made her—in fancy if not in fact—an adultress. Moral blame, from which his mother was freed, was shunted to his wife. Ruskin's own later summary of *The Stones of Venice* confirms that he had this theme in mind. In *The Crown of Wild Olive* (1866) he wrote, '*The Stones of Venice* had, from beginning to end, no other aim than to show that the Renaissance architecture of Venice had arisen out of, and in all its features indicated, a state of concealed national infidelity, and of domestic corruption.' The trip to Scotland which Ruskin, his wife, and Millais took in 1853 strengthened the metaphors, and in later life he accused Millais of infidelity—artistic infidelity he called it[1]—to the Pre-Raphaelite principles as Ruskin had earlier enunciated them. Venice, his wife, and his friend were all guilty of the same crime.

Necessary as Ruskin found it to think of himself as wronged, there were moments when he recognized his own culpability. After the annulment of his marriage he came, by a series of mental leaps, to try a revision of his character. In 1858, while looking at Veronese's *Solomon and Sheba* in Turin, he suddenly felt a wave of sympathy for the 'strong and frank animality' of the greatest artists. He disavowed his earlier religious zeal, and became (though at the urging of his father and of Rose La Touche's mother he didn't publicly say so) quite sceptical. Then, as Wilenski points out, he began to acknowledge that his theory of history in *The Stones of Venice* was mistaken. Writing to Froude in 1864, he stated firmly, 'There is no law of history any more than of a kaleidoscope. With certain bits of glass—shaken so, and so—you will get pretty figures, but what figures, Heaven only knows. . . . The wards of a Chubb's lock are infinite in their chances. Is the Key of Destiny made on a less complex principle?' This renunciation of historical law

---

[1] 'But the spectator may still gather from them some conception of what this great painter might have done, had he remained faithful to the principles of his school when he first led its onset.' (*Fors Clavigera* 79 (July 1877), in *Works* (1903), XXIX, 161.)

was intellectually daring, and emotionally as well, for it meant that he was trying to alter those 'pretty figures' which earlier had enabled him to lock his own conception and marriage into the history of Venice. As part of this change, he resolved to propose marriage to Rose La Touche, and in 1866 he at last did so.[1] Rose La Touche, no mean calendar-watcher herself, said she could not answer for two years, or perhaps for four. Ruskin abided by her verdict with desperation; his diary records the passing of not only these anniversaries but, since she died soon after, of year after year following her death. No one will mock Ruskin's pain, or his struggle to overcome his fears and become as animal as Veronese.

Rose La Touche had been dead less than a year when Ruskin and Wilde met and took walks together. Neither professor nor pupil was reticent, and Wilde probably divined the matters that Ruskin was unwilling to confide. At any rate, the moral law as imparted by Ruskin, even with the softenings he now wished to introduce, was for Wilde sublime—and berserk. In Ruskin, whom everyone called a prophet, the ethical life was noble and yet, in its weird chastity, perverse. Against its rigours life offered an antidote, and what life was had been articulated by Pater, who saw it not in terms of stones but of waters, not of monuments but of rivery passions. Pater was like Wilde in that, at the same age of nineteen, he too had fallen under Ruskin's sway. He soon broke free, his conscience unclenched itself. He surprised a devout friend by nonetheless attempting, although he had lost his faith, to take orders in the Anglican Church. His friend complained to the bishop and scotched this diabolic ordination. The *Studies in the History of the Renaissance*, Pater's first book, doesn't mention Ruskin by name, but uses him throughout as an adversary. Pater's view of the Renaissance did not differ in being more

1 The day he selected for the proposal was probably an effort to change his temperament as well as his luck by another numerological flurry, for it was 2 February, his parents' wedding day. By this symbolism he planned, perhaps, to overcome his revulsion at the thought of both consummation and procreation.

detached; in its way it was just as personal, and it ended in a secular sermon which ran exactly counter to that of *The Stones of Venice*. It is Ruskin inverted. Pater is all blend where Ruskin is all severance. He calls superficial Ruskin's view that the Renaissance was 'a fashion which set in at a definite period'. For Pater it was rather 'an uninterrupted effort of the middle age.' One age was older, one younger, they encountered each other like lovers.

An atmosphere of suppressed invitation runs through Pater's book as an atmosphere of suppressed refusal runs through Ruskin's. The first essay of *Studies in the Renaissance* recounts at length how the friendship of Amis and Amile (in the thirteenth-century story) was so full and intense that they were buried together rather than with their respective wives. Later essays dwell with feeling upon such encounters as that of young Pico della Mirandola, looking like a Phidian statue, with the older Ficino, or that—planned but prevented by murder—of Winckelmann and the still callow Goethe. For Ruskin the Renaissance is an aged Jezebel, while for Pater it is a young man, his hair wreathed in roses more than in thorns, such a youth as Leonardo painted as John the Baptist. In describing this painting, Pater lingers to point out that the saint's body doesn't look as if it had come from a wilderness, and he finds John's smile intriguingly treacherous[1] and suggestive of a good deal[2]—which may be Victorian hinting at the heresy, a specially homosexual one, that Christ and John (not to mention Leonardo and his model) were lovers.

Whatever Ruskin says about strength and weakness, Pater opposes. The decay against which *The Stones of Venice* ful-

[1] Wilde wrote from Algiers in 1895 to Robert Ross, 'The most beautiful boy in Algiers is said by the guide to be "deceitful"; isn't it sad? Bosie and I are terribly upset about it.' (Unpublished text from Sir Rupert Hart-Davis.)
[2] 'It is so with the so-called *Saint John the Baptist* of the Louvre—one of the few naked figures Leonardo painted—whose delicate brown flesh and woman's hair no one would go out into the wilderness to seek, and whose treacherous smile would have us understand something far beyond the outward gesture or circumstances.' (Pater, *The Renaissance*, ed. Kenneth Clark (1961), 118.)

minates is for Pater 'the fascination of corruption', and images of baleful female power, such as Leonardo's Medusa and other 'daughters of Herodias', are discovered to be 'clairvoyant' and 'electric', when Ruskin had found the daughter of Herodias monstrously degraded. Instead of praising the principle of *Noli me tangere*, so ardently espoused by Ruskin, Pater objects to Christian asceticism that it 'discredits the slightest sense of touch.' Ruskin had denounced 'ripe' ornamentation in terms which evoked elements of the adult female body: 'I mean,' he said,

that character of extravagance in the ornament itself which shows that it was addressed to jaded faculties; a violence and coarseness in curvature, a depth of shadow, a lusciousness in arrangement of line, evidently arising out of an incapability of feeling the true beauty of chaste forms and restrained power. I do not know any character of design which may be more easily recognized at a glance than this over-lusciousness. . . . We speak loosely and inaccurately of 'over-charged' ornament, with an obscure feeling that there is indeed something in visible Form which is correspondent to Intemperance in moral habits. . . .

But for Pater overcharged ornament is rather an 'overwrought delicacy, almost of wantonness', or 'a languid Eastern delicious-ness.'

Ruskin strenuously combated what he considered to be a false fusion of classicism and Christianity in the Renaissance. 'It would have been better', he said, 'to have worshipped Diana and Jupiter at once than have gone through life naming one God, imagining another, and dreading none.' Galleries had no business placing Aphrodite and the Madonna, a Bacchanal and a Nativity, side by side. But this juxtaposition was exactly what Pater endorsed. For him European culture was what he called, following Hegel to some extent, a synthesis. To countervail Ruskin's diptych of Venice as virgin of the Adriatic and whore of Babylon, he offered as his Renaissance altarpiece the *Mona Lisa* of Leonardo. His famous description begins, 'The presence that rose beside the waters', and it is clear that he is summoning up not only Lisa, but Venus rising like Ruskin's favourite city from the sea. Lisa has, according to this gospel of Saint Walter, mothered both Mary and Helen, exactly the indiscriminateness, as well as the fecundity, which Ruskin condemned. Pater's heroine, as Salvador Dali has implied by giving her a moustache more suited to Pater, is an androgyne: the activities attributed to her, dealing with foreign merchants and diving in deep seas, seem more male than female. She blends the sexes, she combines sacred and profane. Like Saint John, she has about her something of the Borgias.

Against Ruskin's insistence upon innocence, Pater proffers what he bathetically terms, in the suppressed and then altered and reinstated conclusion to *The Renaissance*, 'great experiences'. He urges his readers to seek out high passions, only being sure they are passions; later, only being sure they are high. The Renaissance is for him the playtime of sensation, even its spiritual aspects being studies in forms of sensation. W. H. Mallock parodied this aspect by having Pater, as the effete 'Mr. Rose' in *The New Republic*, lust for a pornographic book. Something of the extraordinary effect of Pater's *Renaissance* comes from its being exercises in the seduction of young men by the wiles of culture. And yet Pater may not have seduced them in any way except stylistically. When Wilde presented Lord Alfred Douglas to him, the flagrancy of the homosexual relationship was probably, as Lawrence Evans suggests, the cause of the rift between Pater and Wilde which then developed.

Pater and Ruskin were for Wilde at first imagined, and then actual figures; then they came to stand heraldically, burning unicorn and uninflamed satyr, in front of two portals of his mental theatre. He sometimes allowed them to battle, at other times tried to reconcile them. A good example is his first long published work. This was an ambitious review of the paintings in a new London gallery; he wrote it in 1877, his third year at Oxford, for the *Dublin University Magazine*. The article takes the form of a rove through the three rooms, which had been done, Wilde said admiringly, 'in scarlet damask above a dado of dull green and gold.' (Ruskin, who also attended, complained that this décor was 'dull in itself' and altogether unsuited to the pictures.) Upon entering, Wilde immediately belauds Burne-Jones and Holman Hunt as 'the greatest masters of colour that we have ever had in England, with the single exception of Turner' —a compliment to Ruskin's advocacy of Turner and to the sponsorship of the Pre-Raphaelites by both Ruskin and Pater. Wilde then, to praise Burne-Jones further, quotes Pater's remark that for Botticelli natural things 'have a spirit upon them by which they become expressive to the spirit', and as he sweeps through the gallery he finds occasion to savour the same sweet phrase again. He also manages to mention the portrait of Ruskin by Millais, though it was not on exhibition. Reaching the end, he salutes 'that revival of culture and love of beauty which in great part owes its birth to Mr. Ruskin, and which Mr. Swinburne and Mr. Pater and Mr. Symons and Mr. Morris and many others are fostering and keeping alive, each in his peculiar fashion.' He slipped another quotation from Pater into this final paragraph, but a watchful editor slipped it out again.

Wilde's review of the exhibition is not so interesting as Ruskin's, in *Fors Clavigera* 79, which roused Millais to fury and Whistler to litigation. But it did result in Wilde's finally meeting Pater who, having been sent a copy of the review, invited him to call. Their subsequent friendship afforded Wilde a chance to study the student of the Renaissance. He did not lose his admiration, as we can surmise from the poem '*Hélas!*' which he wrote a little later. In it he invokes both of his mentors as if they were contrary forces tugging at him. After owning up to frivolity, Wilde says,

> Surely there was a time I might have trod
> The august[1] heights, and from life's dissonance
> Struck one clear chord to reach the ears of God.

[1] Later 'sunlit'.

The chief reference is to Gothic architecture, celebrated by
Ruskin because, though fraught with human imperfection—
'life's dissonance'—it reached towards heaven. In the next lines
Wilde confesses to having fallen away a little:

> Is that time dead? Lo, with a little rod,
> I did but touch the honey of romance.
> And must I lose a soul's inheritance?

Here he is quoting Jonathan's remark to Saul, 'I did but taste a
little honey with the end of the rod that was in mine hand, and
lo! I must die,' which Wilde remembered Pater's having conspicuously quoted and interpreted in *The Renaissance* in his
essay on Winckelmann. For Pater Jonathan's remark epito-
mizes 'the artistic life, with its inevitable sensuousness,' and is
contrasted with Christian asceticism and its antagonism to
touch.[1] If the taste of honey is a little decadent, then so much the
better. Wilde is less sanguine about this appetite here. But as
Jonathan was saved, so Wilde, for all his alases, expected to be
saved too, partly because he had never renounced the Ruskin
conscience, only forgone it for a time.

The tutelary presences of Pater and Ruskin survived in
Wilde's more mature writings. In *The Picture of Dorian Gray*,
for example, Pater is enclosed (like an unhappy dryad caught
in a tree trunk) in Lord Henry Wotton. Lord Henry's chief sin
is quoting without acknowledgement from *The Renaissance*. He
tells Dorian, as Pater told Mona Lisa, 'You have drunk deeply
of everything . . . and it has all been to you no more than the
sound of music.' He predicts, against the 'curious revival of
Puritanism' (a cut at Ruskin) a new hedonism, the aim of which

---

[1] Compare Ruskin, *Diaries* (1959), III, 972, for 1 January 1878: 'And now,
thinking of the mischief done to my own life and to how many hundred
thousand, by dark desire, I open my first text as I Corinthians VII.i. ['It is good
for a man not to touch a woman. Nevertheless . . . let every man have his own
wife, and let every woman have her own husband.'] And yet the second verse
directly reverses the nobleness of all youthful thought, expressed in a word by
Dr. King: "Not to marry that they may be pure; but to be pure that they may
marry."'

will be 'experience itself, and not the fruits of experience.' It will 'teach man to concentrate himself upon the moments of a life that is but a moment.' These are obvious tags from the Conclusion to *The Renaissance*. Lord Henry's advice to Dorian, 'Let nothing be lost upon you. Be always searching for new sensations,' was so closely borrowed from the same essay that Pater, who wrote a review of the book, was at great pains to distinguish Lord Henry's philosophy from his own. Wilde seems to have intended not to distinguish them, however, and to offer (through the disastrous effects of Lord Henry's influence upon Dorian) a criticism of Pater.

As for Ruskin, his presence in the book is more tangential. The painter Hallward has little of Ruskin at the beginning, but gradually he moves closer to that pillar of aesthetic taste and moral judgement upon which Wilde leaned, and after Hallward is safely murdered, Dorian with sudden fondness recollects a trip they had made to Venice together, when his friend was captivated by Tintoretto's art. Ruskin was of course the English discoverer and champion of Tintoretto, so that the allusion is specific. The ending of *Dorian Gray* executes a Ruskinesque repudiation of a Pateresque career of self-gratifying sensations. Wilde defined the moral in so witty a way as to content neither of his mentors: in letters to newspapers he said *Dorian Gray* showed that 'all excess, as well as all renunciation, brings its own punishment.' Not only are Hallward and Dorian punished by death, but, Wilde asserted, Lord Henry is punished too. Lord Henry's offence was in seeking 'to be merely the spectator of life. He finds that those who reject the battle are more deeply wounded than those who take part in it.' The phrase 'spectator of life' was one that Wilde used in objecting to Pater's *Marius the Epicurean*. However incongruous his conception of himself as activist, with it he lorded it over his too donnish friend. For Pater, while he touted (sporadically at least) the life of pleasure, was careful not to be caught living it. He idealized touch until it became contemplation. He allowed only his eye to participate in the high passions about which he loved to expatiate. Dorian at least had the courage to risk himself.

In *Dorian Gray* the Pater side of Wilde's thought is routed, though not deprived of fascination. Yet Hallward, when his ethical insistence brings him close to Ruskin, is killed too. In 'The Soul of Man under Socialism', also written in 1891, Wilde superimposes Ruskin's social ethic upon Pater's 'full expression of personality', fusing instead of destroying them. In *Salome*, to which we are led at last, the formulation is close to *Dorian Gray*, with both opposites executed. Behind the figure of Iokanaan lurks the image of that perversely untouching, untouchable prophet John whom Wilde knew at Oxford. When Iokanaan, up from his cistern for a moment, cries to Salome, '*Arrière, fille de Sodome! Ne me touchez pas. Il ne faut pas profaner le temple du Seigneur Dieu,*' a thought of Ruskin, by now sunk down into madness, can scarcely have failed to cross Wilde's mind. By this time Wilde would also have recognized in the prophet's behaviour (as in Ruskin's) something of his own, for after his first three years of marriage he had discontinued sexual relations with his wife. Iokanaan is not Ruskin, but he is Ruskinism as Wilde understood that pole of his character. Then when Salome evinces her appetite for strange experiences, her eagerness to kiss a literally disembodied lover in a relation at once totally sensual and totally 'mystical' (Wilde's own term for her), she shows something of that diseased contemplation for which Wilde had reprehended Pater. Her adaptation, or perversion, of the Song of Songs to describe a man's rather than a woman's beauty also is reminiscent of Pater's *Renaissance* as well as of Wilde's predisposition. It is Salome, and not Pater, who dances the dance of the seven veils, but her virginal yet perverse sensuality is related to Paterism.

Admittedly the play takes place in Judea and not in Oxford. Wilde wanted it to have meaning outside his own psychodrama. Yet Wilde's tutelary voices from the university, now fully identified as forces within himself, seem to be in attendance, clamouring for domination. Both Iokanaan and Salome are executed, however, and at the command of the tetrarch. The execution of Salome was not in the Bible, but Wilde insisted upon it.[1] So at the play's end the emphasis shifts suddenly to Herod, who is seen to have yielded to Salome's sensuality, and then to the moral revulsion of Iokanaan from that sensuality, and to have survived them both. In Herod Wilde was suggesting that *tertium quid* which he felt to be his own nature, susceptible to contrary impulses but not abandoned for long to either.

Aubrey Beardsley divined the autobiographical element in Herod, and in one of his illustrations gave the tetrarch the author's face. Herod speaks like Wilde in purple passages about peacocks or in such an epigram as, '*Il ne faut pas regarder que dans les miroirs. Car les miroirs ne nous montrent que les masques.*' Just what Wilde thought his own character to be, as distinct from the alternating forces of Pater and Ruskin, is implied in a remark he made in 1883 to George Woodberry, who promptly relayed it to Charles Eliot Norton. Wilde told Woodberry that Ruskin 'like Christ' bore the sins of the world, but that he himself was 'always like Pilate, washing his hands of all responsibility.' Pilate in the story of Christ occupies much the same role as Herod in the story of John the Baptist. In other letters Wilde continues to lament his own weakness, yet with so much attention as to imply that it may have a certain fibre to it. In March 1877 he wrote, 'I shift with every breath of thought and am weaker and more self-deceiving than ever,' and in 1886 he remarked, 'Sometimes I think that the artistic life is a long and lovely suicide, and am not sorry that it is so.' What he more and more held against both his mentors was a vice they shared equally, that of narrowness. To keep to any one form of life is

---

[1] Gomez Carrillo says that the play was originally to be entitled *La Décapitation de Salome*, thus slighting St. John by precisely equating the two deaths. (Gomez Carillo, *En Plena Bohemia*, 214.)

limiting, he said in *De Profundis*, and added without remorse, 'I had to pass on.'

Herod too passes on, strong in his tremblings, a leaf but a sinuous one, swept but not destroyed by successive waves of spiritual and physical passion, in possession of what Wilde in a letter calls 'a curious mixture of ardour and of indifference. I myself would sacrifice everything for a new experience, and I know there is no such thing as a new experience at all . . . I would go to the stake for a sensation and be a sceptic to the last!' Here too there are martyrdom and abandonment, with a legal right to choose and yet stay aloof. Proust had something of the same idea when he said of Whistler's quarrel with Ruskin that both men were right.[1] In that same reconciling vein Wilde in *De Profundis* celebrates Christ as an artist, and the artist as Christ. And in Wilde's last play, when Jack declares at the end, 'I've now realized for the first time in my life the vital Importance of Being Earnest,' he is demonstrating again that Ruskin's earnestness, and Pater's paraded passionateness, are for the artist not mutually exclusive but may, by wit, by weakness, by self-withholding, be artistically, as well as tetrarchically, compounded.

---

[1] 'Plus je pense aux théories de Ruskin et de Whistler, plus je crois qu'elles ne sont pas inconciliables. Whistler a raison de dire, dans *Ten o'Clock*, que l'Art est distinct de la Morale. Et pourtant, Ruskin émet aussi une vérité, d'un autre plan, quand il dit que tout grand art est moralité.' (Marcel Proust, *Lettres à une amie* (Marie Nordlinger) (Manchester, 1942), 85.)

4 The Critic as Artist as Wilde

Wilde is the one writer of the nineties whom everyone still reads, or more precisely, has read. The mixture of frivolity and pathos in his career continues to arrest us. That career displays its self-conjugation in Wilde's own terms of 'The Critic as Artist'.

In 1914 Henry James could complain that there was not enough criticism about to give novelists their bearings, while T. S. Eliot and Saul Bellow have since regretted, for different reasons and in different tones of voice, that there is now too much. The obtrusive place of the critic today can be related to a methodological emphasis which is conspicuous in other disciplines as well. But Wilde was one of the first to see that the exaltation of the artist required a concomitant exaltation of the critic. If art was to have a special train, the critic must keep some seats reserved on it.

Wilde reached this conclusion by way of two others. The first is that criticism plays a vital role in the creative process. If this sounds like T. S. Eliot admonishing Matthew Arnold, Wilde had expressed it, also as an admonition to Arnold, almost thirty years before. The second is that criticism is an independent branch of literature with its own procedures. 'I am always amused', says Wilde, 'by the silly vanity of those writers and artists of our day who seem to imagine that the primary function of the critic is to chatter about their second-rate work.' And he complains that 'The poor reviewers are apparently reduced to be the reporters of the police-court of literature, the chroniclers of the doings of the habitual criminals of art.' In protesting the independence of criticism, Wilde sounds like an ancestral Northrop Frye or Roland Barthes. These portentous comparisons do indeed claim virtue by association, and such claims may be broadened. André Gide found Nietzsche less exciting because he had read Wilde, and Thomas Mann in one of his *Last Essays* remarks almost with chagrin on how many of Nietzsche's aphorisms might have been expressed by Wilde, and how many of Wilde's by Nietzsche. What I think can be urged for Wilde, then, is that for his own reasons and in his own way he laid the basis for many critical positions which are still debated in much the same terms, and which we like to attribute to more ponderous names.

When Wilde formulated his theories the public was more hostile to criticism than it is now, and Wilde was flaunting his iconoclasm, his contempt for the unconsidered and so uncritical pieties of his age. This in fact was his mode: not to speak for the Victorians, or for the prematurely old writers who dithered that they were the end of an era, as if they must expire with the 1800s. Wilde proposed to speak for the young, with even excessive eagerness. His own age was always a little embarrassing for him, because he had already spent three years at Trinity College, Dublin, when he went up to Oxford. He was not above a little deception on this score. In 1877, when he was twenty-three, he sent a poem to Gladstone with a letter saying, 'I am little more than a boy.' And in a poem written that year he spoke of his 'boyish passion' and described himself as 'one who scarce has seen some twenty summers'. This line, in turn, he repeated in his poem 'The Sphinx', finished when he was forty. Even in court he injudiciously testified he was two years younger than he was, so that he sounds a little like Falstaff shouting to Bardolph during the robbery, 'They hate us youth.' Wilde's mode was calculated juvenescence, and the characters in his books are always being warned by shrewder characters of the danger of listening to people older than themselves. To help reduce that danger, Wilde's characters are invariably parentless. The closest kin allowed is an aunt.

Like Stendhal, Wilde thought of himself as a voice of the age to be, rather than of the one that was fading. Yet like anyone else writing criticism in the nineteenth century, he had to come to terms with the age that had been, and especially with everybody's parent, Matthew Arnold. Wilde sought Arnold's approbation for his first book, *Poems*, 1881, which he sent with a letter stressing their shared Oxonian connections. These extended, though he wisely did not enforce the claim, to their both having won the Newdigate. Actually their prize-winning poems offer a contrast of manners, Arnold's being just as determined to appear older as Wilde's younger than his years. Arnold replied politely.

But by 1881 Arnold was genuinely old, and seven years later, in 1888, he was dead. Wilde's only book of criticism, *Intentions*, was written during the three years following Arnold's death and published in 1891, as if to take over that critical burden and express what Arnold had failed to say. Yeats thought the book 'wonderful' and Walter Pater handsomely praised it for carrying on, 'more perhaps than any other writer, the brilliant critical work of Matthew Arnold.' Pater's encomium is a reminder, however, not to ignore *him*. There are not two but three critical phases in the late nineteenth century, with Pater transitional between Arnold and Wilde.

In 1864, lecturing from the Oxford Chair of Poetry on 'The Function of Criticism at the Present Time', Arnold declared—to everyone's lasting memory—that the 'aim of criticism is to see the object as in itself it really is.' This statement went with his demand for 'disinterested curiosity' as the mark of the critic; its inadvertent effect was to put the critic on his knees before the work he was discussing. Not everyone enjoyed this position.

Nine years later Walter Pater wrote his preface to *Studies in the History of the Renaissance*. Pretending to agree with Arnold's definition of the aim of criticism, he quoted it, then added, 'the first step towards seeing one's object as it really is, is to know one's impression as it really is, to discriminate it, to realise it distinctly.' But Pater's corollary subtly altered the original proposition; it shifted the centre of attention from the rock of the object to the winds of the perceiver's sensations. It made the critic's own work more important as well as more subjective. If observation is still the word, the critic looks within himself as often as out upon the object.

Wilde had been Pater's disciple, and in *Intentions* eighteen years later he tweaks Arnold's nose with the essay which in its first published form was entitled, 'The True Function and Value of Criticism: with Some Remarks on the Importance of Doing Nothing.' Here Wilde rounded on Arnold by asserting that the aim of criticism is to see the object as it really is not. This aim might seem to justify the highly personal criticism of Ruskin and Pater, and Wilde uses them as examples; his contention goes beyond their practise, however; he wishes to free critics from subordination, to grant them a larger share in the production of literature. While he does not forbid them to explain a book, they might prefer, he said, to deepen a book's mystery. (This purpose is amusing but out of date now: who could deepen the mystery of *Finnegans Wake*?) At any rate, their context would be different from that of the creative artist. For just as the artist claimed independence of received experience (Picasso tells us that art is 'what nature is not'), so the critic claimed independence of received books. 'The highest criticism', according to Wilde, is 'the record of one's own soul.' More closely he explained that the critic must have all literature in his mind and see particular works in that perspective rather than in isolation. Thus he, and we as well,

shall be able to realise, not merely our own lives, but the collective life of the race, and so to make ourselves absolutely modern, in the true meaning of the word modernity. For he to whom the present is the only thing that is present, knows nothing of the age in which he lives. To realise the nineteenth century, one must realise every century that has preceded it and that has contributed to its making.

Through knowledge the critic might become more creative than the creative artist, a paradox which has been expressed with more solemnity by Norman Podhoretz about literature of the present day.

Wilde reached these formulations of his aesthetic ideas late in his short life. They were latent, however, in his earliest known essay, 'The Rise of Historical Criticism', which he wrote as a university exercise. While praising historians for their scrupulousness, Wilde finds the core of history to be the wish not merely to paint a picture, but to investigate laws and tendencies. He celebrates those historians who impose dominion upon fact instead of surrendering to it. Later he was to say much more boldly, 'The one duty we owe to history is to rewrite it,' and to praise Herodotus as father not of history but of lies. It is part of his larger conception that the one duty (or better, whim) we owe nature, reality, or the world, is to reconstruct it.

When Wilde turned to literary as distinguished from historical criticism, he at first was content to follow Pater. Wilde was won by Pater's espousal of gemlike flames and of high temperatures both in words and in life. Next to him Arnold sounded chilly, never so Victorian as when he was cogently criticizing Victorianism. That word 'impression', with which Pater sought to unlock everything, became a favourite word in both Wilde and later in Arthur Symons, and was only arrested by Yeats in the 1890s because he could not bear so much impermanence and insisted on a metaphysical basis—the *Anima Mundi*—for transitory moods.[1] Like the word 'absurd' today, though without a systematic philosophy behind it, the word 'impression' agitated against pat assumptions and preconceptions.

[1] See below, p. 105.

Pater's vocabulary shapes the initial poem 'Hélas!' of Wilde's book of verse, published when he was twenty-five.

> To drift with every passion till my soul
> Is a stringed lute on which all winds can play,
> Is it for this that I have given away
> Mine ancient wisdom, and austere control?

To call the poem 'Hélas!', to sigh in a foreign language, alerts us that the confession to follow will luxuriate in its penitence. The Biblical archaisms which occur later offer compunction suitably perfumed. 'To drift' may well put us off as weak; on the other hand, 'to drift with every passion' is not so bad. As its image of passivity, the poem offers 'a stringed lute on which all winds can play'. For the Romantics the Aeolian harp was a favourable image because it harmonized man and nature. Here the winds are winds of temptation, rather than gusts of Lake Country air. The rhetorical question which begins, 'Is it for this?' sounds reproachful enough, yet the phrases 'ancient wisdom' and 'austere control'—self-congratulatory since Wilde never had either—are so vague as to constitute a stately but equally unenergetic alternative to drifting.

The word 'drift' comes down from Oxford in the 1870s. It occupies a prominent position in Pater's *Studies in the History of the Renaissance,* and specifically in the notorious conclusion to that book. This 'Conclusion' was included in the edition of 1873, but omitted in 1877, when Wilde was at Oxford, on the ground that it 'might possibly mislead' the young, who accordingly thronged to be misled by the first edition. It was the boldest thing Pater ever wrote; he drew upon the scientific work of his day to deny the integrity of objects. Physical life is now recognized, he says, to be a concurrence of forces rather than a group of things; the mind has no fixities either. He hits upon a metaphor of liquidity such as William James and Bergson were to adopt a little later in characterizing consciousness as a river or stream; Pater says more balefully that consciousness is a whirlpool, an image which later both Yeats and Pound relished. In our physical life, Pater grants, we sometimes feel momentarily at rest; in our consciousness, however, altering the whirlpool image, he finds 'nothing but the race of the mid-stream, a drift of momentary acts of sight and passion and thought.' To drift is not so wanton, then, as inevitable. To guide our drifting we should rely not on sights or thoughts, in Pater's view, but on 'great passions'. 'Only be sure it is passion,' he puts in as a *caveat*. He urges his readers to recognize that 'not the fruit of experience, but experience itself, is the goal.' 'Our one hope lies in getting as many pulsations as possible into the given time.' This attempt to render experience in terms of quantitatively measurable pulsations sounds a little like *Principles of Literary Criticism,* but Pater's tone is not like Richards's; he plays on the flute for the young to follow him.

When Pater at last decided to reprint this 'Conclusion' (in 1888), he toned it down a little. In *Marius the Epicurean* (1885), also later, the word 'drift' is again prominent, but this time is pejorative instead of merely descriptive. To suit his later and more decorous manner, Pater, in reviewing *Dorian Gray,* complained of the book's 'dainty Epicurean theory' because, he said:

A true Epicureanism aims at a complete though harmonious development of man's entire organism. To lose the moral sense therefore, for instance, the sense of sin and righteousness . . . is to lose, or lower, organisation, to become less complex, to pass from a higher to a lower degree of development.

The letting-go, as well as the drawing-back, of Pater are both evident in Wilde; his work celebrates both impulses, balancing or disporting with them. In a letter of March 1887, written four years before '*Hélas!*', he informs an Oxford friend:

I have got rather keen on Masonry lately and believe in it awfully—in fact would be awfully sorry to have to give it up in case I secede from the Protestant Heresy. I now breakfast with Father Parkinson, go to St Aloysius, talk sentimental religion to Dunlop and altogether am caught in the fowler's snare, in the wiles of the Scarlet Woman—

I may go over in the vac. I have dreams of a visit to Newman, of the holy sacrament in a new Church, and of a quiet and peace afterwards in my soul. I need not say, though, that I shift with every breath of thought and am weaker and more self-deceiving than ever.

If I *could hope* that the Church would wake in me some earnestness and purity I would go over *as a luxury*, if for no better reasons. But I can hardly hope it would, and to go over to Rome would be to sacrifice and give up my two great gods 'Money and Ambition'.

In this letter Wilde testifies playfully to the same yearning to be earnest that he shows in '*Hélas!*' and then mocks in his later comedy. He is half-converted to Catholicism, half to Masonry—that these two groups cannot bear each other does not prevent their being equally attractive to him; they have parity as new areas of sensation, to be enjoyed wilfully and passingly. If, as Wilde announced later, 'the best way to resist temptation is to yield to it,' the reason is that having done so, one may pass on to the next and the next, and in this concourse one may keep a residual freedom by not lingering with any single temptation long.

During the four years between writing this letter and writing '*Hélas!*', Wilde had put aside both Catholicism and Masonry. In his sonnet he has in mind chiefly his formal education as contrasted with his romantic self-indulgence. A classicist by training, Wilde considered Hellenism to be the more basic side of his nature, overlaid, but only as a palimpsest conceals the original, by a more modern mode. He berates himself, gently. His new life is made up of 'idle songs for pipe and virelay', a self-accusation[1] which only concedes frivolity, not depravity. Moreover, it is artistic frivolity, a further mitigation. Wilde remembered Pater's comment in the same 'Conclusion' that 'the wisest' instead of living spend their lives in 'art and song'. If it is wrong to drift, and Wilde hedges a little, then it is less wrong to drift gracefully. A 'boyish holiday' is also not the most offensive way to spend one's time, especially if one likes boys.

[1] See above, pp. 54–5.

The sestet of the poem restates the issue, with new dashes of metaphor. The poet then asks histrionically, 'Is that time dead?' He won't say for sure, but again he sweetens his offence: he has but touched with Jonathan's rod the honey of romance. The last question is not so much despairing as hopeful. Wilde felt he was superior to both classical and romantic modes, because he could manipulate both: he said in his essay on the English renaissance that this variability was the strength of the new movement in letters to which he belonged. He thought he had physiological as well as artistic support for his method, because 'the desire of any very intensified emotion [is] to be relieved by some emotion that is its opposite.' He shifts therefore from foot to foot in other poems besides '*Hélas!*' 'The Sphinx' begins with a fascinated invocation of the sphinx and ends with a strident rejection of her. Wilde summarizes his state or rather his flow of mind in a letter:

Sometime you will find, even as I have found, that there is no such thing as a romantic experience; there are romantic memories, and there is the desire of romance—that is all. Our most fiery moments of ecstasy are merely shadows of what somewhere else we have felt, or of what we long some day to feel. So at least it seems to me. And, strangely enough, what comes of all this is a curious mixture of ardour and of indifference. I myself would sacrifice everything for a new experience, and I know there is no such thing as a new experience at all. I think I would more readily die for what I do not believe in than for what I hold to be true. I would go to the stake for a sensation and be a sceptic to the last! Only one thing remains infinitely fascinating to me, the mystery of moods. To be master of these moods is exquisite, to be mastered by them more exquisite still. Sometimes I think that the artistic life is a long and lovely suicide, and am not sorry that it is so.

Life then is a willed deliquescence, or more exactly, a progressive surrender of the self to all the temptations appropriate to it.

What Wilde needed was not to avoid the precious occasions

of evil in '*Hélas!*' but to approach more enterprising ones. Yet after his *Poems* appeared in 1881 he was at check for almost six years. He kept busy; he went on a lecture tour for a whole year to America; he returned to England and went lecturing on; he tried unsuccessfully for a post as schools inspector such as Matthew Arnold had; erratically still, he married in 1884 and took up husbanding, begetting two children born in 1885 and 1886. Then in 1887 Wilde began the publications by which he is known. He wrote a volume of stories, and one of fairy tales, then one of criticism, then five plays, besides editing from 1887 to 1889 a magazine, *Woman's World*—a patrician ladies' magazine. It would seem that something roused him from the pseudo-consolidation of marriage and lectures, which were dilettantism for him, to genuine consolidation which seemed dilettantism to others.

This something appears in the original version of *The Picture of Dorian Gray*, published in *Lippincott's Magazine* (July 1890). Wilde emphasizes more there than in the final version the murder of the painter Basil Hallward by Dorian; it is the turning-point in Dorian's experience, a plunge from insinuations of criminal tendency to crime itself. The murder at once protects the secret of his double life and vents his revulsion against the man who wants him innocent still. In *Lippincott's* Wilde specifies: 'It was on the 7th of November, the eve of his own thirty-second birthday, as he often remembered afterwards. . . .' Then when the novel was published as a book, Wilde altered this date: 'It was on the ninth of November, the eve of his own thirty-eighth birthday, as he often remembered afterwards.'

Altering Dorian's age would be gratuitous if Wilde had not attached significance to his own thirty-second year which began in 1886. The passage must have been autobiographical, and such a conjecture receives support from Robert Ross, who boasted that it was he, at the age of seventeen, who in 1886 first seduced Wilde to homosexual practices.[1] (Dorian's Sibyl Vane was also

[1] Wilde also regarded Ross as his first lover, as unpublished evidence confirms.

seventeen.) Wilde evidently considered this sudden alteration of his life a pivotal matter, to be recast as Dorian's murder of Hallward. He himself moved from pasteboard marriage to the expression of long latent proclivities, at some remove from the 'ancient wisdom' and 'austere control' to which he had earlier laid claim as his basic nature. Respectability, always an enemy, was destroyed in his own house. The first work which came out of the new Wilde was, appropriately. 'Lord Arthur Savile's Crime', in which murder is comically enacted and successfully concealed.

From late in the year 1886, then, Wilde was able to think of himself, if he wanted to, as criminal. Up to that time he could always consider himself an innocent misunderstood; now he lived in such a way as to confirm suspicions. Instead of challenging Victorian society only by words, he acted in such a way as to create scandal. Indiscreet by nature, he was indiscreet also by conviction, and he waged his war somewhat openly. He sensed that his new life was a source of literary effect. As he wrote later of Thomas Wainewright: 'His crimes seem to have had an important effect upon his art. They gave a strong personality to his style, a quality that his early work certainly lacked.' He returned to this idea: 'One can fancy an intense personality being created out of sin,' and in 'The Soul of Man Under Socialism,' he thought that 'Crime . . . under certain conditions, may seem to have created individualism.' In 'The Portrait of Mr W. H.' (1889), he made Shakespeare's sonnets depend upon a similarly forbidden love affair, with an actor the same age as Ross. Thomas Mann's Tonio Kröger speaks of a banker who discovers his literary talent by committing a serious crime for which he is put in prison. The artist-criminal is implicit in romantic and symbolistic theories of art, but Wilde anticipates the explicitness on this subject of both Mann and Gide, as he does that of Cavafy in 'Their Beginning' or of Auden in *About the House*:

Time has taught you
　　　　how much inspiration
　　your vices brought you. . . .

Wilde might have discounted the sinfulness of his conduct and
applied to himself his own epigram: 'Wickedness is a myth invented by good people to account for the curious attractiveness
of others.' But he was quite content to think of himself as sinful.

He now succeeded in relating his new discoveries about himself to aesthetic theory. His only formal book of criticism, *Intentions,* has the same secret spring as his later plays and stories.
Ostensibly he is accustomed to say that the spheres of art and of
ethics are absolutely distinct and separate. But occasionally,
overtly or covertly, he states that for the artist crime does pay, by
instilling itself in his content and affecting his form. Each of the
four essays that make up *Intentions* is to some degree subversive,
as if to demonstrate that the intentions of the artist are not
strictly honourable. The first and the last, 'The Decay of
Lying' and 'The Truth of Masks', celebrate art for rejecting
truths, faces, and all that paraphernalia in favour of lies and
masks. Wilde doesn't do this in the romantic way of extolling
the imagination, for while he uses that word he is a little chary
of it; the imagination is itself too natural, too involuntary, for
his view of art. He prefers lying because it sounds more wilful,
because it is no outpouring of the self, but a conscious effort to
mislead. 'All fine imaginative work', Wilde affirms, 'is self-
conscious and deliberate. A great poet sings because he chooses
to sing.' On the other hand, 'if one tells the truth, one is sure,
sooner or later, to be found out!' 'All bad poetry springs from
genuine feeling.' Wilde celebrates art not in the name of Ariel,
as the Romantics would, but in the name of Ananias.[1]

He finds art to have two basic energies, both of them subversive. One asserts its magnificent isolation from experience,
its unreality, its sterility. He would concur with Nabokov that
art is a kind of trick played on nature, an *illicit* creation by man.

[1] But see below, p. 89.

'All art is entirely useless,' Wilde declares. 'Art never expresses anything but itself.' 'Nothing that actually occurs is of the smallest importance.' Form determines content, not content form, a point which Auden also sometimes affirms and which is often assumed by symbolists. With this theory Wilde turns Taine upon his head; the age does not determine what its art should be, rather it is art which gives the age its character. So far from responding to questions posed by the epoch, art offers answers before questions have been asked. 'It is the ages that are her symbols.' Life, straggling after art, seizes upon forms in art to express itself, so that life imitates art rather than art life. '. . . This unfortunate aphorism about Art holding the mirror up to nature, is', according to Wilde, 'deliberately said by Hamlet in order to convince the bystanders of his absolute insanity in all art-matters.' If art be a mirror, we look into it to see—a mask. But more precisely, art is no mirror; it is a 'mist of words', 'a veil'.

Sometimes the veil is pierced. This indifferent conferral of forms upon life by art may have unexpected consequences which implicate art instead of isolating it. In 'The Decay of Lying' Wilde speaks of 'silly boys who, after reading the adventures of Jack Sheppard or Dick Turpin, pillage the stalls of unfortunate applewomen, break into sweetshops at night, and alarm old gentlemen who are returning home from the city by leaping out on them in suburban lanes, with black masks and unloaded revolvers.' In *Dorian Gray* the effect is more sinister; Dorian declares he has been poisoned by a book, and while Lord Henry assures him that art is too aloof to influence anybody, Dorian is felt to be right. Art may then transmit criminal impulses to its audience. Like Whitman, Wilde could and did say, 'Nor will my poems do good only, they will do just as much evil, perhaps more.'

The artist may be criminal and instil his work with criminality. Wilde's second essay in *Intentions* is 'Pen, Pencil and Poison'. He uses Thomas Wainewright as the type of the artist. We need not expect to find a beautiful soul; Wainewright was instead 'a forger of no mean or ordinary capabilities, and . . . a subtle and secret poisoner almost without rival in this or any age.' Among his interesting tastes, Wainewright had 'that curious love of green, which in individuals is always the sign of a subtle artistic temperament, and in nations is said to denote a laxity, if not a decadence of morals.' When a friend reproached him with a murder, he shrugged his shoulders and gave an answer that used to be identified as camp: 'Yes; it was a dreadful thing to do, but she had very thick ankles.' Wilde concludes that 'the fact of a man being a poisoner is nothing against his prose,' and 'there is no essential incongruity between crime and culture.' Wainewright's criminal career turns out to be strictly relevant to his art, fortifying it and giving it character. The quality of that art it is too early to judge, Wilde says, but he clearly believes that Wainewright's personality achieves sufficient criminality to have great artistic promise.

'The Critic as Artist' is the most ambitious of the essays in *Intentions*. It too conveys the notion that art undermines things as they are. The critic is the artist's accomplice in crime, or even masterminds the plot in which they are mutually engaged. Criticism overcomes the tendency of creation to repeat itself; it helps the artist discover unused possibilities. For at bottom, Wilde says, criticism is self-consciousness; it enables us to put our most recent phase at a distance and so go on to another. It disengages us so we may re-engage ourselves in a new way.

From this argument Wilde proceeds to find criticism and self-consciousness to be as necessary as sin. 'What is termed Sin is an essential element of progress'; without it, he holds, the world would stagnate or grow old or become colourless.

By its curiosity [there is Arnold's word with Wilde's meaning], Sin increases the experience of the race. Through its intensified assertion of individualism it saves us from monotony of type. In its rejection of the current notions about morality, it is one with the higher ethics.

By a dexterous transvaluation of words, Wilde makes good and evil exchange places. Even socially sin is far more useful than martyrdom, he says, since it is self-expressive rather than self-repressive. The goal of man is the liberation of personality; when the day of true culture comes, sin will be impossible because the soul will be able to transform

into elements of a richer experience, or a finer susceptibility, or a newer mode of thought, acts or passions that with the common would be commonplace, or with the uneducated ignoble, or with the shameful vile. Is this dangerous? Yes; it is dangerous—all ideas, as I told you, are so.

What muddies this point of view in Wilde is his looking back to conventional meanings of words like sin, ignoble, and shameful. He is not so ready as Nietzsche to transvaluate these, though he does reshuffle them. His private equation is that sin is the perception of new and dangerous possibilities in action as self-consciousness is in thought and criticism is in art. He espouses individualism, and he encourages society to make individualism more complete than it can be now, and for this reason he sponsors socialism as a communal egotism, like the society made up of separate but equal works of art.

Meantime, before socialism, what should be thought of the criminal impulses of the artist? Increasingly in his later writings, Wilde spreads the guilt from the artist to all men. If we are all insincere, masked, and lying, then the artist is prototype rather than exception. If all the sheep are black, then the artist cannot be blamed for not being white. Such an exculpation is implied in three of Wilde's plays after Salome—Lady Windermere's Fan, A Woman of No Importance, An Ideal Husband. Wilde allows his characters to be found guilty, but no guiltier than others, and more courageous in their wrongdoing.

Even as he defends them, he allows them to be mildly punished. Half-consciously, Wilde was preparing himself for another abrupt shift in his experience, such as he had made in 1886.

It would be false to say that Wilde wanted to go to prison, yet the notion had frequently crossed his mind. He had always associated himself with the *poètes maudits*, always considered obloquy a certificate of literary merit. In 'The Soul of Man under Socialism' he had opposed suffering, yet acknowledged that the Russian novelists had rediscovered a great medieval theme, the realization of man through suffering. More particularly, in a review of a new book of poems by Wilfrid Scawen Blunt in 1889, he began: 'Prison has had an admirable effect on Mr. Wilfrid Blunt as a poet.' It was like the effect of crime on Wainewright. Blunt had been merely witty and affected earlier, now his work had more depth. Mr. Balfour must be praised, Wilde says jestingly, since 'by sending Mr. Blunt to gaol . . . [he] has converted a clever rhymer into an earnest and deep-thinking poet.' Six years later, just before his own disgrace, Wilde wrote in 'The Soul of Man under Socialism', 'After all, even in prison a man can be quite free.' These hints indicate that Wilde was prepared, or thought he was, for trial and prison, and expected he would derive artistic profit from them. He had no idea of running away, even on a boyish holiday, whatever his friends might say. Instead he accepted imperial authority as readily as Christ had done—a precedent he discovered for himself, though hardly the first or last in hot water to do so. Blunt's poems written in prison were called *In Vinculis*, and Wilde's letter to Douglas from prison, which we know by Ross's title as *De Profundis*, was originally entitled by Wilde *Epistola: In Carcere et Vinculis*.

Hélas! Wilde's literary career was not transmogrified by prison as he hoped, but his experiences there, which were so much worse than he anticipated, gave him his final theme. '*La prison m'a complètement changé*,' he said to Gide at Berneval; '*je comptais sur elle pour cela*.' As before, he made no effort to exonerate himself by saying that his sins were venial or not sins at all. Defences of homosexual or 'Uranian' love were common enough at this period; except once at his trial, he did not make

them. But he reached for the main implication of his disgrace
through a double negative; though men thought he was unlike
them, he was *not*. He was a genuine scapegoat.

This ultimate conception of himself was never put into an
essay, but it is involved in his *De Profundis* letter to Douglas,
and in *The Ballad of Reading Gaol*. Both are predictably full of
imagery of Christ. Before this Wilde had depreciated pity as a
motive in art; now he embraced it. The hero of his poem is a
man who has murdered his mistress and is about to be hanged
for his crime. Wilde identifies himself closely with this prisoner.
The poem's tenor is that the prisoners are humanity, all of whom
are felons:

> Yet each màn kills the thing he loves,
>   By each let this be heard,
> Some do it with a bitter look,
>   Some with a flattering word,
> The coward does it with a kiss,
>   The brave man with a sword! . . .
>
> Some love too little, some too long,
>   Some sell, and others buy;
> Some do the deed with many tears,
>   And some without a sigh:
> For each man kills the thing he loves,
>   Yet each man does not die.

This poem was chosen for the *Oxford Book of Modern Verse*
by Yeats, but he removed what he regarded as the commentary,
including these stanzas. His effort to improve the poem evokes
sympathy; it must be said, however, that whatever the quality
of the bare narrative that Yeats prints, for Wilde—as for D. H.
Lawrence and most readers—the commentary was the excessive
and yet determining part of the poem. During the six years before his imprisonment he had demonstrated first that the artist
was basically and usefully criminal, and second that criminality
was not confined to artists, but was to be found as commonly
among members of the Cabinet. Where most men pretend to a

virtue they don't have, the artist, fully aware of his own sins, takes on those they don't acknowledge. The purpose of sin has subtly shifted in Wilde's mind—it is no longer a means for the artist of extending the boundaries of action, it is a means for him to focus and enshrine guilt. He has the courage, exceptional among men, of looking into the heart of things and finding there not brotherly love so much as murder, not self-love so much as suicide. In recognizing the universality of guilt he is like Christ; in revealing his own culpability he plays the role of his own Judas. Wilde, who had written in one of his poems ('Humanidad') that we are ourselves 'the lips betraying and the life betrayed', had in fact brought about his own conviction. The result was that he was remarried to the society from which he had divorced himself; he was no outcast, for he accepted and even sought the punishment which other men, equally guilty, would only submit to vicariously through him, just as all the prisoners suffer with the doomed murderer. By means of submission and suffering he gives his life a new purpose, and writes over the palimpsest once again.

In this concern with social role Wilde has clearly moved away from Pater, and perhaps we can conceive of him as moving towards another writer, Jean Genet. Genet is of course ferocious and remorseless in a way that Wilde was not, and makes much less concession to the world. But the two men share an insistence on their own criminality and on a possible sanction for it. The comparison with Christ has been irresistible for both. As Genet says in *The Thief's Journal*:

Let us ignore the theologians. 'Taking upon Himself the sins of the world' means exactly this: experiencing potentially and in their effects all sins: it means having subscribed to evil. Every creator must thus shoulder—the expression seems feeble—must make his own, to the point of knowing it to be his substance, circulating in his arteries, the evil given by him, which his heroes choose freely.

Wilde in *De Profundis* remembered having remarked to Gide

that 'there was nothing that . . . Christ had said that could not be transferred immediately into the sphere of Art, and there find its complete fulfilment.' And again, Genet speaks like Wilde of the courage required to do wrong, saying: 'If he has courage, the guilty man decides to be what crime has made him.' He wishes to obtain 'the recognition of evil'. Both writers envisage a regeneration which can come only from total assumption of their proclivities and their lot; as Genet puts it:

I shall destroy appearances, the casings will burn away and one evening I shall appear there, in the palm of your hand, quiet and pure, like a glass statuette. You will see me. Round about me there will be nothing left.

Wilde summons for this sacred moment a red rose growing from the hanged man's mouth, a white one from his heart. He had terrified André Gide by trying to persuade that strictly reared young man to authorize evil,[1] as to some extent in the *acte gratuit* Gide did, and it is just such authorization that Genet asserts with more fierceness than Wilde.

In his criticism and in his work generally, Wilde balanced two ideas which, we have observed, look contradictory. One is that art is disengaged from actual life, the other that it is deeply incriminated with it. The first point of view is sometimes taken by Yeats, though only to qualify it, the second without qualification by Genet. That art is sterile, and that it is infectious, are attitudes not beyond reconciliation. Wilde never formulated their union, but he implied something like this: by its creation of beauty art reproaches the world, calling attention to the world's faults through their very omission; so the sterility of art is an affront or a parable. Art may also outrage the world by flouting its laws or by picturing indulgently their violation. Or art may seduce the world by making it follow an example which

[1] See below p. 100.

seems bad but is discovered to be better than it seems. In these various ways the artist forces the world towards self-recognition, with at least a tinge of self-redemption.

Yet this ethical or almost ethical view of art co-exists in Wilde with its own cancellation. He could write *Salome* with one hand, dwelling upon incest and necrophilia, and show them as self-defeated, punished by execution and remorse. With the other hand, he could dissolve by the critical intellect all notions of sin and guilt. He does so in *The Importance of Being Earnest,* which is all insouciance where *Salome* is all incrimination. In *The Importance of Being Earnest* sins which are presented as accursed in *Salome* and unnameable in *Dorian Gray* are translated into a different key, and appear as Algernon's inordinate and selfish craving for—cucumber sandwiches. The substitution of mild gluttony for fearsome lechery renders all vice harmless. There *is* a wicked brother, but he is just our old friend Algernon. The double life which is so serious a matter for Dorian or for The Ideal Husband, becomes a harmless Bunburying, or playing Jack in the country and Ernest in town. In the earlier, four-act version of the play, Wilde even parodied punishment, by having a bailiff come to take Jack to Holloway Prison (as Wilde himself was soon to be taken) not for homosexuality, but for running up food bills at the Savoy. Jack is disinclined, he says, to be imprisoned in the suburbs for dining in town, and makes out a cheque. The notion of expiation is also mocked; as Cecily observes: 'They have been eating muffins. That looks like repentance.' Finally, the theme of regeneration is parodied in the efforts of Ernest and Jack to be baptized. (By the way, in the earlier version Prism is also about to be baptized, and someone comments, 'To be born again would be of considerable advantage to her.') The ceremonial unmasking at the play's end, which had meant death for Dorian Gray, leaves everyone barefaced for a new puppet show, that of matrimony. Yet amusing as it all is, much of the comedy derives from Wilde's own sense of the realities of what are being mocked. He was in only momentary refuge from his more usual cycle which ran from scapegrace to scapegoat.

During his stay in prison Wilde took up the regeneration theme in *De Profundis* and after being freed he resumed it in *The Ballad of Reading Gaol*. But he was too self-critical not to find the notion of rebirth a little preposterous. When his friends complained of his resuming old habits, he said, 'A patriot put in prison for loving his country loves his country, and a poet in prison for loving boys loves boys.' But to write about himself as unredeemed, unpunished, unreborn, to claim that his sins were nothing, that his form of love was more noble than most other people's, that what had happened to him was the result merely of legal obtuseness, was impossible for Wilde. So long as he had been a scapegrace the door to comedy was still open; once having accepted the role of scapegoat the door was closed. He conceived of a new play, but it was in his earlier mode and he could not write it. Cramped to one myth, and that sombre and depleted, Wilde could not extricate himself. There was nothing to do but die, which accordingly he did. But not without one final assertion of a past enthusiasm: he allowed himself to be converted to Catholicism the night before his death.

5 Corydon and Ménalque

Most literary transactions of the nineteenth century, say those of Stendhal and Byron, or of Baudelaire and Poe, were conducted entirely through print. But André Gide, in his association with Wilde, had the advantage of dealing with the living man rather than only with books. This was perhaps as well, because Gide did not much care for Wilde's writings,[1] and told him so, receiving in reply Wilde's famous *mot*, 'Would you like to know the great drama of my life? I have put my genius into my life; I have put only my talent into my works.' But in fact the distinction between Wilde's life and works could not be so finely drawn: his writings plagiarized from his conversation, and his conversation from his writings.

During seven years Gide and Wilde had five spurts of acquaintance. They first met about 26 November 1891, by which time Wilde had turned thirty-seven and Gide was barely twenty-two. We know almost too well the schedule of their meetings, which occurred nearly every day, often for hours on end, during three weeks. The second one was at the poet Hérédia's, on the 28th. Then Pierre Louÿs, at Gide's request, arranged a small dinner for Wilde at the Café d'Harcourt (Place

[1] Even in later life, Gide lamely defended Wilde's plays as covert revelations of his psychology (*Journal, 1889–1939* (Paris, 1941), 389). Earlier, his comments on Wilde's writings had been so contemptuous that Proust, himself no Wilde fan, had urged him to modify them.

de la Sorbonne) on the 29th, probably with Stuart Merrill making a fourth. Perhaps at Wilde's counter-invitation, Gide met him again at five o'clock next day; the two men dined with Stuart Merrill on the 2nd December, with Marcel Schwob at Aristide Bruant's on the 3rd. These were presumably some of the three-hour dinners at which, according to Gide in a letter to Valéry of December 1891, Wilde talked so well he seemed to be Baudelaire or Villiers. On the 6th they were at the house of Princess Ouroussoff, who claimed—in the midst of one of Wilde's verbal flights—that she saw a halo round his head. To follow out this social calendar doggedly, there was dinner for Gide and Wilde at Schwob's on the 7th, at Bruant's again on the 8th. Gide's daybook records (says Jean Delay) the single name 'Wilde' in large letters for the 11th and 12th; on the 13th Princess Ouroussoff entertained them both again for dinner, along with Henri de Régnier; and on the 15th Gide and Schwob met with Wilde once more, after which Gide went to the country to visit relations, and Wilde, a few days later, went back to London. For Wilde this social round was almost routine, but for Gide it was a complete change; ordinarily he did not frequent either the Café d'Harcourt or Aristide Bruant's, and did not meet so many people in a year.

The second phase of their acquaintance was more clouded— a brief and unexpected encounter in Florence in May 1894. Gide, convalescing from illness, bumped into Wilde accompanied by Lord Alfred Douglas. Their liaison was already notorious, so in his correspondence with Paul Valéry Gide said nothing of the meeting until several weeks later, and then identified Douglas only as *'un autre poète d'une génération plus nouvelle'*. He did not want to be talked about; in particular he feared the merciless teasing of Pierre Louÿs,[1] who (as much from jealousy as distaste) had broken with Wilde over the

---

[1] Louÿs had already begun a series of practical jokes, such as addressing a letter to Mademoiselle Andrée Gide, which implied his suspicions about Gide's sexual orientation.

Douglas attachment,[1] and would have expected him to do likewise. It seemed to Gide that Wilde was far from pleased to see him this time, an attitude he attributed to Wilde's wish not to be recognized on an amorous excursion. It is possible too that Wilde was less pleased with Gide's company than Gide with his. None the less, he gave him two vermouths and told him four stories and, being about to vacate after two weeks a flat he had taken for a month, he offered it to Gide, who accepted.

The acquaintance was resumed in Algeria in January of the following year, the year of Wilde's downfall. Gide was in Blidah, where he had gone presumably to be titillated (but at a discreet distance) by Arab boys. He was checking out of his hotel to go back to Algiers when he suddenly noticed the names of Wilde and Douglas on the register. His first impulse was to leave more quickly. He even set off for the station on foot, carrying his bags, but thought better of it, as he relates, and brought them back again. The three men met and spent the evening together; Gide went on to Algiers next day. He was joined there by Wilde, momentarily on the outs with Douglas. On 30 January occurred the most dramatic moment of their relationship. Wilde took Gide to a café, where Gide was captivated by a young Arab boy playing the flute. Outside Wilde asked him, 'Dear, *vous voulez le petit musicien?*' and Gide, in 'the most choked of voices', said yes. Wilde burst into laughter and made the arrangements. Gide had previously had only one homosexual experience, but he now felt that he had discovered what was normal for him. The next morning Wilde left for England, and as it turned out, for obloquy and prison.

---

[1] Louÿs had been in London from May to July 1892, and on that occasion was indulgent to the male homosexuals whom he met, finding their manners courtly. He would later write about Lesbianism with equal or greater indulgence. But the liaison of Wilde with Douglas was evidently too flagrant for his tastes, and he told Wilde that a choice must be made between Douglas's friendship and his own. When Wilde refused to change his ways, Louÿs would have nothing more to do with him, and Wilde said sadly, '*Je voulais avoir un ami; je n'aurai plus que des amants.*' (Gide, *Si le grain ne meurt, Œuvres Complètes* (Paris, 1932–9) X, 408.)

Following his release from prison, in 1897, he went to Berne-val, and there received an unannounced visit from Gide on 19 June. After that, since both men were living mostly in Paris, it might be supposed that they met often, but in fact Gide mentions only two encounters, both in 1898. Wilde was said to be going downhill, and Gide had completed his apprenticeship. They met the first time by accident, and Gide's instant fear of being compromised was only too patent. Wilde insisted that they not hide behind a pillar; he paid grandly for the drinks, then took Gide aside to say, '*Je suis absolument sans ressources.*' Another meeting was followed by a letter of 10 December asking Gide for 200 francs; a letter of 14 December indicates that the money was given. Two years later Wilde relieved Gide of possible future importunities by dying. This then is the skeletal history of what was, as I shall try to indicate, a momentous association.

That Gide, in the early days of their friendship, was over-whelmed by Wilde is certified by many sources. The writer Jules Renard, who as a man with a beard found the clean-shaven faces of both Gide and Wilde offensive (he emphasizes, in separate descriptions, that each was '*imberbe*'), met Gide at Marcel Schwob's on 23 December just after Wilde had left Paris. He thought the young Gide was in love with Wilde. But Gide's inclinations, as they clarified themselves later, were unequivo-cally for boys, not men of middle age. As for Wilde, he liked Gide, but apparently preferred the company of Louÿs and of Schwob, whose help he solicited for his play in French, *Salome*. Yet if their relations did not crystallize into love, some other process occurred which was vital to Gide although in all his reminiscences he never made it quite clear.

The relation between them was probably very much like that described in *The Picture of Dorian Gray*, between Dorian and Lord Henry Wotton. 'To project one's soul into some gracious form, and let it tarry there for a moment; to hear one's own intellectual views echoed back with all the added music of passion and youth; to convey one's temperament into another as though it were a subtle fluid or a strange perfume; there was a real joy in that. . . .' It has sometimes been said that Wilde was describing here his relation with Douglas, but the writing of the novel—most of it anyway—antedated his meeting with Douglas. Dorian Gray is based rather on Lucien de Rubempré of Balzac; their last names rhyme and their first names resemble each other, just as Lord Henry's surname Wotton seems to be an anglicized version of Lucien's seducer, Vautrin. (Wilde said, 'One of the greatest tragedies of my life is the death of Lucien de Rubempré,' a remark for which he was reproved by Proust in *A la Recherche du temps perdu*.) The seduction of Lucien's mind by Vautrin in a diligence *en route* from the country to Paris in *Illusions perdues* is marked by a good deal of byplay over cigars, which Wilde transposes into cigarettes in his own book. In effect, Wilde spiritually seduced Gide or—what comes to the same thing—Gide chose to feel he had done so. Until that time Gide had gone through life in a dream, like a sleepwalker. Now he suddenly woke up to find himself on a sloping roof. It was well to have an outside agent to blame, or to thank. He did not need to have been a close student of Goethe, though he was one, to rejoice at finding somebody to play Mephisto to his Faust or Faust to his Margarete, and Wilde was just in time to take the job.

The stages in this seduction are marked in Gide's correspondence and journal. At first he was simply dazzled: in a letter of 28 November 1891, to Paul Valéry, he describes meeting 'l'*esthète* Oscar Wilde' along with others, and then comments, '*O, admirable, admirable, celui-là.*' But the tone quickly changes as he chooses to find himself imperilled. A week later he represents Wilde as besieging him, and tells Valéry (4 December), 'Wilde contrives piously to kill what remains to me of soul, because he says that to know an essence, one must suppress it; he wants me to miss my soul. The effort to destroy a thing takes its measure. Everything constitutes itself only by being rendered void . . . etc.'

This idea was good enough for Gide to restate it five years later in *Les Nourritures terrestres,* where he declares, '. . . on certain evenings I was mad enough almost to believe in my soul, I felt it so near escaping from my body.' He adds scrupulously, 'Ménalque said this too.' And in 1924 (24 August), in his journal for *Les Faux-Monnayeurs,* he writes, 'we name things only when we are breaking with them' and then adds that this 'formula . . . may well presage a new departure.' In fact, his notion in that book, that the devil should circulate in it incognito, his reality growing stronger the less the other characters believe in him, is like a corollary to Wilde's theorem. Beyond the evocation of a rather stagey devil, Gide's remarks reflect his eagerness to abandon the idea of a self which should be sequential and predictable, and to accept fits and starts as his natural medium.

When Wilde had left Paris in 1891, Gide almost ceased to write letters—a sure sign of turmoil in this relentless correspondent. After an interval he communicated with Valéry, 'Forgive my being silent: since Wilde I only exist a little.' He was conscious of something gone out of him, out of his existence, out of his innocence. This feeling of being 'devirginated', and too easily, persisted, and stirred in him some resentment. (Wilde was probably also fatigued by this quick spiritual takeover.) Gide begins his journal of 1 January 1892, two weeks after his last encounter with Wilde, by a solemn verdict: 'Wilde, I believe, did me nothing but harm. In his company I had lost the habit of thinking. I had more varied emotions, but had forgotten how to bring order into them.' He plunged back with relief into his readings in philosophy. The damage was evidently not permanent. Paul Valéry had anticipated as much by joking about Wilde, even when Gide was enraptured, as a 'symbolic mouth *à la* Redon which swallows a mouthful and mechanically transforms it at once into a satanic aphorism.'

Those who knew Gide well discovered behind his apparent timidity and awkwardness a good deal of resilience. At the very moment he appeared to be most swayed by someone, he was most likely to defect. This was the experience of Paul Claudel who fancied he had brought Gide to the verge of conversion to Catholicism, only to read with consternation *Les Caves du Vatican* with an epigraph from *L'Annonce faite à Marie* in the latest *Nouvelle Revue française*. Gide knew this tendency in himself and called it *se déprendre*—casting loose.

The image of Wilde as spiritual seducer was typed in Gide's mind. In artistic retrospect, at least, it suited him to think of Wilde, or of Wildism, as diabolic. In his autobiography, *Si le grain ne meurt*, Gide prefaces the brilliant section that recounts his meeting with Wilde in Algeria by saying, 'it has occurred to me lately that an actor of considerable importance—the Devil—may well have played a part in the drama. . . .' Of course one of the joys of the autobiographer is that he can disport with what Beckett calls 'the ethical yoyo', a prop much less detectable in the original proceedings, and some of this diabolism is after the fact. But that he had experienced from the start such an intimation is indicated not only by his statements in 1891, but by a letter to his mother sent from Algeria in 1894, in part with the object—now becoming habitual with him—of alarming her. He has just met again, he says, Oscar Wilde, 'that terrifying man, the most dangerous product of modern civilization—always, as in Florence, escorted by the young Lord Douglas, both of them on the index in London and Paris, and, if this place were not so remote, the most compromising company one could have.' Of Douglas he comments, 'Impossible to know the value of this young Lord, whom Wilde seems to have depraved down to his marrow—after the fashion of a much more terrifying Vautrin (I find) than Père Goriot's—because he does everything under the pretext of aestheticism.' The notion that Wilde had depraved Alfred Douglas is ludicrous—the opposite is more plausible, since Douglas was already being blackmailed by male prostitutes when he and Wilde became friends—but Gide's eagerness to find another in the same plight as he might be himself prompted this misjudgement. His description of Wilde's uproarious and unstoppable laughter when Gide agreed to take on the flute-player seems intended to make it infernal: 'He enjoyed his joke like a child and like a devil.' The truth is more likely to have been less theatrical, that Wilde found Gide prissy—as he was (that very afternoon he had informed Wilde that if they should meet in London or Paris he would not recognize him). Gide did not see that joke. On the other hand, he concealed from Wilde a counter-joke, that he had already had a homosexual experience with an Arab boy; so he had the unsmiling satisfaction of pretending to an innocence he did not possess. If Wilde was the Devil, Gide saw fit to flatter him.

I would suggest then that Gide sustained, and never quite abandoned, a view of Wilde as Luciferian, debauched and debauching. He describes how Wilde, like Ménalque 'insolent with wealth', threw money to the Arab boys who pursued him around Algiers and then boasted, *'J'espère . . . avoir bien démoralisé cette ville.'* Gide found him shocking. Wilde's prodigalities of expression, or of expenditure, became pronunciamentos, to be discountenanced. But after Wilde's fall in 1895, it was impossible to keep whole-heartedly to this view of him. Gide's visit to Berneval must have been motivated in the main by Gide's inveterate curiosity: was Wilde still throning it now he was in hell? Gide must have been astonished to find the ne'er-do-well turned into the suffer-all, no longer victimizer but victim. Still, further meetings even with Christ might be embarrassing. The sight of Wilde in Paris some months later made Gide look for cover. It took him much of his life to compromise himself, as if the most copious disclosure of his own propensities might expiate his earlier reluctance to accept Wilde's without blushing.

When Gide wrote his first memorial essay on Wilde a year after the latter's death, he gave a memorable picture of his friend, but skirted the central issue of their relationship. Not only did he omit the flute-player in Algiers, he also omitted any account of the meeting in Florence when Wilde had given him his flat on the Arno. This act of indifferent bounty lacked the quality of 'theatre', and was also incompatible with diabolism: the devil offers fair words but never shelter. Yet Gide remembered this flat (from which after a brief stay he transferred to a *pensione*) well enough to set a scene in *Les Nourritures terrestres* in it. I suspect that the history of their friendship could have been written quite differently, with less pride before Wilde's fall and less fall after the pride. Greek tragedy is hard to resist. It appears also that Gide sometimes misinterprets Wilde, as when he reports the comment Wilde made to him at Berneval about *Les Nourritures terrestres:* 'Listen, dear, you've got to make me a promise now. *Les Nourritures terrestres* is good . . . it's very good. . . . But dear, promise me: from now on don't write *I* any more . . . In art, don't you see, there is no first person.' Gide interpreted this to mean that the artist should always wear a mask, and contrasted his own pursuit of sincerity. But that this was not Wilde's sense of it is demonstrated by a letter to Douglas written by Wilde at the same time: 'André Gide's book fails to fascinate me. The egoistic note is, of course, and always has been to me, the primal and ultimate note of modern art, but *to be an Egoist one must have an Ego*. It is not everyone who says, "I, I" who can enter the Kingdom of Art.' He thought Gide was lacking not in mask but in what lay beneath the mask, in flamboyant selfhood, and was therefore unable to achieve the symbolic relation to his age which true egoists like Byron and Wilde had attained. Perhaps, however, he was understood by Gide better than he allowed, since Gide speaks regretfully later of a 'complaisance towards myself' which he felt he had exhibited in *André Walter,* and commends Goethe for the way in which the 'I' in Goethe's work 'at once magnifies itself'. A thinness in the visionary speaker of *Les Nourritures terrestres,* and a resultant loss in persuasiveness, suggest that Wilde was right.

Gide never said explicitly what evangel Wilde had imparted to him, but in the character Ménalque, who appears in both

Les Nourritures terrestres and *L'Immoraliste,* there is clearly a bow
of sorts to Wilde, though an ironic one, especially in the later
book. The narrator feels for Ménalque more than friendship,
but less than love. Ménalque is a man who no longer lives under
the old dispensation. Rather than being dissolute, he is uncon-
strained. Gide represents him as much older, and I may mention
that each time he met Wilde he noted how terribly he had aged
since their last encounter. The section about Ménalque was
published in the review *L'Ermitage* before the rest of *Les Nourritures terrestres.* and in the earlier version Ménalque was approxi-
mately Wilde's age; in the later version Gide heaped on another
decade, perhaps to qualify the allusion. Ménalque is a grandfather then, but a newborn one, an elderly apostle of youthful
sensation. If Wilde recognized this very unsmiling portrait of
himself, he gave no hint. Wilde's main influence on the book
came from his faith in himself as bearer of a new gospel to be
transmitted above all to the young; Gide took over this role for
his own; it is he who tutors Nathanaël, and Ménalque is rele-
gated to the lesser part of precursor.

Besides this fictional transformation of Wilde, Gide wrote
about him non-fictionally many times. In 1905 he was prompted
by the posthumous appearance of *De Profundis,* which gave an
image obverse to that of Wilde as tempter, to write a second
memorial essay. It also spurred him to his defence of homosexuality as more natural, besides being more rewarding, than
heterosexuality, in *Corydon,* which he began about 1908 and
published three years later. In the same way, his reading of
Alfred Douglas's *Oscar Wilde and Myself* in 1918 was a spur to
writing his autobiography so he could 'unmask' Douglas. Gide's
finest tribute to Wilde may however be not what he published,
distinguished though that is, but the fact that he cut out of his
journal the pages which dealt with the first three weeks of their
friendship. The main document about the psychic possession
of Gide by Wilde is therefore a missing one—a truly symbolist
piece of evidence. Mallarmé used to speak of the flower which

should be '*L'Absente de tous bouquets*', and the obliterated section of Gide's journal is the Absent of all documents. We know it, as Wilde said we might know the soul, by its having been eliminated.

I want to speculate on exactly what Wilde's message to Gide may have been, and why it had so disturbing an effect. It is easy to be deceived—one might suppose that the regress in *Les Faux-Monnayeurs*, frame within frame within frame, might have had its inception in similar manœuvring in Wilde's narrative, 'The Portrait of Mr. W.H.' But already in *Les Cahiers d'André Walter*, before he knew Wilde's work, Gide had posed an author writing about an author. Much in common between the two men comes from their equal saturation in a literary movement which sought, by imbedding symbol within symbol and perspective within perspective, to reach 'the mind's native land', as Mallarmé called it. Yet speculation about the missing pages is possible, and need not be too risky, since we have Gide's formal essays on Wilde which, for all their evasions, are highly informative, and we have one remark from their conversation which Wilde himself recorded. There are, besides, the works of Wilde and Gide written at about this time. No doubt much of what passed between them was unspoken, a matter of assumptions, of smiles, of calculated disdain or indifference, of exclusion. The subject of homosexuality, for example, was not mentioned —Gide attests—although it must have been at least as present behind the scenes as the Devil in *Les Faux-Monnayeurs*.

In trying to reconstruct the missing pages of Gide's journal, or some of the points recorded in them, one is helped by remembering the atmosphere in which the two men met. For Wilde the year 1891 had been glorious, the more so because his life had not always been like that. For some time after he went down from Oxford in 1878, he had remained on the periphery of literature, lecturing to Americans, publishing lush verses, reviewing bad books, attending openings, a dandy, a man about town, a target of *Punch*, a near-bankrupt, high-living from hand to mouth. It was not until after 1886 that Wilde found his theme,

as a direct sequel to a homosexual affair—his first—in that year
with Robert Ross.[1] The effect on Wilde was in fact much the
same as the effect of homosexuality on Gide: it gave both men a
secret life, a hidden message, and a motive to seek more radical
ideas, more adventurous modes. It was only much later, in the
1920s, that Gide would make his secret history public, and
would emphasize that Wilde never did as much.

Yet Wilde was daring enough to court public disfavour. In
April he published his novel, *The Picture of Dorian Gray*, much
expanded from its serial form. Although Gide disclaimed
knowledge at this time of Wilde's works, his journal for 3
January 1892 contains this entry: 'Our whole life is spent in
sketching an ineradicable portrait of ourselves . . . we flatter
ourselves; but later our terrible portrait will not flatter us. We
recount our lives and lie to ourselves, but our life will not lie;
it will recount our soul, which will stand before God in its
usual posture.' If Gide had not read *Dorian Gray*, at least he knew
the plot. In May of 1891 Wilde published *Intentions*, and promulgated many heterodox doctrines, including the central,
anti-Aristotelian one (quoted by Gide repeatedly afterwards)
that nature imitates art, not art nature. Wilde also made in April
a surprising incursion into political thought with 'The Soul of
Man under Socialism'. In December 1891 his *Lady Windermere's
Fan*—with its rebuff to puritans—was in rehearsal. At the very
time that he and Gide were meeting in Paris, also, he was
writing his scandalous new play, *Salome,* which, he joked, would
establish him as a French author. Sometime during this year
Wilde met Alfred Douglas and, at the time he met Gide, he was
about to begin a romance that, in the annals of homosexual love,
occupies a position like that of Yeats and Maud Gonne (which
had begun two years earlier) in heterosexual history. Wilde
amused Henri de Régnier by saying that he had been married
three times, once to a woman and twice to men. This marriage,
with Douglas, was to be his last.

[1] See above pp. 69–70.

The Wilde that Gide met had then sorted out his world. If he took no single stand on the great entities which were the subject of his talk, such as religion, art, life, that was because as a disciple of Pater he had learned the danger of rigidity. He knew, however, how to bend them to express his personality. One must be '*disponible*' (available), as Gide was to say. He experienced no difficulty, for example, in being a symbolist (he praised Mallarmé and got praised back) and a socialist at the same time, any more than he experienced difficulty in admiring Pater and Ruskin together, though one was all infection and the other all contraception. To turn words upon their heads was to overturn the state.

Gide, for his part, could have no such feeling of having arrived, even if he had published his first book and had like Wilde won Mallarmé's admiration. Religion, art, and life were for him three perplexities. In literature, for example, he aspired to be to the novel what Mallarmé was to poetry and Maeterlinck to drama. But secretly he was defecting from symbolism and would begin to satirize the movement as too self-contained. His first book, *Les Cahiers d'André Walter,* was a symbolist one, and like Villiers's *Axël,* depicted its lovers edging over from matter to spirit. It ended with the death of the beloved and the madness and death of the lover. Gide's secret hope—which seems rather absurd now—was that it would persuade his cousin Madeleine Rondeaux to marry him, but she had no sooner read it than she flatly refused. The transfiguration of the flesh on which the book kept verging did not appear to her to promise connubial felicity. Nor was the book entirely to his own taste. He was impelled in his next work to satirize symbolism under the aspect of Narcissus in *Le Traité du Narcisse,* which he published just at the time of his first meetings with Wilde. His Narcissus is obliged to accept image over act, when he would prefer act over image.

If Wilde read Gide on Narcissus, he probably found this fable precious. At any rate, he told him his own. (Most symbolist writers began with narcissi and ended with roses, like T. S. Eliot after them.) According to Wilde,

When Narcissus died, the flowers of the field were desolate and asked the river for some drops of water to weep for him. 'Oh!' answered the river, 'if all my drops of water were tears, I should not have enough to weep for Narcissus myself. I loved him.' 'Oh!' replied the flowers of the field, 'how could you not have loved Narcissus? He was beautiful.' 'Was he beautiful?' said the river. 'And who should know better than you? Each day, leaning over your bank, he beheld his beauty in your waters.' 'If I loved him,' replied the river, 'it was because, when he leaned over my waters, I saw the reflection of my waters in his eyes.'

The name of this story, said Wilde, was 'The Disciple'. The point was that there are no disciples—a sharp lesson from the master. People are suns, not moons.

Wilde's conquest of Gide was partly by parable. But he had precepts as well. He must have turned quickly to religion as soon as he realized that Gide was of Huguenot ancestry. He would complain later to Alfred Douglas that Gide was a French Protestant, and that, he said, is the worst kind, except of course for the Irish Protestant. But Irish Protestantism, at least in Dublin, had long since spent its force. (Once Arthur Balfour asked Wilde his religion and Wilde replied, 'Well, you know, I don't think I have any. I am an Irish Protestant.') Wilde thought Gide still dominated by inhibitions that sprang from his religious training. He complained of Gide's lips that they were too straight and therefore supplied further confirmation of a puritan temperament. I suspect that Wilde broached the subject of religion to Gide in 1891, as he had broached it to Bernard Berenson a year before, by saying, 'Tell me at once. Are you living with the Twenty Commandments?' The reason I think he said this or something like it is that in *Les Nourritures terrestres* Gide begins one section with the question, 'God's commandments, are there ten of you or twenty?' Nothing could have so completely pervaded Gide's consciousness as the disclosure that the Biblical terrain, on which he and his ancestors had trod so confidently, was mined with boobytraps.

If, as is likely, Wilde was apprised of Gide's domination by his mother, and by her piety, he would have quoted now, as he did in 'The Soul of Man under Socialism', Christ's question, 'Who is my mother?' Gide, in his developing filial revolt, would favour a comparable quotation, 'Woman, what have I to do with thee?' More to the point, Wilde approached Gide at a party at Hérédia's and asked, 'Would you like me to tell you a secret? . . . but promise me not to tell it to anyone. . . . Do you know why Christ did not love his mother?' He paused. 'It's because she was a virgin!' To Gide, himself a virgin and destined to remain one for another year, the idea that purity might be monstrous could not fail to cause some agitation. Up to now under his mother's thumb, he began to behave towards her with calculated ferocity, hinting, with less and less disguise, at the homosexuality which he knew she would abhor. The conviction of Wilde may well have been for her the moment of total disclosure. Jean Delay suggests that it killed her.

Gide discussed Wilde's attitude towards Christianity in the first essay he wrote after Wilde's death. He somewhat misrepresents Wilde there, and his version has been accepted too unquestioningly. Gide declares that Wilde posed pagan naturalism against Christian miracles so as to put Christianity out of countenance. If Wilde had done only this, he would be doing no more than Swinburne. But the examples Gide gives require a different interpretation: Wilde generally prolongs the scene of the miracle, and adds a new fiction and further meaning to the original. It is a fifth gospel, the gospel according to Saint Thomas, as he says of Renan's life of Jesus. For example, in Wilde's version of the raising of Lazarus, Christ comes upon a young man weeping and asks why. The man replies, 'Lord, I was dead and you brought me back to life. What else should I do but weep?' This is not pagan naturalism, but the novelist amending—as Yeats would say—'What was told awry/By some peasant gospeller.' Gide forgets he is borrowing from Wilde when, in his autobiography, he speaks of 'that kind of abominable anguish that Lazarus must have felt after his escape from the tomb.' His own play about King Saul, which was the first of his works to interest Wilde much, was a similar extension, and variant, of Biblical narrative, in this case by depicting Saul as in love with David. Gide understandably preferred not to think of Wilde's method as being so close to his own as it in fact was. Once he had received the initial impetus, he had no need for further tutelage, and could vie with Wilde in rewriting both Testaments to take account of homosexuality.

Yet Wilde had something else to propose, something even more useful to Gide, a way of bridging the divide between art and life, and so of allaying the dissatisfaction of Narcissus with a world of images rather than of acts. By this theory the artist sets forth models of experience which people rush to try out. And as his supreme artist Wilde had the ingenious idea of naming Christ. For Christ urged others to live artistically, and lived artistically himself. 'His entire life is the most wonderful of poems,' Wilde said. 'He is just like a work of art himself.' Gide's journal contains a note written the month after he had first come to know Wilde, and it reads, 'A man's life is his image.' In Wilde's work this is a habitual theme, in Gide's it is a new one.

That Wilde did talk in this vein to Gide is also confirmed by De Profundis, where Wilde remarks, 'I remember once saying to André Gide, as we sat together in some Paris café, that while Metaphysics had but little interest for me, and Morality absolutely none, there was nothing that either Plato or Christ had said that could not be transferred immediately into the sphere of Art, and there find its complete fulfilment. It was a generalisation as profound as it was novel.' For Gide, a young man bent upon the exculpation of his instincts yet addicted to Biblical quotation, this idea was like an explosive device. In 1893 he writes in his journal, 'Christ's saying is just as true in art: "Whosoever will save his life (his personality) shall lose it." ' He proceeded with this translation of Christianity to a higher level, and even projected a book to be entitled, *Christianisme contre le Christ*. Wilde also, if he had lived, might well have taken over Christianity as he took over socialism; to one of his friends he projected a book that would rescue his religion from its adherents and be, as he said, 'the Epic of the Cross, the Iliad of Christianity'.

To some extent he carried out this plan, first in 'The Soul of Man under Socialism', and then in his *De Profundis* letter. In the first, Wilde insisted that Christ taught the importance of the individual and, a Pater before the fact, urged total self-expression. 'Know thyself!' was written over the portal of the antique world . . . the message of Christ to man was simply, 'Be thyself.' In *Les Nourritures terrestres*, Gide similarly insists that 'Know thyself' is 'a maxim as pernicious as it is ugly', a phrase which itself suggests Wilde's aesthetic-ethical blend. 'Whoever observes himself arrests his development.' The family and personal property, being impediments to self-expression, must go. Gide was willing to be rid of his mother (as Wilde was not) and to spend his inheritance, as Wilde would have done if only he had had one. Wilde held that art 'is the most intense form of individualism that the world has known', so the better the artist the more perfect his imitation of Christ. The artistic life is a guide to conduct. Gide was to complain in *Les Faux-Monnayeurs* that symbolism offered an aesthetic but no ethic. Wilde brought the two together before Gide did.

The way in which art affects life was a subject that Wilde brooded over. What he says in *Intentions* is that life would repeat itself tediously were it not for the daemonic changes which art forces upon it. Art would be repetitious too, if it were not for the critical impulse which impels the artist to new and subversive modes of thinking and feeling. Wilde is willing to see this idea through, and he finds the impulse to destroy at work in the artist along with the urge to create. One of his early letters speaks of the artistic life as 'a long and lovely suicide', because the artist must sheer away one after another of his formulations.[1] Unlike Yeats, who said that works of art beget works of art, Wilde holds that works of art murder works of art. He put this idea to Gide in the form of one of his best fables:

There was a man who could think only in bronze. And one day this man had an idea, the idea of joy, of the joy which dwells in the moment. And he felt that he had to tell it. But in all the world, not a single piece of bronze was left; for men had used it all. And this man felt that he would go mad if he did not tell his idea. And he thought about a piece of bronze on the grave of his wife, of a statue he had made to ornament the tomb of his wife, the only woman he had loved; it was the statue of sadness, of the sadness which dwells in life. And the man felt that he would go mad if he did not tell his idea. So he took the statue of sadness, of the sadness which dwells in life; he smashed it, he melted it down, and he made of it the statue of joy, of the joy which dwells only in the moment.

That one work of an artist rejects another, that each is a statement made contingent upon later repudiation, is the lesson here. Gide adopted this conception, too, as he declares in a letter to Francis Jammes of 6 August 1902: 'Each of my books is an immediate reaction *against* the preceding one. No one of them ever completely satisfied me, and I never dance on more than one foot *at a time*: the main thing is to dance well all the same; but with every book I change feet, as one is tired from having danced, and the other from having rested all that time.' He was just as fond of having his books murder each other, and he proposed that Wilde's *De Profundis* was the opposite of *Intentions,* as if he recognized that Wilde had subjected himself to the same law. He must also have been aware that 'The Soul of Man under Socialism' is killed by *Salome* as certainly as *L'Immoraliste*—that hollow victory of the flesh—is killed by *La Porte etroite*—that hollow victory of the spirit.

For Wilde this oscillation is a cardinal principle; it can be observed at work within each book as well as between books.

[1] See above, p. 68.

In *Dorian Gray*, Wilde writes that 'Nothing can cure the soul but the senses just as nothing can cure the senses but the soul.' (Gide writes likewise in *Les Nourritures terrestres*, 'I owed the health of my body only to the irremediable poisoning of my soul.') Wilde in *Salome* reinterprets the Biblical legend to put both Salome and Iokanaan to death. Virtue itself becomes a kind of sin, a debauchery of the spirit not be to exalted over other forms of debauchery. Gide was delighted to embrace this view. In Wilde it finds many instances, such as *Lady Windermere's Fan*, in which Lady Windermere moves from strident virtue to abandon, and cither way is chastened, like Herod in *Salome*.

The fact that Wilde was already tilting from one extreme to another at the time that he met Gide entitles us, I think, to question the interpretation of Gide's development which Jean Delay proposes in his admirable account of Gide's youth. Professor Delay, himself a psychiatrist, argues that Gide suffered from an inferiority complex which left him in a constant state of indecision, so that in self-defence he made ambiguity his literary method. The theory might be more convincing if it were not that Wilde, who was more confident than Gide was timid, developed the same method and may even have inculcated Gide with it. Wilde's prior example would indicate that the term 'inferiority complex' explains nothing, since that was one complex Wilde did not have.

It must also be said that to the extent Gide and Wilde employ ambiguity, they follow in a literary tradition which extends at least to Keats and his theory of Negative Capability. The pressure of literature may outdo that of the Id. Nor would it appear that the final effect of either Gide or Wilde is one of indecision. With whatever postulate of physical or spiritual reality they begin each work, the object is to effect an undeception, whether of the characters or of the reader. There is a perpetual unmasking.

I have left to the end the question of whether or not Wilde was a satanic force as Gide sometimes credited him with being. In some unpublished notes which Delay prints, Gide remarked

that Wilde was always trying to get him to authorize evil. I have
no doubt that Wilde proposed to Gide a transformation of the
usual meanings of good and evil, such as later on Gide would
find in Nietzsche. Wilde must have said to Gide what he had
written in 'The Soul of Man under Socialism', that crime may
advance life, and what he said in 'Pen, Pencil and Poison', that
the artist is a kind of criminal. But it was no part of Wilde's
scheme to eliminate good and evil altogether, or to endorse
crime for crime's sake. He reconstitutes these terms, like all the
others he touches, but he does not erase them. If he did, there
could be no epigrams, nor any of those simple reassertions of
moral feeling with which his works, like Gide's, almost always
end. What Wilde was urging upon Gide may have sounded
to Gide like the authorization of evil, but Wilde probably was
mischievously prodding him to avoid the evil of self-suppres-
sion, from which the young man appeared to be suffering. It
has to be said, also, that Wilde could not have been so solemnly
baleful as Gide at moments makes him out. If he played Mephisto for a few moments, he would then say with Lord Dar-
lington in *Lady Windermere's Fan,* 'As a wicked man I am a
complete failure. Why, there are lots of people who say I have
never done anything wrong in the whole course of my life. Of
course they only say it behind my back.'

What Wilde provided for Gide, at a crucial moment in the
latter's youth, was a way of extricating himself from an aestheticism which had not yet come to grips with love, religion, or
life, and from a religion which offered safety only in return
for inhibition. He did this not by rejecting aesthetics or ethics;
instead he turned sacred things inside out to make them secular,
and secular things inside out to make them sacred, he showed
souls becoming carnal and lusts becoming spiritual. He also
showed the aesthetic world not isolated from experience, but
infused into it. This was the new Hellenism of which Wilde
liked to speak. Gide developed it with more coherence if less
originality.

6 Discovering Symbolism

Literary movements pass their infancy in inarticulate disaffection, but mature when they achieve a vocabulary. Late in the nineteenth century, the problem was to find a word. In 1899 it was found. Arthur Symons's *The Symbolist Movement in Literature* and W. B. Yeats's *The Wind among the Reeds* were published in London, and as if to show that the need was both international and interdisciplinary, Freud's *Interpretation of Dreams* was published in Vienna. In dissimilar ways the three books recorded the search for a psychic reality which challenged external reality and offered to fix half-glimpsed meanings in a systematic way.

Symbolism was the term that brought together the rumours of new literature that had drifted slowly into England, chiefly from France, since 1875, when Mallarmé, whose '*L'Après-midi d'un faune*' was about to rouse the French public to derision, paid a visit to Swinburne. As a term it was not in common use, although it was officially proposed by Jean Moréas as a name for the movement in 1886. In England the rumours that attended it were a little sinister—of corrupt lives, enigmatic or opaque or morally ambiguous writings, so that it remained easy until Arthur Symons's book to regard the practitioners as manifestations of what Max Nordau called 'degeneration'. Symons did not wish wholly to give up the idea of some taint, but his principal emphasis was on symbolism as a saner literature than what preceded it. Writers who had been hesitating towards a new conception of their work, in which poetry claimed something of its ancient awe, offered not merely words but signs and portents, and made life reach its goal in being transformed into a book, now sensed affinities with each other. The Pre-Raphaelites had presented their work as the iconography of unutterable doctrines, but the symbolists offered formulations, though these were extraordinarily gnomic.

No doubt it was a little embarrassing to Symons that he had to represent as his *avant-garde* a group of writers who were anything but young. Of those he discussed, Nerval was not so much symbolism's father as its grandfather (its father was Baudelaire), having died in 1855; five of his other examples (Laforgue, Villiers, Rimbaud, Verlaine, and Mallarmé) had died between 1887 and 1898. The only two living exponents of symbolism in his book were Maeterlinck and Huysmans, neither of them fledglings. But the lives and works of all these writers retained enough flamboyance to satisfy the need for strange, novel creatures, and Symons turned the scandal that hung over them into a glamour previously reserved for the English Romantic poets.

Before Symons the main middleman between English and French culture had been George Moore. Moore went to Paris in the late 1870s and met Villiers de l'Isle-Adam, Mallarmé, Verlaine, and others. Many of these, as well as Rimbaud, are remembered in his *Confessions of a Young Man* (1888). It was Moore who introduced Huysmans' *À Rebours* (1884), before Wilde created a parallel to the book in Dorian Gray's library (1890). As he was prone to boast, Moore also wrote the first articles in English—none of them much good—on Rimbaud, Laforgue, and Verlaine, collecting them in 1891 in his *Impressions and Opinions*. Edmund Gosse was to follow him by writing the first English essay on Mallarmé in his *Questions at Issue* (1893). This was the year that Verlaine came to England in

November to lecture at Oxford; a little later, in March 1894, Mallarmé also lectured at Oxford and at Cambridge. The same month Villiers's *Axël* was produced in Paris for the first time; among the audience was Yeats, who grasped the sense if not the words and instantly classed it among his 'sacred books'. Translations of the symbolist writers began to appear in the middle nineties, and when Verlaine died in 1896 and Mallarmé two years later, Symons saw how he might reverently collocate what Moore and others had only grazed with the ends of rather disdainful fingers.

Half-consciously Symons had been preparing himself for this undertaking. A Cornishman born in Wales, who prided himself on not being English, he came to London while still young and set himself promptly to the task of showing that the English, rather than he, were the provincials. In no time he was more cosmopolitan than anybody. He was the son of a Methodist preacher, so it was perhaps inevitable that he should be drawn towards 'diabolism', and should write juvenile poems about Judas, Cain, and the pleasures of opium. As he passed out of adolescence he shifted his subject to 'the Juliets of a night', as in poems like 'Stella Maris'. He told Verlaine that 'Stella Maris' was '*un peu osé*' for an English review, and it was '*un peu osé*' that Symons always aspired to be. In youth as in age, he longed to write verse that should be Baudelairean and *faisandé*. But when pressed he had a line of retreat ready, and would say that the poems represented imaginings rather than acts. His biographer, Roger Lhombreaud, is inclined to accept this view. Symons delighted in a brisk succession of love affairs, perhaps unconsummated, with ballet dancers and circus performers, in the tradition of Huysmans' Des Esseintes. He amazed Yeats by confiding, 'I have never been in love with a serpent-charmer before.' Yet he also admired Yeats's single, unsatisfied love for Maud Gonne, and was ready to try hopelessness himself. Rhoda Bowser, though she eventually married him, gave him a number of hopeless years first.

Symons had by nature a curiosity about all feelings and a sense that his own might be more varied than deep. For a time he took hashish, he boasted, presumably to taste his way to new thresholds. But excess did not really suit him. With Yeats he tried the experiment of taking two glasses of whisky every night before retiring, in the hope that addiction might result. It did not, and after the prescribed term of the experiment, a month, both men returned to the beverage they preferred— hot water.

By the time he was twenty Symons had begun to make a career as a literary critic and editor of texts. He familiarized himself with all the arts, popular and unpopular, and frequented the music hall as much as the opera house. Books, especially foreign ones, attracted him like poised women. His response was always urbane and unsurprised, expressed in a style (learned from Pater) at once feather-preening and attentive. He quickly made himself useful to the *Athenaeum* and other magazines as a reviewer. In 1896, at the age of thirty-one, he became founder and editor of the *Savoy*. By this time he was known as the principal interpreter of foreign writers, like Valery Larbaud in Paris in the 1920s.

His interest in France was consolidated by a trip to Paris in 1889 with Havelock Ellis as his companion. They visited Mallarmé on one of his *mardis*, and met also Huysmans, Maeterlinck, and other prominent writers. Villiers, whom they had hoped to see, disobliged them by dying shortly before their arrival, but Symons wrote an obituary article on him for Oscar Wilde's *Woman's World* in the same year. This was not only the first article in English on Villiers, but also the first of Symons's studies of the symbolist group. The visit confirmed his pleasure in an international ambiance, and the next year and regularly thereafter he returned to Paris. In 1890 Charles Morice introduced Symons to Verlaine, and Verlaine's trip to England was largely the result of Symons's arrangements, memorialized by Verlaine in an attractive poem.

What Symons lacked as a critic was the ability to generalize
—his remarks are better than his conclusions—yet paradoxically
the importance of his book on symbolism was its ruling
generalization. That the movement should be called 'symbolist'
was not at first clear to him. In an essay of 1893 he preferred,
while dismissing the question as of little consequence, to use the
word 'decadent' rather than 'symbolist'. He may have felt the
necessity of being cautious, since George Moore had contemptuously scoffed at symbolism as just 'saying the opposite
of what you mean', and Wilde, who held that all art was 'surface and symbol', joked about symbolism as 'a new and fascinating disease'. But Wilde's fall in 1895 put decadence out of
favour, and at this point Symons began to accept the view of
Yeats, that symbolism was springlike rather than autumnal, and
stood for the imagination's recovery of its lost authority over
the body and the material world.

The two men became acquainted about 1891 in the Rhymers' Club, the group of poets who met at the Cheshire Cheese.
Calling themselves rhymers rather than poets, the members
dreamed mostly of writing pure poems. Any programme, any
commitment outside literature was suspect. Symons was better
at listening to general statements than at imparting them, but
his critical professionalism made him throw out statements such
as, 'We are concerned with nothing but impressions.' The
Rhymers greeted this kind of remark with silence, and Symons
would attempt to explain that a nomadic life was best for an
artist, because impressions were much thicker away from home.
At this point, as Max Beerbohm indicates, he might well have to
submit to reproof from Yeats, equally distant from home but
inveterately nostalgic. Yeats would insist that 'an artist works
best among his own folk and in the land of his fathers.' The
building blocks of art were not impressions, but rather eternal
moods or states of mind. Since both points of view found little
support in the Cheshire Cheese, Symons and Yeats talked a good
deal to each other. Late in 1895 their friendship was consolidated

when Yeats moved into rooms connected with Symons's in Fountain Court, and during a crucial period of over a year they shared food, friends, and ideas.

At this time Yeats impressed Symons with the view that the movement was symbolist—he called it symbolic—and that its being so was of consequence. Yeats, like several French writers of this school, had come to symbolism through occult study and experiment. The images on which he had concentrated in connection with magical meditation, in the hope of eliciting their secret powers, were close kindred of images in verse. The process of improving his poetry had become for him a matter of intensification of his metaphors. He had so meditated over images in his early poems that by the time he re-used them, 'they had become true symbols,' he wrote in 1908. And in the preface to his *Poems* (1895), he says he had wished to add 'some new heraldic images' to 'that majestic heraldry of the poets', which constituted 'the ritual of the marriage of heaven and earth'. The turning of images to symbols, the emblazoning of a heraldic ritual, indicate that by 1894 he was consciously designing an organized scheme of images, a symbology. The three-volume edition of Blake on which he and Edwin Ellis had laboured in the early nineties had given him an example of concatenated and clamant images, and he looked for such a pattern in other men's work as well as in his own.

Yeats's life became another area, contiguous with his verse, in which he might mine for symbols. His love affair with Maud Gonne, which began in 1889, may at first have seemed like other people's; but as it became clear that the condition under which it could persist was that it should not be consummated, the beloved's image was held at symbol's length, her terrestrial body became a celestial rose, and she came to represent eternal beauty or the spirit of Ireland or the Shekinah, a cabbalistic version of the splendour of God. Maud Gonne seems to have fostered this symbol-diffusion by telling him that they were

symbolically married.[1] Yeats could easily confuse her with
Ireland, not so much with the actual country as with 'the poor
old woman' who traditionally stood for it. In his play *Cathleen
ni Houlihan*, Maud Gonne—symbol of a symbol—would take
her part. With Miss Gonne, too, he was contriving and renew-
ing, in an Irish mystical order of his devising, the symbols which
might some day bring independence—if not literal at least
symbolical. Political defeat, like amorous defeat, might be overcome by 'Mental Fight' (as Blake called it), by the establishment
of symbolic powers which would make the body politic (like
his mistress's body) unimportant:

> Some had no thought of victory
> But had gone out to die
> That Ireland's mind be greater,
> Her heart mount up on high . . .
>
> ('Three Songs to the One Burden')

[1] It may be useful to summarize briefly Yeats's relationship with Maud Gonne
during their youth. When they first met in 1889, she was already in love with
Lucien Millevoye, a French newspaper editor. Millevoye ardently supported the
political ambitions of General Boulanger, and Maud Gonne carried secret
messages about Europe to promote the cause. But in 1889, his oven having
cooled, Boulanger fled from France, and she turned to the Irish independence
movement. Yeats, deeply enamoured, gathered her into his own activities;
together they organized Irish libraries, practised magic in the Golden Dawn,
and planned a national literature. Oblivious of Millevoye's existence, Yeats felt
encouraged by her to think that since they were spiritually married, some day
spirit might become matter.

Meanwhile Maud Gonne had borne Millevoye a child, but to her intense
distress the child died. She questioned Yeats and his friend George Russell on
what might happen to the soul of a dead child, and Russell oraculated that it
was often reborn in the same family. Then occurred one of the most macabre
events in Pre-Raphaelite passion. As Yeats's *Memoir* (the first draft of part of his
Autobiographies) recounts, Maud Gonne brought Millevoye down to the dead
infant's vault so that its soul might be reconceived. Another child, Iseult, was
in fact evoked.

It was probably during the infancy of the second child that Maud Gonne's
prolonged absence in France gave Yeats a respite from his love. About 1895
Mrs. Olivia Shakespear, a cousin of Lionel Johnson and a minor novelist,
whose daughter was to marry Ezra Pound, rescued Yeats from 'youth's dreamy
load', or as he calls it in cold prose, from 'unctuous celibacy'. The affair began
in embarrassment, as Yeats tells with amusement, and came to a sudden end
when Maud Gonne once more required his attention.

Even after her marriage to Major John MacBride in 1903, she continued to

This symbolism was not entirely gratifying, but it suited Yeats's desire for extremities of thought and feeling.

The strength of these conceptions bent Symons and his magazine, the *Savoy*, towards symbolism too. Although the *Savoy* is often treated as if it were just one short-lived sensation in the decade-long anecdote of the nineties, Yeats's programmatic inclinations gave it shape and substance. He himself supplied the centre with three essays on Blake which related Blake to Mallarmé and offered a theory of symbolical art. He contributed also his stories, 'The Tables of the Law' and 'Rosa Alchemica', in which the narrator declares that for his mind 'symbolism was a necessity', and several emphatically symbolic poems like 'The Secret Rose'. Symons for his part translated some poems of Mallarmé as reinforcement.

He now began to surrender his word 'impressions' as a key to the new literature. In 1896 Symons wrote a preface for a new edition of his book of verse, *Silhouettes*, at a time when he and Yeats were travelling together in the west of Ireland. This time he shifts from impressions to 'moods', but he then defends his poems as the depiction of moods for their own sake. This is good and bad Yeats, for to Yeats the moods embodied fundamental energies, while to Symons they simply evidenced a strong emotional life. What distinguishes Yeats's theory also is that it implies continuity, as Symons's implies discontinuity, and later he was to reprove Symons for sponsoring *isolated* lyrical moments. By Yeats's lights, the images had to be contagious.

Mostly at Yeats's urgency, then, Symons decided to publish a book on the French writers as members of a group. Yeats's phrase in the *Savoy*, 'the symbolical movement', was too general; by calling it the 'symbolist movement', Symons made

---

occupy his thoughts. She and MacBride were soon separated. In a journal of Yeats which has not been published, it is made clear that at least once, about 1907, his unrequited love for Maud Gonne found requital. 'The first of all the tribe lay there,' as he was afterwards to boast in a poem.

it more French and doctrinaire. With this key he tried to establish the contours of an aesthetic system that could bind the
separate essays he had published between 1895 and 1898 on
Huysmans, Mallarmé, Nerval, Rimbaud, Villiers, Verlaine, and
Maeterlinck. He retouched them, added an essay on Laforgue,
then wrote an introduction and conclusion to embody the new
insight he had reached—the perception of singleness of purpose
among these disparate talents. He dedicated his book to Yeats
as the leading practitioner in English of the symbolist school.

Symons offers a definition of symbolism as 'a form of expression, essential but arbitrary, until it has obtained the force of a
convention, for an unseen reality apprehended by the consciousness.'[1] But he did not bind it down too closely; if he had,
some of the impact of his book would have been lost, and some
of the writers he denominated as symbolists would have had
marginal claims for inclusion. In the essays on Nerval and
Villiers, he treats symbolism as the perception of a reality which
is opposite to the world of appearance; in those on Mallarmé
and Maeterlinck, he situates this reality just over appearance's
borders instead of far away; with Rimbaud and Verlaine, on the
other hand, he interprets symbolism as the perception of the
visible world with visionary intensity; for Huysmans it is rather
the perception of that world's organic unity. In other words,
Symons includes among the symbolists those who reject the
world, those who see an unseen universe impinging upon the
world, those who accept the world so totally they see it with
new eyes, those who regard it as reflecting a quasi-divine order.
Yeats never felt that Symons correctly understood the inter-

[1] Awkward as this definition is, it is probably better than the more laicized one
which Edmund Wilson provided in *Axel's Castle* (1931), 'Symbolism may be
defined as an attempt by carefully studied means—a complicated association of
ideas represented by a medley of metaphors—to communicate unique personal feelings.' In *The Background of Modern Poetry* (1951), J. Isaacs proposed
instead, 'Symbolism is an attempt through a subtly articulated pattern of metaphors, to offer some facets of contemporary sensibility.' This is more accurate,
but too humble. For 'some facets of contemporary sensibility' might be sub-
stituted 'hidden aspects of consciousness or experience'.

penetration of the symbolic and real worlds, and the essay, 'The Symbolism of Poetry', which he wrote in part as a corrective, offers a much more thoroughgoing claim for a 'buried reality' as controlling the world. Yet he himself varied: sometimes he affirmed the autonomy of imaginative symbols as 'self-born mockers of man's enterprise' ('Among School-Children'), sometimes he regrets their ineffectuality within actual life as being merely symbolic—'an agony of flame that cannot singe a sleeve' ('Byzantium'), and sometimes he appears to relish their fall from spirit to matter 'for desecration' (*The King of the Great Clock Tower*).

In our day some of Symons's subtleties in his book may easily be overlooked. His style is delicate and insinuating. For him these writers are participants in 'a sacred ritual', a Yeatsian phrase, and each of them is a renunciant, who gives up contentment for the sake of his art and its mysterious relations to the unseen powers. Although occasionally Symons proffers a date, his portraits are almost timeless, like those of purely fictitious characters in his book, *Spiritual Adventures*. These men are so strange that it is almost conjectural that they lived at all. Symons discovers them, and they discover him, finally turning, or almost turning, into some of those moods of his, struggling fitfully for expression, then dying out. Their lives pass as in a dream; their behaviour, odd or objectionable, makes the dream richer. So personal is the book, so intricate the bond writer offers to reader, that we almost concede to Symons for a moment his claim at the end, that symbolist writers may help to reconcile us to death by guaranteeing the endurability of imaginative experience.

Yeats was content for the time to let Symons offer the discursive account of symbolism, while he himself presented example rather than precept. He gathered those images together which best expressed his sense of a twilit meshing of material and spiritual. Common images such as rose, lily, star, and bird were given meanings which flowed between the two

worlds, with now one now the other dominant. These were
reinforced by uncommon images, such as the boar without
bristles and the Valley of the Black Pig, and the whole dyed
Irish. He wove *The Wind among the Reeds* out of the varying
intangibility and corporeality of things.

With this book Yeats set the method for the modern movement, as in 1898 Wordsworth's and Coleridge's *Lyrical Ballads*
shaped the Romantic movement. It was not that the early
Yeats poems were as good, but they had an extraordinary consistency of colour and a powerful interrelation. They were not
merely poems but talismans in a *grimoire*. Wordsworth's theme
had been the renewal of man's bond to nature; Yeats's was the
uncovering of a secret nature in which all outward things took
their character from internal pressures. The mighty presence
which for Wordsworth was outside man was for Yeats inside,
and all the scenic elements, such as stars, sea, winds, and woods,
became emblematic of forces operative within the mind as upon
things. At the pinnacle of Yeats's early symbolism was the rose
of beauty, which in certain circumstances might flower from
the cross of suffering. The meaning of rose and cross varied
according to the context, but in general the rose moves between
the unnamed Maud Gonne and some unnameable principle of
timelessness and totality.[1] The cross is not only the emblem of
suffering, of Christ's passion which is mimicked by every
lover's 'passion', but is also representative of discord, incom-
pleteness, temporality. Some juncture of the two is constantly
being heralded. It is not easy in this volume to know whether
Yeats is addressing a human or superhuman being, or whether
such a distinction is any use; as he said later in 'Upon a Dying
Lady', 'I have no speech but symbol, the pagan speech I made

[1] The rose is not neglected in later symbolist poets. In Pound's *Cantos*, the 'rose
in the steel dust' is a kind of illumination immanent in natural life but elicited
by the poet; in Molly Bloom's monologue in Joyce's *Ulysses*, the rose stands
(mostly) for love; in Eliot's *Little Gidding*, the union of the fire and the rose is
paradisal. Yeats, with his gardenful of roses, implies all these meanings in one
or another poem.

when I was young.' The poet would like to be translated to spirit, or to have his love translated to matter, but there is some pleasure in her apotheosis even if it proves irremediable.

The Wind among the Reeds and *The Symbolist Movement in Literature* quickly became known among the writers who were to carry on their tradition. Joyce praised Yeats's book lavishly and quoted from Symons's; Pound imitated the poems, and acknowledged Symons as the principal middleman between France and England; T. S. Eliot said in 1930 of Symons's work, 'I myself owe Mr. Symons a great debt; but for having read his book I should not, in the year 1908, have begun to read Verlaine; and but for reading Verlaine, I should not have heard of Corbière.' (Laforgue was an even stronger influence.) Though Eliot did not like Yeats's verse, he saw it as the extreme of nineties work, a point of departure. Yeats departed from it, too. Although the word 'symbolism', so laboriously arrived at, quickly became *démodé*, the literary fashions implied by it kept a firm grip on the principal poets for fifty years.

7 Two Faces of Edward

Victoria stayed too long, Edward arrived too late. By the time the superannuated Prince of Wales became king, it was evident that a change would take place in literature; it took place, but Edward has somehow never received credit for it, and the phrase 'Edwardian literature' is not often heard. We have to fall back on it, though, because there is no neat phrase in English, like 'the nineties', to describe the first ten years of a century. The word 'Edwardian' has taken its connotations from social rather than literary history. Just what it means is not certain, beyond the high collars and tight trousers which flouted Victorian dowdiness then, and which later became for a time the pedantic signs of juvenile delinquency. Perhaps 'pre-war courtliness' is the closest we can come to the meaning of Edwardian outside literature, sedate Victorianism in better dress. The meaning was present enough to Virginia Woolf for her to declare that 'on or about December 1910,' that is, in the year of Edward's death, 'human character changed.' Edward 'the Peacemaker' had to die before the world could become modern, and she pushed the dead Edwardians aside to make room for the lively Georgians. The distinction was more relevant, however, for describing Virginia Woolf's own accession to purposiveness than George's accession to rule.

While the late Victorians seem to have relished the idea that they were the last, the Edwardians at once declined to consider themselves as stragglers, ghostly remains of those Englishmen who had stretched the Empire so far. The Edwardians had, in fact, a good deal of contempt for the previous reign, and an odd admiration for their own doughtiness. In the midst of the general melancholy over Victoria's death, her son said sturdily, 'The King lives.' To Virginia Woolf the hated Edwardian writers were Bennett, Galsworthy, and Wells, yet even these writers laboured under the apprehension or misapprehension that they were trying something new. Lascelles Abercrombie, in one of the few essays on Edwardian literature, finds the period to be only the decorous extension of tradition, and in his essay is detectable that faintly patronizing note which occurs also in biographies of Edward that prove the king was a worthy man. So for Abercrombie the writers of this time were engagingly discreet; they drew in literature, as Edward in life, upon an ample wardrobe, and perhaps dared to go so far as to leave unbuttoned the lowest button on their literary waistcoats.

That the Edwardians have been discounted is understandable, I think, because of the prevalence of a sociological assumption. If the birth of modern literature is dated back to the century's first decade, what happens to our conviction that it was the Great War which turned the tables? At any cost we have to confine the beginning of the century to the infancy or adolescence of modern writers, so that only when the guns boomed did they become old enough to discern the nature of the world. The admonitory fact, however, is that most of the writers whom we are accustomed to call modern were already in their twenties or older when King Edward died. In 1910 Eliot was twenty-two, Lawrence and Pound were twenty-five, Joyce and Virginia Woolf were twenty-eight, Forster was thirty-one, Ford Madox Ford thirty-seven, Conrad fifty-three, Shaw fifty-four, Henry James sixty-seven. Bennett, Galsworthy, and Wells were in their forties. To dismiss most of the writers I have named as either too young or too old to be Edwardians, as if only men of middle age counted in literary fashion, is one of those historical simplicities like denying that the twenties were the twenties because so many people didn't know the twenties were going on. Neither age nor self-consciousness determines the private character of a period; if anything does, it is the existence of a community between young and old experimental writers. Such a community existed in the Edwardian period. It was a community which extended not only across the Irish Sea but, spottily at least, across the Channel and the Atlantic; so, if I extend Edward's dominions occasionally to countries he did not rule, it is only to recover the imperial word 'Edwardian' from an enforced limitation.

If a moment must be found for human character to have changed, I should suggest that 1900 is both more convenient and more accurate than Virginia Woolf's 1910. In 1900, Yeats said with good-humoured exaggeration, 'everybody got down off his stilts; henceforth nobody drank absinthe with his black coffee; nobody went mad; nobody committed suicide; nobody joined the Catholic Church; or if they did I have forgotten.' That there was pressure upon them to change was something that the writers of this time were distinctly aware of; it is not only Yeats whose attitudes take a new turn; it is also lesser writers. Even John Masefield was once asked how it had happened that his poetry had moved from the nostalgic rhythms of his early work to the more athletic ones of 'The Everlasting Mercy', and he replied simply, 'Everybody changed his style then.' The Edwardians came like Dryden after Sir Thomas Browne, anxious to develop a more wiry speech. Their sentences grew more vigorous and concentrated. I will not claim for the Edwardians' work total novelty—that can never be found in any period, and many of their most individual traits had origin in the nineties or earlier. But in all that they do they are freshly self-conscious. What can be claimed is that there was a gathering of different talents towards common devices, themes, and attitudes, and King Edward at least did nothing to impede it.

What strikes us at once about Edwardian literature is that it is thoroughly secular, yet so earnest that secularism does not describe it. It is generally assumed that in this period religion was something to ignore and not to practise. Edwardian writers were not in fact religious, but they were not ostentatiously irreligious. In the Victorian period people had fumed and left the churches; in the Edwardian period, becalmed, they published memoirs or novels describing how strongly they had *once* felt about the subject. This is the point of Gosse's *Father and Son* (1907) as well as of Samuel Butler's *The Way of All Flesh* (written earlier, but published in 1903). It was also part of the subject of Joyce's *A Portrait of the Artist as a Young Man*, much of it written in 1907–8, as it is of Yeats's first autobiographical book, *Reveries over Childhood and Youth*, written just before the war. In all these books the intensity of rebellion is past, an incident of an unhappy childhood (and the vogue of having had an unhappy childhood may well have begun with the Edwardians) succeeded by confident maturity.

Because they outlived their passionate revolt, writers as different as Yeats and Joyce are sometimes suspected now of having been reverted Christians or at least demi-Christians. Certainly they no longer make a fuss about being infidels. And they are suspected of belief for another reason, too. Almost to a man, Edwardian writers rejected Christianity, and having done so, they felt free to *use* it, for while they did not need religion they did need religious metaphors. It is no accident that the Catholic modernists, with their emphasis upon the metaphorical rather than the literal truth of Catholic doctrines, became powerful enough in the first years of the century to be worth excommunicating in 1907. There were other signs of a changed attitude towards religion: the comparative mythologists tolerantly accepted Easter as one of many spring vegetation rites;

William James's *The Varieties of Religious Experience*, published
in 1902, made all varieties equally valid.

In creative writers, this new temper appears not in discussion
of religion, which does not interest them, but in vocabulary.
Religious terms are suddenly in vogue among unbelievers.
Yeats calls up God to be a symbol of the most complete thought.
Joyce in *A Portrait* allows the infidel Stephen to cry out
'Heavenly God!' when, seeing a girl wading, he experiences
'an outburst of *profane* joy'. Elsewhere, as in *Ulysses*, he asks
what difference it makes whether God's name be Christus or
Bloom, and Jesus is allowed into *Finnegans Wake* as one of
Finnegan's many avatars. Ezra Pound, newly arrived in London
in 1908, immediately writes a canzone to celebrate 'The Yearly
Slain', a pagan god, and then a ballad to celebrate the 'Goodly
Fere', who turns out to be Christ made into a Scottish chap. All
deaths of all gods roused Pound to the same fervour. There was
no need to attack with Swinburne the 'pale Galilean', or to say
with Nietzsche that 'God is dead'; as a metaphor God was not
dead but distinctly alive, so much so that a character in Granville-Barker's play *Waste* (1906–7) asks sardonically, 'What is
the prose for God?' T. S. Eliot, if for a moment he may be
regarded as an Edwardian rather than as a Rooseveltian, in
'Prufrock' (written in 1910) used John the Baptist and Lazarus
as if they were characters like Hamlet, and even in his later life,
after becoming consciously, even self-consciously Christian, he
used the words 'God' and 'Christ' with the greatest circumspection, while unbelievers used the words much more casually,
their individual talents more at ease in his tradition than he himself. D. H. Lawrence, the same age as Pound, writes his 'Hymn
to Priapus' in 1912, yet remains attracted by images of Christ
and is willing enough, in spite of his preference for older and
darker gods, to revise Christianity and use its metaphors. In *The
Rainbow* (begun the same year), Tom Brangwen and his wife,
when their physical relationship improves, experience what Lawrence variously calls 'baptism to another life', 'transfiguration',

and 'glorification'. In later life Lawrence would give Christ a
new resurrection so he could learn to behave like the god Pan,
and in poems such as 'Last Words to Miriam' the cross becomes emblematic of the failure to cohabit properly, an interpretation which I should like to think of as Edwardian or at
least post-Edwardian. Even H. G. Wells played for a time with
the notion of a 'finite God', 'the king of man's adventures in
space and time,' though in the end he granted, too unimagina-
tively, that he had been guilty of 'terminological disingenuousness'.

To accept Christianity as one of a group of what Gottfried
Benn calls 'regional moods', or to rewrite it for a new, pagan
purpose, seemed to the Edwardians equally cogent directions.
For the first time writers can take for granted that a large part of
their audience will be irreligious, and paradoxically this fact
gives them confidence to use religious imagery. They neither
wish to shock nor fear to shock. There is precision, not impiety,
in Joyce's use of religious words for secular processes. About
1900, when he was eighteen, he began to describe his prose
sketches not as poems in prose, the fashionable term, but as
'epiphanies', showings-forth of essences comparable to the
showing-forth of Christ. *Dubliners* he first conceived of in 1904
as a series of ten *epicleseis*, that is, invocations to the Holy Spirit
to transmute bread and wine into the body and blood of Christ,
a sacramental way of saying that he wished to fix in their
eternal significance the commonplace incidents he found about
him. To moments of fullness he applied the term 'eucharistic'.
When Stephen Dedalus leaves the Catholic priesthood behind
him, it is to become 'a priest of eternal imagination, transmut-
ing the daily bread of experience into the radiant body of everlasting life.' One did not have to be a defected Irish Catholic to
use terms this way. Granville-Barker's hero in *Waste* wants to
buy the Christian tradition and transmute it. Proust, searching
for an adjective to express his sense of basic experiences, calls
them 'celestial'. Yeats, a defected Protestant, wrote in 1903 that

his early work was directed towards the transfiguration on the mountain, and his new work towards incarnation. The artist, he held, must make a Sacred Book, which would not be Christian or anti-Christian, but would revive old pieties and rituals in the universal colours of art instead of in the hue of a single creed.

The re-establishment of Christianity, this time as outer panoply for an inner creed, was not limited to a few writers. In the Edwardian novels of Henry James the words he is fondest of are 'save' and 'sacrifice', and these are secular equivalents for religious concepts to which in their own terms he is indifferent. In the novels of E. M. Forster, mostly written before Edward died, there is exhibited this same propensity. Forster usually reserves his religious imagery for the end of his novels. In the last pages of *Where Angels Fear to Tread,* his first novel (1905), Forster writes of Philip, 'Quietly, without hysterical prayers or banging of drums, he underwent conversion. He was saved.' *The Longest Journey* (1907) concludes with Stephen Wanham undergoing 'salvation'. In *A Room with a View* (1908), there is a 'Sacred Lake', immersion in which, we are told, is 'a call to the blood and to the relaxed will, a passing benediction whose influence did not pass, a holiness, a spell, a momentary chalice for youth.' At the end the heroine derives from Mr. Emerson, who has 'the face of a saint who understood', 'a sense of deities reconciled, a feeling that, in gaining the man she loved, she would gain something for the whole world.'

Even allowing that writers always incline to inflated language for their perorations, Forster obviously intends his words momentously, almost portentously. He is not for Christ or Pan, but with profoundly Edwardian zeal, for the deities reconciled. Some of the same images appear with much the same meaning in his contemporaries. A character in Granville-Barker calls for 'A secular Church'. Shaw's *Major Barbara* (1905) makes similar use of the theme of salvation with its earnest fun about the Salvation Army. Let us be saved, Shaw says, but with less

Christian noise and more Roman efficiency. Forster's 'chalice' is like the chalice in Joyce's 'Araby' (written in 1905), which is a symbol of the boy's love for his sweetheart. The 'Sacred Lake' with its subverting of Christian implication is like *The Lake* in George Moore's novel (1905), in which the priest-hero immerses himself in the lake not in order to become Christian, but to become pagan. Forster's deflection of familiar Christian phrasing in having his heroine feel that, in gaining the man she loves she gains something for the whole world, is cognate with Joyce's heroine in 'The Dead' (written in 1907), who says of her pagan lover, 'I think he died for me,' a statement which helps to justify the ending of that story in a mood of secular sacrifice for which the imagery of barren thorns and spears is Christian yet paganized. I do not think it would be useful to discriminate closely the slightly varying attitudes towards Christianity in these examples: the mood is the same, a secular one.

Yet to express secularism in such images is to give it a special inflection. The Edwardians were looking for ways to express their conviction that we can be religious about life itself, and they naturally adopted metaphors offered by the religion they knew best. The capitalized word for the Edwardians is not 'God' but 'Life': 'What I'm really trying to render is nothing more nor less than Life,' says George Ponderevo, when Wells is forty-three; 'Live,' says Strether to Little Bilham, when Henry James is sixty; 'O life,' cries Stephen Dedalus to no one in particular when Joyce is about thirty-four; 'I am going to begin a book about Life,' announces D. H. Lawrence, when he is thirty. It does not much matter whether life is exciting or dull, though Conrad is a little exceptional in choosing extraordinary incidents. Arnold Bennett is more usual in his assurance that two old women are worth writing *The Old Wives' Tale* (1908) about. The Edwardians vied with each other in finding more and more commonplace life to write about, and in giving the impression of writing about it in more and more common speech. In Ireland there is the most distinct return to simple men for revelation, in the peasant drama, in Lady Gregory's collection of folklore, in Moore's and Joyce's short stories; but there is a good deal of it in England too, in Arthur Morrison for example. It is connected with an increasing physicality in writers like Lawrence and Joyce, as if they must discuss the forbidden as well as the allowed commonplace. In Lawrence and in Yeats there is the exaltation of spontaneous ignorance, the gamekeeper in the one and the fisherman in the other held up as models to those who suppose that wisdom is something that comes with higher education. In 1911 Ford Madox Ford calls upon poets to write about ash-buckets at dawn rather than about the song of birds or moonlight. While Henry James could not bring himself to joy in ash-buckets, he too believed that by uninhibited scrutiny the artist might attract life's secrets.

The Edwardian writer granted that the world was secular, but saw no reason to add that it was irrational or meaningless. A kind of inner belief pervades their writings, that the transcendent is immanent in the earthy, that to go down far enough is to go up. They felt free to introduce startling coincidences quite flagrantly, as in *A Room with a View* and *The Ambassadors*, to hint that life is much more than it appears to be, although none of them would have offered that admission openly. While Biblical miracles aroused their incredulity, they were singularly credulous of miracles of their own. As Conrad said in his preface to *The Shadow-Line,* 'The world of the living contains enough marvels and mysteries as it is; marvels and mysteries acting upon our emotions and intelligence in ways so inexplicable that it would almost justify the conception of life as an enchanted state.' The central miracle for the Edwardians is the sudden alteration of the self; around it much of their literature pivots. In 1907 Yeats began work on *The Player Queen*, a dramatic statement of his conviction that, if we pretend hard enough to be someone else, we can become that other self or mask. That was the year, too, when Joyce planned out the miraculous birth of his hero's mature soul as the conclusion of *A Portrait of the Artist,* and when J. M. Synge, in *The Playboy of the Western World,* represented dramatically the battle for selfhood. At the end of Synge's play, Christy Mahon is the true playboy he has up to now only pretended to be, and his swagger is replaced by inner confidence. In *The Voysey Inheritance* (1905) Granville-Barker brings Edward Voysey to sudden maturity when, like the hero of that neo-Edwardian novel of James Gould Cozzens, *By Love Possessed,* he discovers the world is contaminated and that he may nonetheless act in it. Lawrence's heroes must always shed old skins for new ones. In Conrad's *Lord Jim* (1900), the struggle for selfhood is the hero's quest, a quest achieved only with his death. In Henry James's *The Ambassadors* (1903), the miracles among which Strether moves at first are phantasmagoric, but there is no phantasmagoria about the miracle which finally occurs, the release of Strether from ignorance to total understanding. Though the dove dies in another of James's novels of this time (1902), her wings mysteriously extend beyond death into the minds of the living, to alter their conduct miraculously. The golden bowl (1904) is cracked and finally broken, but by miracle is recreated in the mind.

Miracles of this sort occur in surprising places, even in H. G. Wells. In *Kipps* the hero is transformed from a small person named Kipps into a bloated person named Cuyps and finally into a considerable person named Kipps. He is himself at last. Less obviously, such a change takes place in George Ponderevo in *Tono-Bungay.* It is part of Wells's favourite myth of human achievement, and trying to express that George Ponderevo says, 'How can I express the values of a thing at once so essential and so immaterial?' To do so he falls back upon the words 'Science' or 'Truth', words as reverberant for Wells as 'chalice' for Forster or 'eucharist' for Joyce. Selfhood—the crown of life, attained by a mysterious grace—forced the Edwardians into their grandest metaphors. It will not seem strange that Bernard Shaw's mind hovers continually about it, as in *Man and Superman* (1901–3) and *Pygmalion* (1912), where miracles as striking and as secular as those in Synge, Joyce, or Yeats, take place. Perhaps we could distinguish two kinds of such miracles: the kind of Shaw and Wells, in which a victory in the spirit is accompanied usually by some material victory, and the kind of James, Lawrence, Conrad, Yeats, and Joyce, in which a victory in the spirit is usually accompanied by some defeat. Shaw complained vigorously to Henry James that James's kind of miracle was not 'scientific'.

If the secular miracle is usually the climax of Edwardian writings, there is also a thematic centre, usually some single unifying event or object, some external symbol which the Edwardians bear down upon very hard until, to use Conrad's unprepossessing phrase, they 'squeeze the guts out of it'. So Forster's *A Room with a View* is organized round the title; Lucy Honeychurch, viewless at first, must learn to see; Forster plays upon the word 'view' at strategic points in the novel, and at the end Lucy attains sight. In Conrad's *Nostromo* (1904) the central motif is silver, established, by Conrad's custom, in the first chapter: silver civilizes and silver obsesses, a two-edged sword, and the different attitudes that silver inspires control the action of the book. The meaning of the hero's name, Nostromo, becomes as ambiguous as silver; a lifetime of virtue is balanced against an ineradicable moral fault, and Nostromo dies an example of Conrad's fallen man, partially at least saved by misery and death. In *The Man of Property* (1906), John Galsworthy, somewhat under Conrad's influence, developed the very name of Forsyte into a symbol, and as if fearful we might miss it, he keeps reminding us that the Forsytes were not only a family but a class, a state of mind, a social disease. The use of a symbolic nucleus in these books seems to justify itself by its public quality, a whole society being measured in terms of it. In *The Golden Bowl,* one of those demonstrations of method which Forster found too extreme, Henry James not only invokes the bowl itself several times in the novel, but keeps invoking its atmosphere by repeating the words 'gold' and 'golden'. Verbal iteration is a means by which Edwardian novelists make up for the obliquity of their method, the complexity of their theme, and give away some of their hand. So Conrad in *Lord Jim* speaks of his hero's clothing, on the first page, as 'immaculate', and at the last he is 'a white speck', all the incongruities of the book pointed up by the overemphasis on stainlessness. Joyce plays on a group of words in *A Portrait,* 'apologise', 'admit', 'fall', 'fly', and the like, expanding their meaning gradually through the book. The pressure of this Edwardian conception of novel-writing is felt even in the work of Lawrence. In his first book, written in 1910, Lawrence is still rather primitive in his use of key words. He changed his title from *Nethermere* to *The White Peacock,* and then laboriously emphasized his heroine's whiteness and introduced discussion of the pride of peacocks. By the time he started *The Rainbow* two years later, he had developed this technique so far as to use the words 'light' and 'dark', and the image of the rainbow itself, obsessively, and he does not relax this method in *Women in Love* or his later books. He even does what most Edwardians do not do, writes his essay 'The Crown' to explain what light, dark, and rainbow signify.

A good example, too, is Joyce's transformation of *Stephen Hero* (1904–5) into *A Portrait of the Artist as a Young Man* (chiefly 1907–8). Between writing the two books he read a good deal of Henry James, George Moore, and others, and quite possibly caught up Edwardian habits from them. *Stephen Hero* was to a large extent a Victorian novel, with an interest in incident for its own sake; so Joyce was particularly pleased when he composed the scene in which Stephen asks Emma Clery to spend the night with him. But two or three years later he expunged that scene: it had become irrelevant to his central image. For by then he had decided to make *A Portrait* an account of the gestation of a soul, and in this metaphor of the soul's growth as like an embryo's he found his principle of order and exclusion. It gave him an opportunity to be passionately meticulous. In the new version the book begins with Stephen's father and, just before the ending, it depicts the hero's severance from his mother. From the start the soul is surrounded by liquids, urine, slime, seawater, amniotic tides, 'drops of water' (as Joyce says at the end of the first chapter) 'falling softly in the brimming bowl.' The atmosphere of biological struggle is necessarily dark and melancholy until the light of life is glimpsed. In the first chapter the foetal soul is for a few pages only slightly individualized, the organism responds only to the most primitive sensory impressions, then the heart forms and musters its affections, the being struggles towards some unspecified, uncomprehended culmination, it is flooded in ways it cannot understand or control, it gropes wordlessly towards sexual differentiation. In the third chapter shame floods Stephen's whole body as conscience develops; the lower bestial nature is put by. Then, at the end of the penultimate chapter, the soul discovers the goal towards which it has been mysteriously proceeding—the goal of life. It must swim no more but emerge into air, the new metaphor being flight. The last chapter shows the soul, already fully developed, fattening itself for its journey until at last it is ready to leave. In the final pages of the book, Stephen's diary, the style shifts with savage abruptness to signalize birth. The soul is ready now, it throws off its sense of imprisonment, its melancholy, its no longer tolerable conditions of lower existence, to be born.

By making his book the matrix for the ontogeny of the soul, Joyce achieved a unity as perfect as any of the Edwardians could achieve, and justified literally his description of the artist as like a mother brooding over her creation until it assumes independent life. The aspiration towards unity in the novel seems related to the search for unity elsewhere, in psychology for example, where the major effort is to bring the day-world and the night-world together. Edwardian writers who commented on history demonstrated the same desire to see human life in a synthesis. In 1900 Joyce announced in his paper on 'Drama and Life' that 'human society is the embodiment of changeless laws,' laws

which he would picture in operation in *Finnegans Wake*. H. G.
Wells insisted later that 'History is one', and proceeded to outline it. Yeats said, 'All forms are one form,' and made clear in
A Vision that the same cyclical laws bind the lifetime of a
person, a civilization, or an idea; and this perception of unity
enabled him, he said, to hold 'in a single thought reality and
justice.'

When they came to state their aesthetic theories, the Edwardians bore down hard on the importance of unity. To choose
one among a multitude of their sources, they were to some extent making English the tradition of the *symbolistes* of whom
Arthur Symons had written in 1899. Aggressively and ostentatiously, the Edwardians point to their works as microcosms characterized by the intense apprehension of the organic unity of all
things. They felt justified in subordinating all other elements to
this node of unity. Events of the plot can be so subordinated,
for example, since, as Virginia Woolf declares, life is not a series
of gig lamps symmetrically arranged but a 'luminous halo'.
Short stories and novels begin to present atmospheres rather
than narratives; and even when events are exciting in themselves,
as in Conrad and often in James, the artist's chief labour goes
to establish their meaning in a painstaking way, and he will
often set the most dramatic events offstage or, rather than present them directly, allow someone to recollect them. Time can
be twisted or turned, for unity has little to do with chronology.
What subject-matter is used becomes of less importance because
any part of life, if fully apprehended, may serve. As Ford Madox
Ford says in describing the novel of this period, 'Your "subject"
might be no more than a child catching frogs in a swamp or the
emotions of a nervous woman in a thunderstorm, but all the
history of the world has gone to putting child or woman where
they are. . . .' Since characters are also subsidiary to the sought-
after unity, there is a tendency to control them tightly. Few
Edwardian characters can escape from their books. Galsworthy's
plays are called *Strife* (1909) or *Justice* (1910), as if to establish

letters. These letters have not survived. But aside from the flexibility of style and mind so notable in Pattison, so lacking in Casaubon, it is now clear, from a letter of George Eliot published in the *Times Literary Supplement* on 12 February 1971 by Professor Gordon S. Haight, that as early as 1846 she was already diverting her friends by concocting the terms of a pedant's proposal of marriage. Casaubon's letter balances precariously on the questions of whether he is seeking a wife or someone to read to him, and of whether he is actuated by love or myopia; the proposal of 'Professor Bücherwurm', which George Eliot pretends to relay to Charles Bray, similarly hinges on the ambiguity of the Professor's securing as his bride someone to translate his books from German. In 1846 George Eliot did not know Pattison, and evidently she had no need to know him in order to evolve Casaubon's letter.

To consider other possible models for Casaubon is to turn up many of George Eliot's acquaintances. Pedantry was not a scarce commodity among them. Ideally the culprit should combine arid learning with sexual insufficiency. This felicitous blend is unexpectedly hard to find. No doubt the laws of Middlemarch, rather than those of experience, demanded that Casaubon's mind symbolize his body, and his body his mind. If George Eliot drew details from models, she used more than one. For sexual low pressure, Herbert Spencer was probably the best example, and Beatrice Webb saw enough resemblance to refer to him as Casaubon. George Eliot knew Spencer well, and may have been perplexed for a time at his failure to marry anyone, herself included. But if his nubility was in doubt for her, his ability was not; it is only a later age that wishes Spencer had been Casaubon enough to finish fewer books. Besides, Spencer came to regard George Eliot as the greatest woman who ever lived, an accolade she would not have so meagrely rewarded.

For the author of the 'Key to all Mythologies', a closer prototype is Dr. R. H. Brabant. It was he whom the novelist Mrs. Eliza Lynn Linton, well acquainted with both him and George cowardice of the European Kurtz, and that the confrontation with Marlow, captain of English ships and master of English prose, bearer of an indisputably English name, was symbolically rehabilitative. To commit suicide is to yield to the mind's jungle, to write is to colonize with the efficiency so highly regarded by Marlow. Kurtz and Marlow meet in the 'heart of darkness' as in the recesses of Conrad's mind: one dies, the other contrives to be reborn. Conrad did not let this theme rest: his return to it in *Lord Jim* and other works must have been a pricking and stanching of the old wound.

This preliminary example may embolden an inquiry into two characters, and their possible prototypes, in *Middlemarch*. George Eliot, contrary to T. S. Eliot, made no claims for the impersonality of the artist. She confided that her first work of fiction, *Scenes of Clerical Life,* drew upon family reminiscences, and many characters from her other books have been pursued to prototypes in her experience, often with her help. She worked from models then, probably habitually.

Like George Eliot herself, Dorothea had two husbands. Of the two, it is Mr. Casaubon who has deserved and attracted attention. He is a pedant of such Saharan aridity that the temptation to identify him has not often been resisted. Among the proffered candidates, the one most mentioned is Mark Pattison, rector of Lincoln College, Oxford. He had three points of *rapport*: an unhappy marriage with a wife much younger than himself, friendship with George Eliot, and the authorship of a life of the Swiss scholar (of the sixteenth century) Isaac Casaubon. George Eliot obviously borrowed from him the name of his subject, but other resemblances are tenuous, as if the price she paid for the one liberty was not to take others. John Sparrow, the most resolute supporter of Pattison as Casaubon's archetype, has rested his case largely on a passage in Sir Charles Dilke's unpublished autobiography, in which Dilke, later married to Mrs. Pattison, states that Casaubon's marriage proposal and Dorothea's answer were based closely on the equivalent Pattison was nondescript. It would seem that the motive power of the story must have come from some other region than the Congo.

This area may be guessed at with the help of a fact first pointed out in Jocelyn Baines's life of Conrad. The correspondence of Conrad's uncle, Thaddeus Bobrowski, discloses that Conrad, at the age of nineteen, did not—as he always said afterwards—fight a duel and suffer a bullet wound. What happened instead was that he gambled away at Monte Carlo some money his uncle had sent him, and then in self-disgust shot himself. This attempted suicide was probably the central event of Conrad's life. In the light of it, the qualities on which Marlow prides himself in *Heart of Darkness*—his rivetlike tenacity, his patience, his coolness under pressure—were the exact opposites of those displayed by the young Conrad. From the moment that he inflicted this wound, Conrad must have regarded it—and its scar—as a sign and symbol of a propensity to give way, to abandon himself. To call his villain Kurtz (German for 'short') was to memorialize this phase of his life when he was not yet Joseph Conrad but still Konrad Korzeniowski—a name prone to be shortened to Korz.

When recovered from his wound, Conrad went to England and sailed on an English coastal vessel. By this time or not long afterwards he had determined to slough off his old life, language, weakness. He decided to present himself no longer as a European but as an Englishman. In the 1880s he took and passed the three examinations which confirmed his navigational skill and executive capacity. If 1875 was the year that he virtually died, 1886 was the year of his virtual resurrection, for during it he qualified as first mate, he became a British subject, and he began to write. Writing was a way of avenging his suicide attempt. Marlow declares, 'mine is the speech that cannot be silenced.' Like Marlow, whose watchword is 'restraint', Conrad must have practised a conscious self-overcoming.

It would seem likely that young Korzeniowski's suicide attempt was extrapolated as the self-abandonment and moral

2 Dorothea's Husbands

A novelist, intent on his art, swallows into it other people along with himself. The living originals of fictional characters are elusive because they have been obliged by the writer to answer purposes not their own. It is as if they were evicted from a universe of free will into a deterministic one. The peril of confusing universes is one to which we have been alerted by fastidious critics and structuralists alike. Yet many novelists are themselves liable to this lapse, and fondly imagine that they have created characters out of people they have known. To follow them a little way is at worst devoted, and at best profitable, since the mode of translating characters from the one universe to the other must be close to basic movements of the mind, and so of critical as well as biographical consequence.

It may be easier to approach George Eliot by way of a writer more patently obsessive. In *Heart of Darkness,* Conrad made avowed use of his own trip to the Congo a dozen years before. Much of the narrative turns out to have an immediate parallel in his experience: Conrad did go to Brussels for his interview, did ship up the Congo River on a steamboat, did rescue a sick agent named Klein who died on the trip back. Yet the story has a quite different feel from the *Congo Diary* and from his letters of the time. And there is an important discrepancy: Klein was no Kurtz, no symbol of spiritual degradation. If anything, he the pre-eminence of theme over character. The heroic hero is particularly suspect. He is undermined not only by Lytton Strachey in *Eminent Victorians* (begun in 1912), but by Joyce, who calls his first novel *Stephen Hero* on the analogy of the ballad 'Turpin Hero', as if to guard by awkwardness against Stephen's being thought too glibly heroic; Granville-Barker writes plays in which the heroes do not deserve the name. The Edwardian male, as he appears in the books of this time, is often passive and put upon, like Maugham's Philip in *Of Human Bondage* (published in 1915 but drafted much earlier) or James's Strether, not only because this is the period of the feminist movement, but because it is the period of the hero's subordination. Concurrently, there is a loss of interest in what the hero does for a living—the emphasis comes so strongly upon their relatively disinterested mental activity that the occupations of Strether, Birkin, or Bloom become shadowy and almost nominal.

The amount of unity which the Edwardians instilled in their work is one of their extraordinary accomplishments. As Edith Wharton aggressively and seriously declared in the *Times Literary Supplement* in 1914, 'the conclusion of [a] tale should be contained in germ in its first page.' Conrad said in his preface to *The Nigger of the 'Narcissus'* that a work of art 'should carry its justification in every line.' There were occasional signs of revolt against this zealous 'desire and pursuit of the whole'.[1] So Wells found Henry James's insistence upon what he aptly called 'continuous relevance' to be objectionable. 'The thing his novel is about is always there,' he said disapprovingly, probably remembering how Joseph Conrad had irritatingly asked several times what Wells's own novels were really *about*. Wells thought himself later to be in favour of irrelevance, but he himself said that 'almost every sentence should have its share in the entire design,' and his best books are not thoughtlessly constructed; they are unified, as I have suggested, by the myth of selfhood.

[1] The title of Frederick Baron Corvo's novel, written in 1909.

The Edwardian aesthetic is fairly closely related to the imagist movement, or part of it. T. E. Hulme had interested Pound and others in his theory of intensive manifolds, that is, of wholes with absolutely interpenetrating parts instead of aggregates of separate elements. Hulme instructed them to place themselves 'inside the object instead of surveying it from the outside.' This position was that which Yeats also insisted upon when he said that the centre of the poem was not an impersonal essence of beauty, but an actual man thinking and feeling. He threw himself into the drama because he saw in it a rejection of externality, even of scenery, and an invitation to the writer to relinquish his self. Henry James was also convinced that the 'mere muffled majesty of irresponsible "authorship"' must be eliminated, and entered the consciousness of his most sensitive characters so thoroughly as to make possible disputes over where *he* stood.

What is confusing about the first imagist manifestoes is that this theory has got mixed up with another, a notion of objectivity and impersonality which, though it receives passing applause from Stephen in *A Portrait*, is not Joycean or Edwardian. Most Edwardian writing is *not* aloof, and the poems Pound praised for their Imagist qualities were poems like Yeats's 'The Magi', or Joyce's 'I hear an army', in which the writer is not at all removed from his image. Pound found a more congenial version of the Edwardian aesthetic in the vorticist movement, for that was manifestly based upon the absorption of the artist into his work, rather than his detachment from it. The word 'vortex' was something of an embarrassment. Pound said, with an obvious allusion to its female symbolism, 'In decency one can only call it a vortex.' But it had the advantage of implying the death of the poet in his poem: the ultimate arrogance of the artist is to disappear. This was the point of view of James and of Yeats as well as of Joyce; Edwardian writers were not much concerned with the artist as were writers of the nineties; they were concerned only with the art. They began to put away their flowing ties. Yeats could never understand the reluctance of some writers to let him improve their poems for them, since to him the work was all. The Edwardian writer is an artist not because he proclaims he is, as Wilde did, but because his works proclaim it. There is much less time for affectation and eccentricity, the point being to get on with the job. As Conrad said in his preface to *The Secret Agent,* 'In the matter of all my books I have always attended to my business. I have attended to it with complete self-surrender.'

Having yielded up his own identity to write his work, the Edwardian wished the reader to make comparable sacrifices. The *hypocrite lecteur* whom Baudelaire had arraigned was the reader who thought he might observe without joining in the work of art. This was to pass through the house like an irresponsible tenant, and the Edwardian novelist was too good a landlord for that. The reader must become responsible, must pay his rent. The sense of the importance of what their books were doing, the sense that only art, working through religious metaphor, can give life value, made the writers free to ask a great deal of their readers, and the literature of the time moved towards greater difficulty, the revival of Donne in 1912 being one of its manifestations, or towards greater importunacy, as in Lawrence. As Henry James remarked to a writer who complained that a meeting of authors was dull, 'Hewlett, we are not here to enjoy ourselves.'

It may seem that, though I have offered to exhibit two faces of Edward, I have in fact shown only one, and that one staring urgently towards the age of anxiety. Yet modern as Edwardian literature was, it was not fully modern. There was a difference in mood, which Yeats hinted at when he said that after 1900 nobody did any of the violent things they had done in the nineties. Can we not detect in this period, so distinguished in many ways, its writers so strict with themselves and with us, a sensible loss of vigour and heat? The Edwardians managed to retain much of the stability of the Victorians, but they did so only by becoming artful where their predecessors had seemed artless. The easy skill of Victorian narrative disappears, and while the Edwardians have good reasons for trying for more awesome effects, their work does not escape the charge of being self-conscious, almost *voulu*. It is the age of prefaces and of revisions. Their secular miracles, which they arranged so graciously, seem too easy now, and the modern equivalents of them, in Malamud or Bellow, for example, are deliberately wrought with far greater restraint. Writers of social protest like Galsworthy seem, as Esmé Wingfield-Stratford points out in *The Victorian Aftermath* (1934), resigned to their own helplessness. H. G. Wells, though so energetic, seems when he is not at his best too devout towards science, towards popular mechanics, and the later history of his writing of novels, which Gordon N. Ray has described, makes us wonder if even earlier he was quite so energetic as he appeared. Bennett presents his slices of life with the assurance of a good chef that life is appetizing, yet he has mastered his ingredients without much flair. *A Portrait of the Artist* is a work of genius, but wanting in gusto; and even Yeats is for much of this time more eloquent than implicated, not so much passionate as in favour of passion. Conrad achieves his effects, yet so laboriously, and with awkward narrators like Marlow who, in spite of his laudable artistic purposes, is a bit of a stick. The repetition of words and images, while helpful to the creation of unity, gives an air of pedantry to this aspiring period; the bird flies, but with leaden wings. I should like to find in George Gissing's book, *The Private Papers of Henry Ryecroft* (1903), a reflection of this diminution of vitality in a period that prided itself on its life. Gissing lived turbulently enough, but in this autobiographical fiction he is at pains to seem full of calm; a writer today might live calmly, but would want his books to be distraught.

The war, for I will not deny that it took place, made everything harder. The Edwardian confidence in artistic sensibility was broken down; the possibility of nothingness seems to replace the conviction of somethingness. Those Edwardian writers who lived through the war found stability less easy to come by. Before the war Yeats could write 'The Magi', with its longing for violence; after the war he wrote 'The Second Coming', in which violence inspires horror. Forster, who had accomplished his secular miracles rather handily in his early books, as by the trick of sending his thinner-blooded characters to lush Italy, descends lower to *A Passage to India*, where there is more brutality, and where the realizations to which he brings his personages are less ample, less reassuring. Pound, content with his troubadours before the war, turns upon himself in *Mauberley* with a strange blend of self-destruction and self-justification. Eliot, after politely mocking Edwardian politeness in 'Prufrock', becomes impolite in *The Waste Land*. Lawrence becomes strident, frantic, exhortatory, almost suffocating his own mind. Virginia Woolf, unable to find herself before the war, discovers at last a tense point round which to organize her books, and this is not so much unity as the threat of the break down of unity. Joyce, content to stay in the conscious mind in his earlier work, descends to a fiercer underworld in the *Circe* episode of *Ulysses,* where Edward VII appears, appropriately now turned to a nightmare figure babbling hysterically of 'Peace, perfect peace'. The miracle of birth was accomplished in *A Portrait of the Artist* without much resistance, but the comparable miracle in *Ulysses,* Bloom's rescue of Stephen in a world where gratuitous kindness seems out of context, is described by Joyce with great circumspection, as if humanistic miracles now embarrassed him. The religion of life keeps most of its Edwardian adherents, but it has begun to stir up its own atheists and agnostics.

8 A Postal Inquiry

Letter-writing imposes its small ceremonies even upon those who disdain the medium. An audience of one requires confrontation too, and even a perfunctory message discloses a little with what candour, modesty, or self-esteem its writer ranks himself in the world. Some accompanying hint of his appraisal of that world is bound to appear in the way he asserts or beseeches a tie with his correspondent, the degree of familiarity he takes for granted, the extent to which he solicits action or approbation, the alacrity and tenacity with which he joins issue. He may present himself in various guises, as machine, badger, deer, spider, bird. Whatever his mode, if he is a practising writer his assembling of words can never be totally negligent; once enslaved by language forever enslaved.

Joyce did not regard the letter or its brazen sister, the postcard, as a literary form of any consequence, but almost every day he burdened mailmen in different parts of his hemisphere with his sedulous correspondence. At letter's length he felt comfortable, and wrote sparely and to the point. His letters adopt a stance which at first may appear the reverse of that in his books. His creative works are humorous, lyrical, daring. These qualities appear from time to time in his correspondence, but its prevailing tenor is wry, terse, pressed down. 'I am in double trouble, mental and material,' he writes, and says in another letter, 'my spiritual barque is on the rocks.' In both of these the statement has a sweep and finality which paradoxically imply that all may not be lost. His summaries of his condition are sometimes more epigrammatic: 'My mouth is full of decayed teeth and my soul of decayed ambitions.' And sometimes he relents a little to joke: 'Well! (as Mr Pater beautifully says) I have reached the low-water mark in Xmases this 'ere time.' He is fond of deflating his life into a vista of ludicrous confusion. As Joyce writes later of Shem, 'O! the lowness of him was beneath all up to that sunk to!' In an early letter he wrote that he could not enter society except as a vagabond, and there is perhaps always a submerged pleasure in his not being an upstanding British subject.

The sense of contradiction between his works and his letters is illusory. The attitude of resignation is not so far removed from that of confidence as it first appears. It contains, in fact, a peremptory note. Underneath themes which are favourites of Joyce from beginning to end—the meticulous exposition of his penury, his physical weakness, or his discouragement—there is the conviction that he expresses rarely because he holds it so unshakeably, that his needs are trivial when weighed with his deserts. The letters simultaneously plead and berate. He tells his brother, 'Do not delay so long executing my requests as I waste a lot of ink.' He demands patronage rather than charity. Joyce's conviction of merit was justified in the event, yet he was imbued with it long before there were publications or even manuscripts to confirm it; confidence in his powers may be said to have antedated their manifestation.

Because of this confidence, he has little patience with those who fail to pay tribute to his talent, and is likely to shift suddenly from supplicant to renunciant. He is regularly on the verge of scorning the help he requires. This readiness to 'doff the world aside' is characteristic of him. He is like Stephen in *A Portrait of the Artist as a Young Man,* who counters his girl's practical questions about his future by making 'a sudden gesture of a revolutionary nature', evidently a dismissal of everything in his present life. Joyce was given to such gestures, as when he went to Paris in 1902 and again in 1903, when he eloped with Nora Barnacle in 1904, when he left Trieste for Rome in 1906 and Rome for Trieste in 1907. A mood of this sort impelled him to write his brother from Trieste, at the age of twenty-three, 'If I once convince myself that this kind of life is suicidal to my soul, I will make everything and everybody stand out of my way as I did before now.' In a letter to his aunt Josephine Murray he threatened to leave his new family as he had left his old one: 'I suppose you will shake your head now over my coldness of heart which is probably only an unjust name for a certain perspicacity of temper or mind.' In later life, angered and pained by his friends' dislike for *Finnegans Wake,* he said he would abandon the writing of the book to James Stephens. Many of these intentions were not carried out; Joyce did not leave his wife, and while Stephens was more or less willing to complete the book, in the end he was mysteriously not called upon. In retrospect, it is clear that Joyce's secret motive in making most of his threats, though not all, was to compel the contrapuntal encouragement which would warrant his not fulfilling them. But the urge to renounce was always present in his mind as a strong possibility, and no doubt reinforced him in repudiating easy solutions to artistic as well as personal problems, thus making possible his elaborate and great solutions. As he said himself of his literary work, he wanted to feel that he had overcome difficulties.

Though his gestures of renunciation, and threats of gestures, might argue that Joyce was as he called Ibsen, an 'egoarch', they must somehow be reconciled with his other qualities. Joyce was gregarious, filial, fraternal, uxorious, paternal, in varying degrees, and surrounded himself with relatives and friends. His letters to his son Giorgio and his daughter Lucia demonstrate his talent, when they were in the dumps, for finding miseries of his own equivalent to theirs, with which he proposed to cheer them up. He needed to return from hours of isolation, it

would seem, and to feel that a few people were in *rapport* with
him. This handshaking (and Joyce ends most of his letters in
Italian with '*una stretta di mano*') affects his work as well, miti-
gating its more savage extremes. Accordingly, in *A Portrait*
Stephen mocks his own gesture of renunciation by comparing it
to 'a fellow throwing a handful of peas up into the air', just as
Lynch mocks Stephen's Flaubertian view of the artist, as a god
paring his fingernails, by suggesting that these too may be
'refined out of existence'. This comic questioning does not dis-
prove the rhetoric, but lightens it, and effects a *rapprochement*
which ostensibly was disdained. The rebel's jokes, many of
them on himself, allow him back into the human family.

   Joyce's lifelong reluctance to comment publicly on his work
gives unusual value to these letters as evocations of his mental
scenery. They do not, however, offer more than fragments of
self-analysis, and we must relate them ourselves. Certain expres-
sions appear often enough to claim special notice. Among them
the word 'artist' thrusts itself forward as a starting-point. Joyce's
conception of himself as artist had origins in his early life; if
A Portrait of the Artist may be said to plead for anything, it is for
the continuity of the artistic temperament almost from infancy.
He apparently first articulated this vocation soon after he passed
from childhood to adolescence. The words 'artist' and 'puberty'
had, in fact, a relation that is several times hinted at in these
letters. As early as the age of fourteen, Joyce said,[1] he began to
go to brothels, initially with a strong sense of guilt. The Church
urged him to master these impulses, but he found himself unable, and at heart unwilling, to do so. At confession he could
find comfort and pardon, but not sanction. He was unwilling
to give up either the spiritual idealism which had sustained him
as a child, or the erotic drive which was agitating his adolescence.
If debauchery was a part of his character, and he sometimes said
it was, then it must be justified. The word 'artist', which in the
late nineteenth century had been invested with a secular awe,

---

[1] To his brother Stanislaus, who noted it down in a diary.

offered a profession which would protect all his soul instead of only its idealistic side, and might yet give it a profane sanctity. He thought of it as denoting something solid, unitary, and radiant, compounding into a new purity the errant flesh and the moral nature.

In early youth Joyce began to formulate the relation of art and the spiritual self into an aesthetic, as his letters testify; this aesthetic would vindicate him by establishing the primacy of the poet over the priest through a system rival to theology's. The artist was to be shown as devoted to integrating human experience on a level higher than the priest's, and without external or supernatural authority to make his work easier. This conscious definition of the principles of his art finds an accompaniment in the letters in Joyce's reiterated insistence that his own behaviour has been defensible and even praiseworthy. He tells his brother that his struggle with conventions 'was not entered into by me so much as a protest against these conventions as with the intention of living in conformity with my moral nature'. He granted contemptuously, 'There are some people in Ireland who would call my moral nature oblique, people who think that the whole duty of man consists in paying one's debts.' He is not less but more moral than other people. A year before he had written Nora Barnacle, 'Six years ago I left the Catholic Church, hating it most fervently. I found it impossible for me to remain in it on account of the impulses of my nature. . . . I made myself a beggar but I retained my pride.' The words 'nature', 'moral nature', and 'pride' stand for him as aspects of the one substance, the artist's soul.

Although Joyce does not bother to mention his moral nature often, his awareness of it lies behind most of his letters. It enables him to assert to Grant Richards that *Dubliners* is 'a chapter of the moral history of my country'. It underlies his criticism of other writers, such as Thomas Hardy. He writes his brother in December 1906 to complain of a book of Hardy's stories called *Life's Little Ironies,* and says:

One story is about a lawyer on the circuit who seduces a servant, then receives letters from her so beautifully written that he decides to marry her. The letters are written by the servant's mistress who is in love with the lawyer. After the marriage (servant is accompanied to London by mistress) husband says fondly, 'Now, dear J. K.-S- &c, will you write a little note to my dear sister, A. B X. etc and send her a piece of the wedding-cake. One of those nice little letters you know so well how to write, love.' Exit of servant wife. She goes out and sits at a table somewhere and, I suppose, writes something like this 'Dear Mrs X— I enclose a piece of wedding-cake.' Enter husband— lawyer, genial. Genially he says 'Well, love, how have you written' and then the whole discovery is found out. Servant-wife blows her nose in the letter and lawyer confronts the mistress. She confesses. Then they talk a page or so of copybook talk (as distinguished from servants' ditto). She weeps but he is stern. Is this as near as T.H. can get to life, I wonder? O my poor fledglings, poor Corley, poor Ignatius Gallaher! . . . What is wrong with these English writers is that they always keep beating about the bush.

In discountenancing Hardy, Joyce was attacking not only a kind of fiction but a way of seeing or failing to see. Hardy appeared to him to lack the directness which he had taught himself by accepting nothing because it had been accepted before. As a result, the characterization in Hardy's stories was a false one based upon conventional ideas of class. Joyce, living with a servant girl himself, was particularly entitled to detect the improbability here. He rejected as well the whole idiom as 'copybook talk'. For Joyce Hardy had lacked the courage to break through, and so was already dated, the moral fault breeding a literary one.

In his first years away Joyce associated artistic intrepidity with political self-consciousness, and he declared himself emphatically to be a 'socialistic artist'. The character of his socialism was never made clear; he mentions Wilde and Lassalle rather than Marx, and planned to translate Wilde's essay on the subject into Italian. He was closest to Wilde in conceiving of socialism as a means of protecting the self and enabling it to be free. The particular abuses in society which made socialism necessary were the property system, which offered no provision for writers; religion, with its burdensome load of belief; and marriage, perpetuating property arrangements and disregarding individual freedom. Joyce does not condescend to argue the case for socialism on an abstract level, but he names rich and church-married Oliver Gogarty as his epitome of the 'stupid, dishonest, tyrannical and cowardly burgher class'. Gogarty appears in the letters as a kind of mythical adversary, a Hayley to Joyce's Blake, and the later use of him as 'Buck Mulligan' was not accidental in the moral scheme of *Ulysses*.

Joyce did not hesitate to disclose that his socialism had a personal motivation, the hope of securing for himself a subsidy from the state. He wrote his brother, 'Some people would answer that while professing to be a socialist I am trying to make money: but this is not quite true at least as they mean it. If I made a fortune it is by no means certain that I would keep it. What I wish to do is to secure a competence on which I can rely, and why I expect to have this is because I cannot believe that any State requires my energy for the work I am at present engaged in.' Stanislaus objected that this socialism was thin, and his brother unexpectedly agreed, 'Of course you find my socialism thin. It is so and unsteady and ill-informed.' But any other system was tyranny, he maintained. Then on 25 February 1907, he reported, 'The interest I took in socialism and and the rest has left me. . . . I have no wish to codify myself as anarchist or socialist or reactionary.' He never calls himself a socialist again.

He gave temporary allegiance to one other political programme, that of *Sinn Féin*; this Irish movement proposed to attack England by an economic boycott, a method which pleased Joyce more than armed revolution. Not joining an army, and annoying England, were equally desirable in his mind. Apart from the Irish language programme, he said he was a nationalist. This interest in *Sinn Féin* also languished after a short time, however. At heart he was incapable of belonging to any political party, but he continued to make war in his own indirect way upon tyrannical authority.

Sometimes the moral note of Joyce's letters is more equivocal. There is, for example, the extraordinary letter he sent his mother from Paris soon after his twenty-first birthday:

Dear Mother Your order for $3^s/4^d$ of Tuesday last was very welcome as I had been without food for 42 hours (forty-two). Today I am twenty hours without food. But these spells of fasting are common with me now and when I get money I am so damnably hungry that I eat a fortune ($1^s/-$) before you could say knife. I hope this new system of living won't injure my digestion. I have no news from 'Speaker' or 'Express'. If I had money I could buy a little oil-stove (I have a lamp) and cook macaroni for myself with bread when I am hard beat. I hope you are doing what I said about Stannie—but I daresay you are not. I hope the carpet that was sold is not one of the new purchases that you are selling to feed me. If this is so sell no more or I'll send the money back to you by return of post. I think I am doing the best I can for myself but it's pulling the devil by the tail the greater part of the time. I expect to be served with my bill (£1-6-0 with oil) any day and then my happiness is complete. My condition is so exciting that I cannot go asleep at night often till four in the morning and when I wake I look at once under the door to see if there is a letter from my editors and I assure you when I see the wooden floor only morning and morning I sigh and turn back to sleep off part of my hunger. I have not gone to Miss Gonne nor do I intend to go. With the utmost stretching your last order will keep me Monday midday (postage half a franc probably)—then, I suppose, I must do another fast. I regret this as Monday and Tuesday are carnival days and I shall probably be the only one starving in Paris.   JIM

On the back of the letter Joyce transcribed a few bars of a song called 'Upa-Upa', which he said was played 'before the queen of some Indian island on occasions of state'.

This letter does not inspire an instant sympathy or a desire to join in singing 'Upa-Upa'. Its young writer is not self-sacrificing, not virtuous, not sensible, although he waves his hand distantly at these attributes. At first we see only self-pity and heartlessness in this assertion of his own needs as paramount. He takes unfair advantage of the fact that his mother's love is large enough to accept even the abuse of it. Yet there are twinges of conscience, sudden moments of concern for her, and there is evidence that he depends upon her for more than money, as if he could not live outside the environment of family affection, badly as he acts within it. The postscript about 'Upa-Upa' is a kind of humorous palinode; it seems to say, 'Never mind. We can still sing.'

Throughout the letter the emphasis is on his Lenten fasts for his art. In other correspondence with her too, Joyce asks his mother to approve his artistic plans while he is fully aware that they are beyond her grasp, just as later he makes the same demands of his less educated wife. He writes that he will publish a book of songs in 1907, a comedy in 1912, and an aesthetic system five years after that. 'This must interest you!' he insists, fearful that she may regard him as a starveling rather than as a starved hero. Her reply to many such pleas is a naked statement of maternal love: 'My dear Jim if you are disappointed in my letter and if as usual I fail to understand what you would wish to explain, believe me it is not from any want of a longing desire to do so and speak the words you want but as you so often said I am stupid and cannot grasp the great thoughts which are yours much as I desire to do so. Do not wear your soul out with tears but be as usually brave and look hopefully to the future.' To his harshness, and the defence of harshness by reference to his art, and the muted note of apology in her son's letters to her, May Joyce responded with a faultless simplicity.

The subdued ferocity of Joyce's letter was consistent enough with his consciousness of the difficulties of the life he had chosen. In his private phantasmagoria, which he never laid aside but had less use for later, he saw the world as giant and himself as Jack. He must evade, hide away in Pola and Trieste, and scheme (in 'silence, exile and cunning'), and one day the world would topple at his feet. To get out of Ireland was a step of this strategy. It was justified in two ways: the loftier was Rousseau's, 'If one wishes to devote one's books to the true benefit of one's country, one must write them abroad.' Joyce rephrased this as, 'The shortest way to Tara is *via* Holyhead.' A Parnell of art, he would 'create a conscience at last in the soul of this wretched race'. He predicted in a 1912 letter to his wife, 'I hope that the day may come when I shall be able to give you the fame of being beside me when I have entered into my Kingdom.' His images of departure evoked balancing images of return, which displayed themselves not only in his trips back to Dublin but in the ironical homecoming of *Exiles*, the 'eternal return' of *Finnegans Wake*, and the saturation of almost all his work in Irish times and places.

The second means of justifying departure was more reactive than independent. Joyce felt he had been 'betrayed' by his countrymen, not of course by all but by those on whom he might have expected to rely, his friends. The letter he wrote to Ibsen when he was eighteen indicates he already expected trouble from this quarter and was set to follow his master's example by 'absolute indifference' to them. But absolute indifference was not his mode. In certain moments he conceded that his decision did not depend upon his friends' behaviour; he wrote his brother that it was 'a youthfully exaggerated feeling of this maldisposition of affairs which urged me to pounce upon the falsehood in their attitude towards me as an excuse for escape'. We may even add that, without meaning to, he courted betrayal. As if to prepare the ground, he made great demands upon his friends, and in asserting his own freedom of action, he hampered theirs, to draw them into what he himself described as 'the Daedalean spell'. He tested their loyalty by making them his creditors, by leaning upon them, by asking their responses to his works and acts. The demands grew greater. His friends were like his readers, who had only to accept one difficult work when he devised another much harder for them to accept, in an ascending series. They, for their part, had never met anyone so enveloping, at once so contemptuous of their abilities and so avid for their allegiances. Their own individuality seemedpardized by Joyce's quiet importunacy. As signs of their resistance multiplied, Joyce saw these as inevitable; he did not recognize that the friendship he required of them was inordinate, yet his own doubts that they would persist in it contributed to that failure of which he then complained.

Sometimes he granted that he might himself be a little at fault, and this admission, rare as it was, lends support to his claim that he could free himself from his preconceptions when necessary. He allowed to Nora Barnacle that he had 'a contemptuous suspicious nature'. His habit of representing himself as worse than he was also offered encouragement to those who wanted to leave him. Before he went away from Dublin with her in 1904, he admitted that he had a propensity 'a little devilish . . . that makes me delight in breaking down people's ideas of me and proving to them that I am really selfish, proud, cunning and regardless of others'. But even as he denigrated his own character, he mustered support for it. So he wrote his brother in a burst of anger, 'My irregularities can easily be made the excuse of your conduct.' Others, with more faults than he, dared not risk his candour. He has only to ask, in self-depreciation, could I deserve more from the world than exile? when the question changes to: could I deserve less? as if to ask, who would want to be anything but an outcast?

His ironies may therefore be said to compete with each other. At one end of the scale he filters self-abasement through mockery; at the other, he approaches grandeur, feels it verging on grandiosity, and turns abruptly away. He wrote to inform his friend in Trieste, Alessandro Francini Bruni, of the magnificent praise which Valery Larbaud had lavished upon *Ulysses*, then wryly concluded: '*Son diventato un monumento—anzi vespasiano!*' ('I have become a monument—no, a vespasian!') When he announced to his brother that his situation in Trieste was a 'voluntary exile', he meant it, though the word 'voluntary' before 'exile' begged the question a little. But when he spoke of his departure with Nora Barnacle from Dublin to Pola as a 'hegira', the mood of self-mockery was in the ascendant.

The title of his autobiographical novel imposed the problem of reconciling two persistent attitudes towards himself. He had named it *Stephen Hero* in ironic allusion, perhaps, to Byron's *Childe Harold* as well as to the ballad of 'Turpin Hero', but the brag, archaically inverted, began to trouble him as too sceptical of its own vain gloriousness. His letters show that he thought about the matter a good deal. He wrote Stanislaus to say flatly, 'the whole structure of heroism is, and always was, a damned lie and . . . there cannot be any substitute for the individual passion as the motive power of everything—art and philosophy included.' All talk of selflessness and social purpose was poppy-cock. In response to a compliment about steadfastness in adversity, he replied, 'I dislike to hear of any stray heroics on the prowl for me.' Yet the issue was not dismissed so flippantly. He had written to Ibsen in 1900 that the quality most admirable in that artist was an 'inward heroism' which had for one aspect the 'wilful resolution to wrest the secret from life', and for another the 'absolute indifference to public canons of art, friends, and shibboleths'. Now, writing to Stanislaus again, he mused, 'Do you not think the search for heroics damn vulgar, and yet how are we to describe Ibsen?' The upshot of these ruminations was that he changed the title of his novel to *A Portrait of the Artist as a Young Man,* a title less likely to be misinterpreted, although the term 'young man' was meant humorously (he wrote Dámaso Alonso) insofar as it was applied to the infant on the first page.

Joyce did regard himself as a hero, but thought it advisable not to say so explicitly; he thought of himself also as in some ways a martyr, but as usual his way of saying so is by seeming to repudiate the idea. Referring to this Christlike resemblance, he wrote his brother, 'I must get rid of some of these Jewish bowels I have in me yet.' And in another letter he said, 'I am not likely to die of bashfulness but neither am I prepared to be crucified to attest the perfection of my art.' The figure pleased him, and a year later he remarked once more, 'I have written quite enough and before I do any more in that line I must see some reason why—I am not a literary Jesus Christ.' But three disavowels of the crown are less convincing than one. Whatever he might say in the cold mutton of letters, Joyce was fascinated by the Christlike analogies of the artist, and developed them fully in *A Portrait of the Artist*. A powerful sacrificial feeling sustained him as he fought for a literary foothold around southern Europe, staving off mosquitoes in Pola, instilling an alien tongue into Triestines, cashing cheques for other people in Rome. But he undercut it with modesty by jokingly or grimly calling attention to his defects and failures.

His behaviour with his books was a similar combination of aloofness and self-advertisement. The enormous pride of the artist was compatible with enormous exertions. He had his own press notices printed up and sent them, with chilling formality, to possible reviewers. He did not condescend to explain his own work, but through letters and conversations he laid down, as he told Harriet Shaw Weaver, the terms in which *Ulysses* was subsequently discussed. He was equally skilful with *Finnegans Wake*. There were earlier schemes which mixed self-exculpation with promotion, such as his letter to the press in 1911, complaining that publishers had broken contracts with him for *Dubliners* because of the book's forthrightness. Another was his public letter in 1919 protesting against mistreatment by the British Consulate General in Zürich. The protest in 1928 against the piracy of *Ulysses*, in which a hundred and fifty eminent men joined, was one of his shrewdest mixtures of publicity with high principle. He could never think of his works as popular, or as popular enough, and he felt justified in overcoming middle-class torpor and hostility by any means he could devise.

Sometimes his epistolary campaigns moved outside literature. One of these was on behalf of the tenor John Sullivan, whom

Joyce regarded as a kind of *alter ego*. Others involved such
schemes of enrichment as importing Irish tweeds to Trieste,
establishing a cinema in Dublin, managing a troupe of actors in
Zürich. These projects had much the same place in Joyce's mind
as the Sardinian silver mines in Balzac's, and like those came to
nothing, though they were also good ideas. His attitude in them
exhibited a combination of effrontery and involvement,
supplication and reserve.

This mixture permeates his letters and is somewhat explained
by them. Joyce often appeared to be cold and aloof, but in his
own view these qualities were less fundamental than others. He
thought of himself most fondly as fragile and vulnerable. Once
this part of his self-portrait becomes visible, other elements take
shape around it. The 'enigma of a manner', which he speaks in
the first draft of *A Portrait* of consciously fabricating, is seen as
an attempt at self-protection. 'Can you not see the simplicity
which is at the back of all my disguises? We all wear masks,' he
writes to Nora Barnacle, and he is pleased, at least temporarily,
when she pierces his 'magnificent poses' and recognizes him to
be an 'impostor'. His asperities show as attempts to overcome
an indulgence to which he feels so apt to become prey, and the
method of his prose books is a kind of absorption of the universe
rather than a facing up to it; he seems to draw it bit by bit inside
him, and conceives of the imagination as a womb.

Joyce liked to think of himself as weak and of others as
stronger than he. Like Shem, he 'disliked anything anyway
approaching a plain straightforward standup or knockdown
row'. Men were stronger physically and women stronger
spiritually. 'I am so helpless tonight, helpless, helpless!' he writes
his wife, and in his poem, 'A Prayer', he begs, 'Take me, save me,
soothe me, O spare me.' This attitude is the one he regularly
assumes in his letters to his wife, and is the more surprising in
that she might have been expected to take it towards him. The
letters to Nora Barnacle Joyce, which make this position plain,
are psychologically the most important he wrote; they move

gradually towards self-surrender as if it were a kind of Ultima Thule.

At first their tone is jaunty, with some of that 'assumed don-giovannism' which he attributed to the young Shakespeare. But within a month of the beginning of their courtship, the tone is solemnized. She must become his mistress, to be sure, but he seems more occupied with something else, that she become his fellow-conspirator against the established order. 'My mind rejects the whole present social order and Christianity— home, the recognised virtues, classes of life, and religious doctrines,' he writes her in August 1904. His intransigence to the world is related to his submission to her. Their elopement must not be sportive but agonized, a sign and portent of his future work. He was aware that to his father, and to many of his friends, the relationship with Nora Barnacle was a misalliance. Though he pretended to be impervious to their criticism, 'their least word', he told her, 'tumbles my heart about like a bird in a storm.' Yet like Heine, as he says, and like others he does not trouble to name, he had the courage to see that the world was wrong about this as about other things. By virtue of being poor and in love with him, Nora became the banned sweetheart of a banned artist. 'It seemed to me that I was fighting a battle with every religious and social force in Ireland for you and that I had nothing to rely on but myself.' Chambermaid and prodigal son might make a match of it; obloquy was a state they might share like pleasures of the bed.

Joyce's affection for Nora Barnacle developed rapidly, though she complained it lagged behind her own. He was already unconsciously altering his role in the affair from active to passive. 'Allow me, dearest Nora,' he wrote her, 'to tell you how much I desire that you should share any happiness that may be mine and to assure you of my great respect for that love of yours which it is my wish to deserve and to answer.' The word 'love' was one that mustered up all his doubts, doubts of his own sincerity, doubts of the emotion itself. To talk of 'spiritual love', he informed Stanislaus, was 'lying drivel', though in a few years he used the phrase without irony. But as he said, he was deeply impressed by the unqualified feeling Nora Barnacle had for him, and the fact that she expressed it without the coyness he had come to expect in girls of his age. 'I never could speak to the girls I used to meet at houses,' he wrote her later. 'Their false manners checked me at once.' Stephen Dedalus represents Shakespeare as equally shy. If Nora was untutored she was also unspoiled, a 'simple honorable soul', and one 'incapable of any of the deceits which pass for current morality'. It was very important for him, knowing with what intricate devices he met most people, to have in her someone he could trust. His reserve, his sense of watching his own dignity, are involved in almost all his other relationships. With Harriet Shaw Weaver, for example, he seems to want not only to act politely towards her, but to see himself as meeting the English Protestant middle class with adequate decorum. A certain gentleness comes through regardless, but almost against his will. With Nora there was the possibility available to him nowhere else, of complete self-revelation, a great relief to a suspicious man. He came to feel that she was more than wife or mistress; she must triple as a symbol of Ireland and a more genuine one than Yeats's Maud Gonne. In her he saw, as he said, 'the beauty and the doom of the race of which I am a child', and he asked her, 'O take me into your soul of souls and then I will become indeed the poet of my race.'

This yielding of himself was not achieved without difficulty. Joyce had to pass through stages of amusement, perplexity, boredom, and even distrust. The last was of course the most serious. In 1909, on his first trip back to Dublin, he was led mistakenly to believe that Nora had been faithless to him during a period which he held sacred, the early months of their love. In a few days he was undeceived, and felt guilty for having so misjudged her. His first letters were filled with remorse: 'What a worthless fellow I am!' But gradually he tried to turn the incident to advantage by ushering her into a greater intimacy. His letters became a turbulent mixture of erotic imagery and apologies for it, the apologies being accompanied by equally extreme flights of adoration. His relationship with her had to counterbalance all his rifts with other people. Having become partners in spiritual love, they must now share an onanistic complicity, agitating each other to sexual climax by means of their letters. In this way Joyce renewed the conspiratorial and passionate understanding that they had had when they first left Ireland together.

These letters of 1909 and 1912 present Joyce with more intensity than any others. Often they transfer habitual attitudes to a different plane; he does not ask her for more money, as he does others, but for more proof of affection. He reminds her constantly of his art, often combining it with love tokens: the first present he brings her from Dublin is a necklace inscribed with a line from one of his poems, and the next is a manuscript of *Chamber Music* laboriously copied out on parchment. His art is the lofty counterpart of that deeper nature which he will divulge otherwise only to her. And he mixes his pleas with tender rebuke, scolding her for scolding him. She is too rude to him, ruder than he deserves. To vary the note, he sometimes delights in acknowledging his faults, including his infidelities with prostitutes, in imagining her as even more merciless to him, as whipping him like the ladies of Sacher-Masoch, and with furs on to complete the picture. 'You have me completely in your power,' he enjoys telling her, pleased to have, as whipping-boy, her undivided attention. Then, to renew his innocence and hers, he leans upon her as if she were a mother, and longs to be her child or even her unborn infant: 'Take me into the dark sanctuary of your womb. Shelter me, dear, from harm!'

Yet one route of distrust remains: he can never quite understand her implacable unlikeness to him. He finds himself suspicious again: 'Are you with me, Nora, or are you secretly against me?' When most allayed, this feeling can tease itself almost pleasurably with a curiosity like John Donne's about her body's life before she knew him, but she cannot reassure him enough: 'I am sure there are finer fellows in Galway than your poor lover but O, darling, *one day* you will see that I will be something in my country.' And he writes again, in a letter three years later, 'Can your friend in the sodawater factory or the priesteen write my verses?' He adores her as 'my beautiful wild flower of the hedges, my dark-blue rain-drenched flower', and compares her to the Virgin, then desecrates this romantic lyricism by naming her his 'fuckbird' instead. One moment he is an angel, the next a frog, and then back again. He likes to boast of his prudishness with men, at whose dirty stories he never even smiles, to give a greater secretive value to his outspokenness with her, and to indicate that this erotic singleness must prove the essential innocence of his nature.

The atmosphere is not one of Catholic guilt, but it is certainly not one of pagan insouciance either. He feels compelled to set images of purity against images of impurity. He dwells upon the association of the sexual and excretory organs, then fears she will consider him corrupt, although he has found learned sanction in Spinoza, yet he also wants corruption to be a part of their love as well as incorruption. 'Are you too, then, like me,' he asks hopefully, 'one moment high as the stars, the next lower than the lowest wretches?' They must share in shame, shamelessness, and unashamedness.

Frank as these letters are, their psychology can easily be misunderstood. They were intended to accomplish sexual gratification in him and inspire the same in her, and at moments they fasten intently on peculiarities of sexual behaviour, some of which might be technically called perverse. They display traces of fetishism, anality, paranoia, and masochism, but before quartering Joyce into these categories and consigning him to their tyranny we must remember that he was capable, in his work, of ridiculing them all as Circean beguilements, of turning them into vaudeville routines. Then too, the letters rebuke such obvious labels by an ulterior purpose; besides the immediate physical goal, Joyce wishes to anatomize and reconstitute and crystallize the emotion of love. He goes further still; like Richard Rowan in *Exiles*, he wishes to possess his wife's soul, and have her possess his, in utter nakedness. To know someone else beyond love and hate, beyond vanity and remorse, beyond human possibility almost, is his extravagant desire.

In later life Joyce evidently wrote Nora in a similar vein, but with more sense of human limitations. Their relationship never achieved the complete understanding for which he had striven. The only letter of importance that has survived was one sent her in April 1922, when against his will she took their two children to Galway. She seems to have said she would not return, and wrote to ask him for money to remain. He replied:

8.30 a.m. Thursday
My darling, my love, my queen: I jump out of bed to send you this. Your wire is postmarked 18 hours later than your letter which I have just received. A cheque for your fur will follow in a few hours, and also money for yourself. If you wish to live there (as you ask me to send two pounds a week) I will send that amount (£8 and £4 rent) on the first of every month. But you also ask me if I would go to London with you. I would go anywhere in the world if I could be sure that I could be alone with your dear self without family and without friends. Either this must occur or we must part forever, though it will break my heart. Evidently it is impossible to describe to you the despair I have been in since you left. Yesterday I got a fainting fit in Miss Beach's shop and she had to run and get me some kind of a drug. Your image is always in my heart. How glad I am to hear you are looking younger! O my dearest, if you would only turn to me now and read that terrible book which has now broken the heart in my breast and take me to yourself alone to do with me what you will! I have only 10 minutes to write this so forgive me. Will write again before noon and also wire. These few words for the moment and my undying unhappy love.

JIM

This letter, written while *Ulysses* was meeting with great success, is humourless and sad like almost all Joyce's love letters. It assumes the old humility of subject to queen, but as usual it is the subject who controls the royal treasury. He is as eager now as fifteen years before to buy furs for her. Each sign of weakness has its implicit limit: he begs for more affection, but is still able to threaten that without it they must part forever. His heart is broken, so she must read his book. His 'undying unhappy love' and his physical collapse are proofs of his dependence upon her, but they are also curiously self-regarding. With all his testimony of surrender, Joyce utterly dominated that scene.

A more complete picture of his mind though not of his emotions can be elicited from his imperfect and rather eerie liaison with Martha Fleischmann in Zürich in 1918 and 1919. Joyce wrote this young Swiss woman quite a few letters, of which four have survived. Their idiom is a less intense copy of that which he employed with his wife; he writes pitiably, with many references to physical weakness, and he prostrates himself before Martha. Though well aware that women are not necessarily susceptible to advances of this sort, Joyce seems to have been able to use no others. The letters make Martha his Virgin and Madonna like Nora before her; he suggests she might be Jewish but asks her not to take offence, since Jesus was born from the womb of a Jewess. And throughout he calls attention to his art, as in his slightly inaccurate remark that, at the age of thirty-five, he was at the same point as Dante when he began the *Divine Comedy* and Shakespeare when he had his affair with the Dark Lady of the Sonnets. He was actually thirty-six.

Joyce knew he was behaving absurdly, but he had never halted any line of action merely to avoid possible folly, and it is not necessary to doubt his statement in one letter that he was passing sleepless nights over her. That he intended only a clandestine affair, however, and so was not offering himself completely, is indicated by his caution in disguising his handwriting by using Greek e's, as Bloom does in writing another

Martha in *Ulysses*. The affair never came to much: the letters, and other information, suggest that Joyce engaged in a good deal of peering through windows at Martha Fleischmann, and that the chief pleasure he arrived at was probably voyeuristic like Earwicker's in the Phoenix Park. He recognized the implicit comedy afterwards by depicting a similar episode in Bloom's day, in which Gerty McDowell, like Martha Fleischmann, has a limp. There also a men's temperance retreat is going on at the Star of the Sea church, and the prayers to the Virgin are amusingly juxtaposed with Bloom's profane adoration of Gerty. Joyce, in turn, seems to have written Martha letters that contained obscene words, and his behaviour also admixed detachment and passion.

The later parody of the emotions does not prove that earlier they were false, and it is unlikely that Joyce laughed at the time. But even though he kept his sense of comedy in abeyance as he clutched tentatively for support at another female figure, it must have existed in reserve as a defence against possible humiliation, ready if called upon to turn amorous defeat into artistic triumph when his original feelings had run their course.

The dip and sway of Joyce's love letters make an amusing counterpoint to his letters to men. With Nora the effort is to rip away pretences, with men Joyce is very bespectacled and walking-sticked. There are exceptions, such as his bantering notes to Frank Budgen and Ezra Pound, but usually he pushes the correspondent away a little by continuing to employ 'Mr' after long association, by pretending some indifference to the things that most oppress him, by half-anticipating defeat in arguments, as with publishers, though he wishes to appear bold and steadfast.

Because of his disinclination to collide with men, or to be informal with more than two or three, Joyce's correspondence with his brother Stanislaus, especially from 1902 to 1912, stands almost by itself as a fairly frank expression of his intellectual position. It is comparable to the letters setting forth his emotional position to Nora. James, as older brother, asserted himself freely, and Stanislaus, as younger, disputed his conclusions but admired most of them; he considered James superior only in literary matters, not in politics or domestic behaviour. The relationship of the two was set from the first as one in which Stanislaus was to pay heavily. The letters make clear that by and large he accepted this arrangement to which he sometimes objected, and that James assumed it as a matter of course. From their correspondence Stanislaus emerges as a solid figure, helpful and cantankerous, roused by his brother to intellectual emulation as well as to envy and impatience.

The hints and declarations in his letters enable us to see Joyce a little as he saw himself. While he considered that rebellion had been for him the beginning of wisdom, a kind of birth of consciousness, he did not regard himself primarily as a rebel. His dominant image of himself was one of delicacy and fragility, of perpetual ill health and ill-luck, of a tenor among basses. It led him to imagine himself as like a deer or a bird or a woman, or like a Gandhian Christ. He reacted against varieties of power by juxtaposing the strong with the weak, Boylan with Bloom or the Ondt with the Gracehoper. Then his wit challenged the powerful masculine energies until they had lost their strength. He wished to protect the lyrical centre of his work by acknowledging with laughter all the absurdities of human conduct through which it must draw its breath. He counters a possible contempt for his almost effeminate delicacy by examining in the fullest and liveliest way its inescapably comic embodiment. Where other writers, like Wells, appear always to be thrusting, Joyce characterized himself more nearly by the parry. Each of his works concludes in a lyrical assertion, which is made possible by the undermining of maleness by comedy, as if brute force had to be overcome by subtler devices. In *Finnegans Wake* the Crimean War is reduced to a scatological joke, the battle of Waterloo to an extravaganza in a waxworks museum, and the World War to a prizefight; in *Ulysses* the Cyclops is defeated;

in *A Portrait* Ireland is left. Joyce's distaste for war, crime, and
brutality relate to this preference for all that is not the bully. His
work is not conceived as a blow in the face, but, his letters help
us to perceive, as a matrical envelopment.

But this appraisal of Joyce which his letters sponsor is not
entirely satisfactory. His disclaimers of masculinity, his assumption of 'feminine' weakness, were secondary manifestations.
After all, strong men have hidden themselves among women
before. His succession of mewing exhortations always sprang
from initial decisions inflexibly pursued. He cared for his
daughter with a solicitude that could be called feminine, but his
delicate coaxing and joking were directed to twist her mind
back to sanity, like a resistant piece of iron. Though he lived in
discouragement like a bad climate, and sporadically thought of
not finishing his books, he needle-and-threaded each one to its
conclusion. As if adjusting himself to his pliant, jointless body,
which was basically tough and wiry, he imagined himself in
the state of being malleable and passive, and commenced to live
there, like a second residence. The mixture of such qualities as
pride and plaintiveness, the flashes of candour amid stretches
of tortuous reticence or confessions that are off the point, lend
his spare self-portraiture in his letters an interest quite different
from that to be found in the shaped nuances of Henry James or
the open-collared eloquence of D. H. Lawrence. An urge to the
immoderate is always there, but at various distances from the
surface. Read in this light, Joyce's letters—the best of them—are
among the most interesting, and insinuating, ever written.

9 'He Do the Police in Different Voices'

Lloyds' most famous bank clerk revalued the poetic currency fifty years ago. As Joyce said, *The Waste Land* ended the idea of poetry for ladies. Whether admired or detested, it became, like *Lyrical Ballads* in 1798, a traffic signal. Hart Crane's letters, for instance, testify to his prompt recognition that from that time forward his work must be to outflank Eliot's poem. Today footnotes do their worst to transform innovations into inevitabilities. After a thousand explanations, *The Waste Land* is no longer a puzzle poem, except for the puzzle of choosing among the various solutions. To be penetrable is not, however, to be predictable. The sweep and strangeness with which Eliot delineated despair resist temptations to patronize Old Possum as old hat. Particular discontinuities continue to surprise even if the idea of discontinuous form—to which Eliot never quite subscribed and which he was to forsake—is now almost as familiar as its sober counterpart. The compound of regular verse and *vers libre* still wears some of the effrontery with which in 1922 it flouted both schools. The poem retains the air of a splendid feat.

Eliot himself was inclined to pooh-pooh its grandeur. His chiselled comment, which F. O. Matthiessen quotes, disclaimed any intention of expressing 'the disillusionment of a generation', and said that he did not like the word 'generation' or have a

plan to endorse anyone's 'illusion of disillusion'. To Theodore
Spencer he remarked in humbler mood, 'Various critics have
done me the honour to interpret the poem in terms of criticism
of the contemporary world, have considered it, indeed, as an
important bit of social criticism. To me it was only the relief of
a personal and wholly insignificant grouse against life. It is just
a piece of rhythmical grumbling.'

This statement is prominently displayed by Mrs. Valerie
Eliot in her excellent decipherment and elucidation of *The
Waste Land* manuscript (1971). If it is more than an expression
of her husband's genuine modesty, it appears to imply that he
considered his own poem, as he considered *Hamlet*, an inade-
quate projection of its author's tangled emotions, a Potemkin
village rather than a proper objective correlative. Yet no one
will wish away the entire civilizations and cities, wars, hordes of
people, religions of East and West, and exhibits from many
literatures in many languages that lined the Thames in Eliot's
ode to dejection. And even if London was only his state of mind
at the time, the picture he paints of it is convincing. His remark
to Spencer, made after a lapse of years, perhaps catches up
another regret, that the poem emphasized his *Groll* at the
expense of much else in his nature. It identified him with a
sustained severity of tone, with pulpited (though brief) citations
of Biblical and Sophoclean anguish, so that he became an
Ezekiel or at least a Tiresias. (In the original version John the
Divine made a Christian third among the prophets.) While
Eliot did not wish to be considered merely a satirist in his earlier
verse, he did not welcome either the public assumption that his
poetic mantle had become a hair shirt.

In its early version *The Waste Land* was woven out of more
kinds of material, and was therefore less grave and less organized. The first two sections had an over-all title (each had its
own title as well), 'He Do the Police in Different Voices', a
quotation from *Our Mutual Friend*. Dickens has the widow
Higden say to her adopted child, 'Sloppy is a beautiful reader

of a newspaper. He do the Police in different voices.' Among
the many voices in the first version, Eliot placed at the very
beginning a long conversational passage describing an evening
on the town, starting at 'Tom's place' (a rather arch use of his
own name), moving on to a brothel, and concluding with a
bathetic sunrise:

> First we had a couple of feelers down at Tom's place,
> There was old Tom, boiled to the eyes, blind . . .
> —("I turned up an hour later down at Myrtle's place.
> What d'y' mean, she says, at two o'clock in the morning,
> I'm not in business here for guys like you;
> We've only had a raid last week, I've been warned twice. . . .
> So I got out to see the sunrise, and walked home.

This vapid prologue Eliot decided, apparently on his own, to
expunge, and went straight into the now familiar beginning of
the poem.

Other voices were expunged by Eliot's friend Ezra Pound,
who called himself the *'sage homme'* (male midwife) of the poem.
Pound had already published in 1920 his own elegy on a shipwrecked man, *Hugh Selwyn Mauberley*. Except in the title, the
hero is unnamed, and like Eliot's protagonist, he is more an
observing consciousness than a person, as he moves through
salons, aesthetic movements, dark thoughts of wartime deaths.
But Mauberley's was an aesthetic quest, and Eliot deliberately
omitted this from his poem in favour of a spiritual one. (He
would combine the two later in *Four Quartets*.) When Eliot was
shown *Mauberley* in manuscript, he had remarked that the
meaning of a section in Part II was not so clear as it might be,
and Pound revised it accordingly. Now he reciprocated.

Pound's criticism of *The Waste Land* was not of its meaning;
he liked its despair and was indulgent of its neo-Christian hope.
He dealt instead with its stylistic adequacy and freshness. For example, there was an extended, unsuccessful imitation of *The Rape
of the Lock* at the beginning of 'The Fire Sermon'. It described

the lady Fresca (imported to the waste land from 'Gerontion' and one day to be exported to the States for the soft-drink trade). Instead of making her toilet like Pope's Belinda, Fresca is going to it, like Joyce's Bloom. Pound warned Eliot that since Pope had done the couplets better, and Joyce the defecation, there was no point in another round. To this shrewd advice we are indebted for the disappearance of such lines as:

> The white-armed Fresca blinks, and yawns, and gapes,
> Aroused from dreams of love and pleasant rapes.
> Electric summons of the busy bell
> Brings brisk Amanda to destroy the spell . . .
> Leaving the bubbling beverage to cool,
> Fresca slips softly to the needful stool,
> Where the pathetic tale of Richardson
> Eases her labour till the deed is done. . . .
> This ended, to the steaming bath she moves,
> Her tresses fanned by little flutt'ring Loves;
> Odours, confected by the cunning French,
> Disguise the good old hearty female stench.

The episode of the typist was originally much longer and more laborious:

> A bright kimono wraps her as she sprawls
> In nerveless torpor on the window seat;
> A touch of art is given by the false
> Japanese print, purchased in Oxford Street.

Pound found the décor difficult to believe: 'Not in that lodging house?' The stanza was removed. When he read the later stanza

> —Bestows one final patronising kiss,
> And gropes his way, finding the stairs unlit;
> And at the corner where the stable is,
> Delays only to urinate, and spit

he warned that the last two lines were 'probably over the mark', and Eliot acquiesced by cancelling them.

Pound persuaded Eliot also to omit a number of poems that

were for a time intended to be placed between the poem's
sections, then at the end of it. One was a renewed thrust at poor
Bleistein, drowned now but still haplessly Jewish and luxurious
under water:

> Full fathom five your Bleistein lies
> Under the flatfish and the squids.
>
> Graves' Disease in a dead jew's/man's eyes!
> Where the crabs have eat the lids . . .
>
> That is lace that was his nose . . .
>
> Roll him gently side to side
> See the lips unfold unfold
>
> From the teeth, gold in gold. . . .

Pound urged that this, and several other mortuary poems, did
not add anything, either to *The Waste Land* or to Eliot's previous work. He had already written 'the longest poem in the
English langwidge. Don't try to bust all records by prolonging
it three pages further.' As a result of this resmithying by *il
miglior fabbro*, the poem gained immensely in concentration.
Yet Eliot, feeling too solemnized by it, thought of prefixing
some humorous doggerel by Pound about its composition.
Later, in a more resolute effort to escape the limits set by *The
Waste Land*, he wrote *Fragment of an Agon*, and eventually,
'somewhere the other side of despair,' turned to drama.

Eliot's remark to Spencer calls *The Waste Land* a personal
poem. His critical theory was that the artist should seek impersonality, but this was probably intended not so much as a
nostrum as an antidote, a means to direct emotion rather than
let it spill. His letters indicate that he regarded his poems as
consequent upon his experiences. When a woman in Dublin[1]
remarked that Yeats had never really felt anything, Eliot asked

---

[1] Mrs. Josephine MacNeill, sometime Irish Ambassador to the Netherlands,
from whom I heard the account.

in consternation, 'How can you say that?' *The Waste Land* compiled many of the nightmarish feelings he had suffered during the seven years from 1914 to 1921, that is, from his coming to England until his temporary collapse.

Thanks to the letters quoted in Mrs. Valerie Eliot's introduction, and to various biographical leaks, the incidents of these years begin to take shape. In 1914 Eliot, then on a travelling fellowship from Harvard, went to study for the summer at Marburg. The outbreak of war obliged him to make his way, in a less leisurely fashion than he had intended, to Oxford. There he worked at his doctoral dissertation on F. H. Bradley's *Appearance and Reality*. The year 1914–15 proved to be pivotal. He came to three interrelated decisions. The first was to give up the appearance of the philosopher for the reality of the poet, though he equivocated about this by continuing to write reviews for philosophical journals for some time thereafter. The second was to marry, and the third to remain in England. He was helped to all three decisions by Ezra Pound, whom he met in September 1914. Pound had come to England in 1908 and was convinced (though he changed his mind later) that this was the country most congenial to the literary life. He encouraged Eliot to marry and settle, and he read the poems that no one had been willing to publish and pronounced his verdict, that Eliot 'has actually trained himself *and* modernized himself *on his own.*' Harriet Monroe, the editor of *Poetry*, must publish them, beginning with 'The Love Song of J. Alfred Prufrock'. It took Pound some time to bring her to the same view, and it was not until June 1915 that Eliot's first publication took place. This was also the month of his first marriage, on 26 June. His wife was Vivien Haigh-Wood, and Eliot remained, like Merlin with another Vivian, under her spell, beset and possessed by her intricacies for fifteen years and more.

What the newlyweds were like is recorded by Bertrand Russell, whom Eliot had known at Harvard. In a letter of July 1915, Russell wrote of dining with them:

I expected her to be terrible, from his mysteriousness; but she was not so bad. She is light, a little vulgar, adventurous, full of life—an artist I think he said, but I should have thought her an actress. He is exquisite and listless: she says she married him to stimulate him, but finds she can't do it. Obviously he married in order to be stimulated. I think she will soon be tired of him. He is ashamed of his marriage, and very grateful if one is kind to her.

Vivien was to dabble in painting, fiction, and verse, her mobile aspirations an aspect of her increasing instability. Ten years later her husband was to describe her to Russell as 'still perpetually baffling and deceptive. She seems to me like a child of 6 with an immensely clever and precocious mind. She writes *extremely* well (stories, etc.) and great originality. And I can never escape from the spell of her persuasive (even coercive) gift of argument.'

Eliot's parents did not take well to their son's doings, though they did not, as has been said by Robert Sencourt, cut him off. His father, president of the Hydraulic Press Brick Company of St. Louis, had expected his son to remain a philosopher, and his mother, though a poet herself, did not like the *vers libre* of 'Prufrock' any better than the free and easy marriage. To both parents it seemed that bright hopes were being put aside for a vague profession in the company of a vague woman in a country only too distinctly at war. They asked to see the young couple, but Vivien Eliot was frightened by the perils of the crossing, perhaps also by those of the arrival. So Eliot, already feeling 'a broken Coriolanus', as Prufrock felt a Hamlet *manqué*, took ship alone in August for the momentous interview.

His parents urged him to return with his wife to a university career in the States. He refused: he would be a poet, and England provided a better atmosphere in which to write. They urged him not to give up his dissertation when it was so near completion, and to this he consented. He parted on good enough terms to request their financial help when he got back to London, and they sent money to him handsomely, as he acknowledged—not handsomely enough, however, to release him from the necessity of very hard work. He taught for a term at the High Wycombe Grammar School, between Oxford and London, and then for two terms at Highgate Junior School. He completed his dissertation and was booked to sail on 1 April 1916 to take his oral examination at Harvard; when the crossing was cancelled, his academic gestures came to an end. In March 1917 he took the job with Lloyds Bank, in the Colonial and Foreign Department, at which he stuck for eight years.

During the early months of their marriage the Eliots were helped also by Russell, who gave them a room in his flat, an act of benevolence not without complications for all parties. Concerned for his wife's health, and fearful—it may be—that their sexual difficulties (perhaps involving psychic impotence on his part) might be a contributing factor, Eliot sent her off for a two-week holiday with Russell. The philosopher found the couple none the less devoted to each other, but noted in Mrs. Eliot a sporadic impulse to be cruel towards her husband, not with simple but with Dostoevskyan cruelty. 'I am every day getting things more right between them,' Russell boasted, 'but I can't let them alone at present, and of course I myself get very much interested.' The Dostoevskyan quality affected his imagery: 'She is a person who lives on a knife-edge, and will end as a criminal or a saint—I don't know which yet. She has a perfect capacity for both.'[1]

The personal life out of which came Eliot's personal poem now began to be lived in earnest. Vivien Eliot suffered obscurely from nerves, her health was subject to frequent collapses, she complained of neuralgia, of insomnia. Her journal for 1 January 1919 records waking up with migraine, 'the worst yet,' and

[1] Russell later claimed that he had given Eliot the idea for some lines in *The Waste Land*. 'After seeing troop trains departing from Waterloo, I used to have strange visions of London as a place of unreality. I used in imagination to see the bridges collapse and sink, and the whole great city vanish like a morning mist. Its inhabitants began to seem like hallucinations, and I would wonder whether the world in which I thought I had lived was a mere product of my own febrile imagination.' (*Autobiography*, II (1968), 18.)

staying in bed all day without moving; on 7 September 1919, she records 'bad pain in right side, very very nervous.' Ezra Pound, who knew her well, was worried that the passage in *The Waste Land*,

> "My nerves are bad to-night. Yes, bad. Stay with me.
> "Speak to me. Why do you never speak? Speak.
> "What are you thinking of? What thinking? What?
> "I never know what you are thinking. Think."

might be too photographic. But Vivien Eliot, who offered her own comments on her husband's verse (and volunteered two excellent lines for the low-life dialogue in 'A Game of Chess'),[1] marked the same passage as 'Wonderful'. She relished the presentation of her symptoms in broken metre. She was less keen, however, on another line from this section, 'The ivory men make company between us,' and got her husband to remove it. Presumably its implications were too close to the quick of their marital difficulties. The reference may have been to Russell, whose attentions to Vivien were intended to keep the two together. Years afterwards Eliot made a fair copy of *The Waste Land* in his own handwriting, and reinserted the line from memory. (It should now be added to the final text.) But he had implied his feelings six months after his marriage when he wrote in a letter to Conrad Aiken, 'I have lived through material for a score of long poems in the last six months.'

Russell commented less sympathetically about the Eliots later, 'I was fond of them both, and endeavoured to help them in their troubles until I discovered that their troubles were what they enjoyed.' Eliot was capable of estimating the situation shrewdly himself. In his poem, 'The Death of Saint Narcissus', which *Poetry* was to publish in 1917 and then, because he withdrew it probably as too close to the knuckle, failed to do so, and which he thought for a time of including in *The Waste Land*,

---

[1] "If you don't like it you can get on with it
What you get married for if you don't want to have children"

Eliot wrote of his introspective saint, 'his flesh was in love with the burning arrows. . . . As he embraced them his white skin surrendered itself to the redness of blood, and satisfied him.' For Eliot, however, the search for suffering was not contemptible. He was remorseful about his own real or imagined feelings, he was self-sacrificing about hers, he thought that remorse and sacrifice, not to mention affection, had value. In the Grail legends which underlie *The Waste Land*, the Fisher King suffers a Dolorous Stroke that maims him sexually. In Eliot's case the Dolorous Stroke had been marriage. He was helped thereby to the poem's initial clash of images, 'April is the cruellest month,' as well as to hollow echoes of Spenser's *Prothalamion* ('Sweet Thames, run softly till I end my song'). From the barren winter of his academic labours Eliot had been roused to the barren springtime of his nerve-wracked marriage. His life spread into paradox.

Other events of these years seem reflected in the poem. The war, though scarcely mentioned, exerts pressure. In places the poem may be a covert memorial to Henry Ware Eliot, the unforgiving father of the ill-adventured son. Vivien Eliot's journal records on 8 January 1919, 'Cable came saying Tom's father is dead. Had to wait all day till Tom came home and then to tell him. *Most terrible.*' Eliot's first explicit statement of his intention to write a long poem comes in letters written later in this year. The references to 'the king my father's death' probably derive as much from this actual death as from *The Tempest*, to which Eliot's notes evasively refer. As for the drowning of the young sailor, whether he is Ferdinand or a Phoenician, the war furnished Eliot with many examples, such as Jean Verdenal, a friend from his Sorbonne days, who was killed in the Dardanelles.[1] But the drowning may be as well an extrapolation of Eliot's feeling that he was now fatherless as well as rudderless.

---

[1] Verdenal has received the posthumous distinction of being called Eliot's lover, but in fact the rumours of homosexuality—not voiced directly in Sencourt's recent memoir but whispered in all its corners—remain unwitnessed.

The fact that the principal speaker appears in a new guise in the last section, with its imagery of possible resurrection, suggests that the drowning is to be taken symbolically rather than literally, as the end of youth. Eliot was addicted to the portrayal of characters who had missed their chances, become old before they had really been young. So the drowned sailor, like the buried corpse, may be construed as the young Eliot, himself an experienced sailor, shipwrecked in or about *l'an trentièsme de son eage,* like the young Pound in the first part of *Hugh Selwyn Mauberley* or Mauberley himself later in that poem, memorialized only by an oar.

It has been thought that Eliot wrote *The Waste Land* in Switzerland while recovering from a breakdown. But much of it was written earlier, some in 1914 and some, if Conrad Aiken is to be believed, even before. A letter to John Quinn indicates that much of it was on paper in May 1921. The breakdown, or rather, the rest cure, did give Eliot enough time to fit the pieces together and add what was necessary. At the beginning of October 1921 he consulted a prominent neurologist, who advised three months away from remembering 'the profit and loss' in Lloyds Bank. When the bank had agreed, Eliot went first to Margate and stayed for a month from 11 October. There he reported with relief to Richard Aldington that his 'nerves' came not from overwork but from an 'aboulie' (Hamlet's and Prufrock's disease) 'and emotional derangement which has been a lifelong affliction.' But, whatever reassurance this diagnosis afforded, he resolved to consult Dr. Roger Vittoz, a psychiatrist in Lausanne. He rejoined Vivien and on 18 November went with her to Paris. It seems fairly certain that he discussed the poem at that time with Ezra Pound. In Lausanne, where he went by himself, Eliot worked on it and sent revisions to Pound and to Vivien. Some of the letters exchanged between him and Pound survive. By early January 1922 he was back in London, making final corrections. The poem was published in October.

The manuscript had its own history. In gratitude to John

Quinn, the New York lawyer and patron of the arts, Eliot presented it to him. Quinn died in 1924, and most of his possessions were sold at auction; some, however, including the manuscript, were inherited by his sister. When the sister died, her daughter put many of Quinn's papers in storage. But in the early 1950s she searched among them and found the manuscript, which she then sold to the Berg Collection of the New York Public Library. The then curator enjoyed exercising seignorial rights over the collection, and kept secret the whereabouts of the manuscript. After his death its existence was divulged, and Valerie Eliot was persuaded to do her knowledgeable edition.

She did so the more readily, perhaps, because her husband had always hoped that the manuscript would turn up as evidence of Pound's critical genius. It is a classic document. No one will deny that it is weaker throughout than the final version. Pound comes off very well indeed; his importance is comparable to that of Louis Bouilhet in the history of composition of *Madame Bovary*. Yeats, who also sought and received Pound's help, described it to Lady Gregory: 'To talk over a poem with him is like getting you to put a sentence into dialect. All becomes clear and natural.' Pound could not be intimidated by pomposity, even Baudelairean pomposity.

> London, the swarming life you kill and breed,
> Huddled between the concrete and the sky;
> Responsive to the momentary need,
> Vibrates unconscious to its formal destiny.

Next to this he wrote 'B-ll-S'.[1] Pound was equally peremptory about a passage that Eliot seems to have cherished, perhaps because of childhood experiences in sailing. It was the depiction at the beginning of 'Death by Water' of a long voyage, a modernizing and Americanizing of Ulysses' final voyage as given by Dante, but joined with sailing experiences of Eliot's youth:

[1] Pound's comments appear in red on the letterpress transcription facing the reproduction of each manuscript page.

> Kingfisher weather, with a light fair breeze,
> Full canvas, and the eight sails drawing well.
> We beat around the cape and laid our course
> From the Dry Salvages to the eastern banks.
> A porpoise snored upon the phosphorescent swell,
> A triton rang the final warning bell
> Astern, and the sea rolled, asleep.

From these lines Pound was willing to spare only

> with a light fair breeze
> We beat around the cape from the Dry Salvages.
> A porpoise snored on the swell.

All the rest was—seamanship and literature. It became clear that the whole passage might as well go, and Eliot asked humbly if he should delete Phlebas as well. But Pound was as eager to preserve the good as to expunge the bad: he insisted that Phlebas stay because of the earlier references to the drowned Phoenician sailor. With equal taste, he made almost no change in the last section of the poem, which Eliot always considered to be the best, perhaps because it led into his subsequent verse. It marked the resumption of almost continuous form.

Eliot did not bow to all his friend's revisions. Pound feared the references to London might sound like Blake, and objected specifically to the lines

> To where Saint Mary Woolnoth kept the time,
> With a dead sound on the final stroke of nine.

Eliot wisely retained them, only changing 'time' to 'hours'. Next to the passage

> "You gave me hyacinths first a year ago;
> "They called me the hyacinth girl"

Pound marked 'Marianne', and evidently feared—though Mrs. Eliot's note indicates that in his last years, when asked, he denied it—that the use of quotation marks would look like an imitation of Marianne Moore. (He had warned Miss Moore of the equivalent danger of sounding like Eliot in a letter of 16 December 1918.) But Eliot, for whom the moment in the hyacinth garden had obsessional force—it was based on feelings, though not on a specific incident in his own life—made no change.

Essentially Pound could do for Eliot what Eliot could not do for himself. There was some reciprocity, not only in *Mauberley* but in the *Cantos*. When the first three of these appeared in *Poetry* in 1917, Eliot offered criticism which was followed by their being completely altered. It appears, from the revised versions, that he objected to the elaborate wind-up, and urged a more direct confrontation of the reader and the material. A similar theory is at work in Pound's changes in *The Waste Land*. Chiefly by excision, he enabled Eliot to tighten his form and get 'an outline', as he wrote in a complimentary letter of 24 January 1922. The same letter berated himself for 'always exuding my deformative secretions in my own stuff . . .' and for going 'into nacre and objets d'art'. Yet if this was necessity for Pound, he soon resolved to make a virtue of it, and perhaps partially in reaction in Eliot's form, he studied out means of loosening his own in the *Cantos*. There was to be no outline. The fragments which Eliot wished to shore and reconstitute Pound was willing to keep unchanged, and instead of mending consciousness, he allowed it to remain 'disjunct' and its experiences to remain 'intermittent'. Fits and starts, 'spots and dots', seemed to Pound to render reality much more closely than the outline to which he had helped his friend. He was later to feel that he had gone wrong, and made a botch instead of a work of art. Notwithstanding his doubts, the *Cantos*, with their violent upheaval of sequence and location, stand as a rival eminence to *The Waste Land* in modern verse.

Notes and Index

Notes

I LITERARY BIOGRAPHY

2   where, . . . his naked back / Katharine Balderston, 'Johnson's
    Vile Melancholy', in *The Age of Johnson: Essays Presented to C. B.
    Tinker*, ed. F. W. Hilles (New Haven, Conn., 1949), 3–14.

5–6 'The child . . . an instant' / Jean-Paul Sartre, *Saint Genet: Actor
    and Martyr*, trans. Bernard Frechtman (New York, 1963; Lon-
    don, 1964), 26–7.

7   'It cannot . . . *par excellence*' / Erik H. Erikson, *Young Man
    Luther* (New York, 1962), 193.

    Luther did not invent . . . medieval schoolmen / Roland
    Bainton, 'Luther: A Psychiatric Portrait', *Yale Review*, XLVIII
    (Spring 1959), 405–10.

8   'He suddenly . . . psychological theory' / Erikson, *Young Man
    Luther*, 23, 37.

9   'All in all . . . in others' / Ibid., 249.

10 'In a list . . . remained celibate' / Leon Edel, *Henry James: The
    Untried Years: 1843–1870* (Philadelphia and London, 1953), 55.

11 'Two forces . . . chaos of feeling' / Edel, *Henry James: The
    Treacherous Years: 1895–1901* (Philadelphia and London, 1969),
    109.

    'The physical habits . . . and anecdotage' / Ibid., 17.

12 'On the way back . . . garden of spring' / George D. Painter,
    Proust: The Early Years (London and Boston, 1959), 16–17.

14 'The "morbid melancholy" . . . intellectual excellence' /
    James Boswell, *Life of Johnson* (Oxford Standard Authors,
    London, 1953), 47–50.

16   'the kick that . . . to direction' / Samuel Beckett, *Murphy*
     (London, 1938), 78.

     to discover . . . with Diderot's . . . prose / Leo Spitzer,
     'The Style of Diderot', in *Linguistics and Literary History* (Princeton, N.J., 1967).

2 DOROTHEA'S HUSBANDS

19   She confided . . . family reminiscences / J. W. Cross, *George
     Eliot's Life* (Edinburgh and London, 1885), II, 66.

     The most resolute . . . Pattison letters / John Sparrow, *Mark
     Pattison and the Idea of a University* (Cambridge, 1967), 9–18;
     Gordon S. Haight, *George Eliot: A Biography* (Oxford and New
     York, 1968), 449, 563–5; *Notes and Queries*, CCXIII (May 1968),
     191–4, 432–5, 469.

21   'never got farther . . . theological dogma' / Eliza Lynn
     Linton, *My Literary Life* (London, 1899), 42.

     'well got up and well preserved' / Ibid., 45.

23–4 'It is Mr. Mackay's faith . . . our religion' / *Essays of George
     Eliot*, ed. Thomas Pinney (London, 1968), 30–1.

24   'rather worse . . . of the place' / *The George Eliot Letters*, ed.
     Gordon S. Haight, 7 vols. (London and New Haven, Conn.,
     1954–6), II, 29, 31.

26   a passage . . . called attention / Barbara Hardy, *The Appropriate Form* (London, 1964), 116–17.

27   'I venture . . . these Utopias' / *Letters*, I, 22.

     advises against . . . 'to my grave' / Haight, *George Eliot*, 23;
     Letters, I, 22.

29   he follows closely . . . 'book of Genesis' / *Essays*, 36.

29–30 'Impossible to . . . sorry for him' / *Letters*, V, 322.

30   more in common with Ladislaw / Matilde Blind, *George Eliot*
     (London, 1883), 184, suggests a connection between Ladislaw
     and Lewes.

     'I should not . . . night from me' / Linton, *My Literary Life*,
     100.

31   'I have had . . . at work again' / Quoted by Haight, *George Eliot*,
     415.

     'Here we had . . . sunshine' / Cross, *George Eliot's Life*, III, 79.

32   'And I remember . . . profoundly sad' / Ibid., III, 431.

33   been to California / J. W. Cross, *Impressions of Dante and of the*

New World . . . (Edinburgh and London, 1893), 277. 'rests on . . . to militarism', x; 'One thing . . . to rivals', 234.

35 'my ideal' . . . 'high calling' / Cross, *George Eliot's Life,* VII, 276.

'he sees . . . life to me' / *Letters,* VII, 211–12.

'Best loved . . . back hair' / Cross, *George Eliot's Life,* VII, 211–12.

36 'And to think . . . clear-sighted?' / Eliza Lynn Linton, 'George Eliot', in *Women Novelists of Queen Victoria's Reign* (London, 1897), 103.

36–7 In another place . . . in mind / Linton, *My Literary Life,* 103.

3 OVERTURES TO 'SALOME'

39 'like a . . . mechanical monotony' / Mario Praz, *The Romantic Agony,* trans. Angus Davidson, 2nd ed. (reissued London and New York, 1970), 201.

40 took care . . . his own *Hérodiade* / See Haskell M. Block, *Mallarmé and the Symbolist Drama* (Detroit, Mich., 1963), 19.

41 the play's culminating moment . . . Heine's *Atta Troll* / Praz, *Romantic Agony,* 313.

Wilde knew . . . in 1888 / Heywood's *Salome* was one of several books discussed in Wilde's review, 'The Poet's Corner', *Pall Mall Gazette,* XLVII: 7128 (20 January 1888), 3.

42 the two turning-points . . . 'to prison' / *The Letters of Oscar Wilde,* ed. Rupert Hart-Davis (London and New York, 1962), 469. Unless otherwise noted, all quotations from Wilde's letters in this essay are from this volume.

The two men . . . Ruskin and Pater / Vincent O'Sullivan, *Aspects of Wilde* (London, 1936), 139.

his 'golden book' / W. B. Yeats, *Autobiography* (New York and London, 1965), 87.

'that book . . . over my life' / Wilde, *Letters,* 471.

'to leap . . . a bat' / Ruskin, *Sesame and Lilies* (London, 1900), 203.

43 'there was . . . a road' / Based on newspaper accounts of Wilde's American tour, 1881–2.

'The dearest memories . . . to see' / Wilde, *Letters,* 218.

44 he duly notified . . . her fidelity / Derrick Leon, *Ruskin, The Great Victorian* (London, 1949), 152.

46 'She became . . . fornication' / Ruskin, *The Stones of Venice* (London, n.d.), I, 150.

46–7 'Now Venice . . . into her grave' / Ibid., 38–9.

47 The Renaissance . . . its connotations / Wallace K. Ferguson, *The Renaissance in Historical Thought* (Cambridge, Mass., 1948), 142–4.

'in memory . . . as ceaseless . . .' / Entry for 30 November 1880, in *The Diaries of John Ruskin*, ed. Joan Evans and J. H. Whitehouse (Oxford, 1959), III, 995.

48 But Daru . . . such consequence / Pierre Daru, *Histoire de la République de Venise* (Paris, 1853), II, 198–9.

49 '*The Stones of Venice* had . . . domestic corruption' / *The Works of John Ruskin*, ed. E. T. Cook and Alexander Wedderburn (London, 1903), XVIII, 443.

he suddenly felt . . . the greatest artists / Ruskin, *Diary*, II, 537, and Notes on the Turin Gallery. Quoted by R. H. Wilenski, *John Ruskin* (London, 1933), 231–2.

'There is no law . . . less complex principle?' / Quoted by Wilenski, *John Ruskin*, 69.

51 the heresy . . . were lovers / See Wilde, *Letters*, 756.

52 'I mean . . . in moral habits' / Ruskin, *The Stones of Venice*, III, 8.

53 as Lawrence Evans . . . / In conversation.

56 'all excess . . . part in it' / To the Editor of the *St. James's Gazette*, 26 June 1890, in Wilde, *Letters*, 259.

'spectator of life' / Ibid., 476.

57 'mystical' (Wilde's own term) / Jean Paul Raymond and Charles Ricketts, *Oscar Wilde: Recollections* (London, 1932), 51.

58 Ruskin 'like Christ . . . all responsibility' / Unpublished letter in the Houghton Library, Harvard.

59 'a curious mixture . . . to the last!' / Wilde, *Letters*, 185.

4   THE CRITIC AS ARTIST AS WILDE

60–1 'I am always amused . . . second-rate work' / *The Artist as Critic: Critical Writings of Oscar Wilde*, ed. Richard Ellmann (New York, 1969; London, 1970), 365. Unless otherwise indicated, quotations from Wilde's criticism in this essay are from this volume.

61 'The poor reviewers . . . criminals of art' / Ibid., 358.

63–4 'shall be able . . . its making' / Ibid., 382.

66 'A true Epicureanism . . . degree of development' / Walter
Pater, 'A Novel by Oscar Wilde', in *Oscar Wilde: A Collection of
Critical Essays* (Twentieth Century Views), ed. Richard Ellmann
(Englewood Cliffs, N.J., 1969), 36.

66-7 'I have got . . . 'Money and Ambition' / Wilde, *Letters*, 30-1.

68 'Sometime you will find . . . that it is so' / Ibid., 185.

73 'By its curiosity . . . the higher ethics' / *The Artist as Critic*, 360.

74 'into elements . . . as I told you, are so' / Ibid., 406-7.

77-8 'Let us ignore . . . choose freely.' 'I shall destroy . . . nothing
left' / Jean Genet, *The Thief's Journal*, trans. Bernard
Frechtman (New York, 1964; London, 1965), 208, 206.

80 'A patriot . . . loves boys' / *Letters*, 705.

5 CORYDON AND MÉNALQUE

81 'Would you . . . into my works' / 'Voulez-vous savoir le
grand drame de ma vie?—C'est que j'ai mis mon génie dans ma
vie, je n'ai mis que mon talent dans mes œuvres.' Gide, *Œuvres
Complètes* (Paris, 1932-9), III, 488.

81-2 Then Pierre Louÿs . . . making a fourth / F. J. L. Mouret, 'La
Première Rencontre d'André Gide et d'Oscar Wilde', *French
Studies*, XVII (January 1968), 37-9.

82 three-hour dinners . . . or Villiers / 'Wilde qui cause et que je
crois Baudelaire ou Villiers . . .' André Gide—Paul Valéry,
Correspondance 1890-1942, ed. Robert Mallet (Paris, 1955), 141,

82 Princess Ouroussoff . . . round his head / Gide, *Si le grain ne
meurt, Œuvres Complètes*, X, 340.

Gide's daybook . . . back to London / Jean Delay, *La Jeunesse
d'Andre Gide* (Paris, 1956), II, 132-3.

'un autre poète . . . plus nouvelle' / Letter of July 1894, in *Correspondance*, Gide–Valéry, 206.

83 It seemed . . . amorous excursion / 'fort peu flatté de la rencontre, car il se croyait clandestin.' Letter to Valéry of July 1894,
cited above.

a flat . . . who accepted / Letter from Gide to his mother,
28 May 1894, quoted in Delay, *Jeunesse*, II, 327.

'the most choked of voices' / 'de quelle voix étranglée.' *Si le
grain ne meurt, Œuvres Complètes*, X, 410-11.

he now felt . . . normal for him / 'à présent je trouvais enfin
ma normale.' Ibid., 414.

84 Following his release . . . on 19 June / Wilde, *Letters*, 616.

'*Je suis absolument sans ressources*' / *Œuvres Complètes*, III, 502.

. . . money was given / Wilde, *Letters*, 769, 771.

He thought . . . with Wilde / Jules Renard, *Journal, 1887–1910* (Paris, 1965), 107 (entry for 23 December 1891).

85   'One of the . . . Lucien de Rubempré' / Wilde, *The Artist as Critic*, 299.

he describes . . . *O, admirable, celui-là*' / Letter from Gide to Valéry, 28 November 1891, in *Correspondance*, 139.

'Wilde contrives . . . rendered void . . . etc.' / 'Wilde s'in-génie à tuer ce qui me restait d'âme, parce qu'il dit que pour connaître une essence, il faut la supprimer: il veut que je regrette mon âme. L'effort pour la détruire est la mesure de toute chose. Toute chose ne se constitue que de son vide . . . etc.' Ibid., 141. (Delay reads *s'ingénie* rather than *s'étudie*.)

86   'on certain evenings . . . from my body' / 'J'espère bien avoir connu toutes les passions et tous les vices; au moins les ai-je favorisés. Tout mon être s'est précipité vers toutes les croy-ances; et j'étais si fou certains soirs que je croyais presque à mon âme, tant je la sentais près de s'échapper de mon corps . . .' *Les Nourritures terrestres* (Gide, *Romans* (Pléiade ed., Paris, 1958), 158.)

'we name things . . . a new departure' / 'On ne donne un nom qu'a ce dont on se sépare . . . si cette formule même ne présagait pas un départ.' *Œuvres Complètes*, XIII, 57.

his notion . . . believe in him / 'J'en voudrais un (le diable) qui circulerait incognito à travers tout le livre et dont la réalité s'affirmerait d'autant plus qu'on croirait moins en lui.' Ibid., 21.

'Forgive . . . exist a little' / Pardonne-moi d'être tu: depuis Wilde je n'existe que très peu.' Letter from Gide to Valéry, Christmas eve 1891, *Correspondance*, 144.

'Wilde, I believe . . . order into them' / 'Wilde ne m'a fait, je crois, que du mal. Avec lui, j'avais désappris de penser. J'avais des émotions plus diverses, mais je ne savais plus les ordonner . . .' Gide, *Journal, 1889–1939* (Pléiade ed., Paris, 1939), 28 (entry for 1 January 1892).

'symbolic mouth . . . satanic aphorism' / '. . . je le vois comme un symbolique bouche à la Redon qui déglutit une bouchée et mécaniquement la transforme aussitôt en satanique aphorisme . . .' Letter from Valéry to Gide, 5 December 1891, in *Corre-spondance*, 142.

87   'it has occurred . . . in the drama . . .' / 'Enfin, s'il m'est récemment apparu qu'un auteur important: le Diable, avait bien pu prendre part au drame, je raconterai néanmoins le drame sans

faire intervenir d'abord celui que je n'identifierai que long-
temps plus tard.' *Si le grain ne meurt, Œuvres Complètes*, x, 345.

'that terrifying man . . . one could have' / 'Il est rentré le soir,
cet homme terrible, le plus dangereux produit de la civilisation
moderne—toujours, comme à Florence, escorté du jeune Lord
Douglas, tous deux mis à l'index de Londres et de Paris, et, si
l'on n'était loin, la société la plus compromettante du monde.'
Quoted by Delay, *Jeunesse*, II, 446.

'Impossible to know . . . pretext of aestheticism' / 'Impossible
de comprendre ce que vaut ce jeune Lord, que Wilde semble
avoir dépravé jusqu'aux moelles—à la façon d'un Vautrin bien
plus terrible (je trouve) que celui du Père Goriot—parce qu'il
fait tout sous prétexte d'esthétisme.' 'Oscar Wilde', quoted
Delay, ibid., 440.

88   'He enjoyed . . . like a devil' / *Si le grain ne meurt*, 'Oscar
Wilde', *Œuvres Complètes*, x, 411.

'J'espere . . . démoralisé cette ville' / *Œuvres Complètes*, III, 487.

89   'Listen, dear . . . no first person' / 'Écoutez, dear, il faut maintenant que vous me fassiez une promesse. *Les Nourritures terrestres*, c'est bien . . . c'est très bien . . . Mais, dear, promettez-moi:
maintenant n'écrivez plus jamais 'JE'. . . . En art, voyez-vous, il
n'y a pas de première personne.' *Œuvres Complètes*, III, 499.

Gide interpreted . . . wear a mask / *Journal*, 1 October 1927,
847–8.

'Andre Gide's book . . . Kingdom of Art' / Wilde, *Letters*, 590.

'complaisance towards myself' / 'Ce dont je souffre le plus en
relisant mes Cahiers, c'est une complaisance envers moi-même
dont chaque phrase reste affadie.' Preface to *André Walter* (1930),
Œuvres Complètes, I, 202.

'at once magnifies itself' / 'Avec lui [Goethe], le "je" tout
aussitôt se magnifie. Le généralité se livre dans l'individuel, ou
plutôt, l'individuel s'affirme en symbole d'une vérité univer-
selle dont il manifeste l'essence.' 'Goethe' in Gide, *Préfaces*
(Neuchâtel et Paris, 1948), 91.

90   'a spur . . . unmask' Douglas / '. . . j'espère ne pas mourir
avant de l'avoir démasqué.' *Journal*, 655.

92   'Our whole life . . . its usual posture' / 'Toute notre vie
s'emploie à tracer de nous-mêmes un ineffaçable portrait . . . on
se flatte; mais notre terrible portrait, plus tard, ne nous flattera
pas. On raconte sa vie et l'on se ment; mais notre vie ne
mentira pas; elle racontera notre âme, qui se présentera devant
Dieu dans sa posture habituelle.' *Journal*, 29.

92 Wilde amused . . . twice to men / Reported by Edmond de
Goncourt in Edmond and Jules de Goncourt, *Journal* (Paris, 1956),
IV, 395 (entry for 30 April 1893): 'Sur le nom d'Oscar Wilde,
Henri de Régnier, qui est chez moi, se met à sourire. J'interroge
ce sourire: "Ah! vous ne savez pas? . . . Du reste, il ne s'en
cache pas. Oui, il s'avoue pédéraste . . . C'est lui qui a dit un
jour: 'J'ai fait trois mariages dans ma vie, un avec une femme
et deux avec des hommes!'"'

93 In literature . . . to drama / 'Donc Mallarmé pour la poésie,
Maeterlinck pour le drame—et quoique auprès d'eux deux, je
me sente bien un peu gringalet, j'ajoute Moi pour le roman.'
Letter from Gide to Valéry, 26 January 1891, in *Correspondance*, 46.

94 According to Wilde, 'When Narcissus died . . . 'The Disciple' /
'Quand Narcisse fut mort, les fleurs des champs se désolèrent et
demandèrent à la rivière des gouttes d'eau pour le pleurer.
—Oh! leur répondit la rivière, quand toutes mes gouttes d'eau
seraient des larmes, je n'en aurais pas assez pour pleurer moi-
même. Narcisse: je l'aimais.
—Oh! reprirent les fleurs des champs, comment n'aurais-tu pas
aimé Narcisse? Il était beau.
—Était-il beau? dit la rivière. —Et qui mieux que toi le saurait?
Chaque jour penché sur ta rive, il mirait dans tes eaux sa
beauté . . .'
Wilde s'arrêtait un instant . . .
'—si je l'aimais, répondit la rivière, c'est que, lorsqu'il se penchait
sur mes eaux, je voyais le reflet de mes eaux dans ses yeux.'
Puis Wilde, se rengorgeant avec un bizarre éclat de rire, ajoutait:
'Cela s'appelle: *Le Disciple*.'
                                     Œuvres Complètes, III, 476–7.

He would complain . . . Irish Protestant / Alfred Douglas,
Without Apology (London, 1938), 274.

(Once Arthur Balfour . . . 'Irish Protestant') / O'Sullivan,
Aspects of Wilde, 65.

94–5 'Tell me at once . . . the Twenty Commandments?' / Professor
Ernest Samuels found this quotation from Wilde in an unpublished letter of Berenson.

'God's commandments . . . or twenty?' / 'Commandements de
Dieu, serez-vous dix ou vingt?' *Œuvres Complètes*, II, 165.

95 'Woman, what . . . to do with thee?' / 'Femme! dit-il à sa
mère qui continue à l'aimer spécialement—femme! qu'y-a-t-il
de commun entre toi et moi?' 'Réfléxions', *Œuvres Complètes*,
II, 432.

'Would you like . . . a virgin!' / 'Voulez-vous que je vous dise un secret? . . . un secret, mais promettez-moi de ne le redire à personne . . . Savez-vous pourquoi le Christ n'aimait pas sa mère? . . . C'est parce qu'elle était vierge!' *Œuvres Complètes,* III, 482.

a fifth gospel . . . to Saint Thomas / Wilde, *Letters,* 479.

96 'that kind of . . . from the tomb' / 'cette sort d'angoisse abominable que dut goûter Lazare échappé du tombeau.' *Œuvres Complètes,* X, 386.

His own play . . . to interest Wilde much / Wilde, *Letters,* 768.

'His entire life . . . of art himself' / Ibid., 477, 487.

'A man's life is his image' / 'La vie d'un homme est son image.' *Journal,* 29.

'I remember . . . it was novel' / Wilde, *Letters,* 476.

96-7 'Christ's saying . . . shall lose it' / '. . . c'est en art qu'est vraie également la parole du Christ: "Qui veut sauver sa vie (sa personnalité) la perdra."' *Journal,* 49.

97 'Christianisme contre le Christ' / *Journal,* 15 June 1914, 420; *Si le grain ne meurt, Œuvres Complètes,* X, 436.

'the Epic . . . Iliad of Christianity' / Coulson Kernahan, *In Good Company* (London, 1917), 223.

'Whoever observes . . . arrests his development' / 'Connais-toi toi-même. Maxime aussi pernicieuse que laide. Quiconque s'observe arrête son développement.' *Romans,* 285.

'a long and lovely suicide' / Wilde, *Letters,* 185.

98 'There was a man . . . only in the moment' / 'Il y avait un homme qui ne pouvait penser qu'en bronze. Et cet homme, un jour, eut une idée, l'idée de la joie, de la joie qui habite l'instant. Et il sentit qu'il lui fallait la dire. Mais dans le monde tout entier il ne restait plus un seul morceau de bronze; car les hommes avaient tout employé. Et cet homme sentit qu'il deviendrait fou, s'il ne disait pas son idée.

'Et il songeait à un morceau de bronze, sur la tombe de sa femme, à une statue qu'il avait faite pour orner la tombe de sa femme, de la seule femme qu'il eût aimée; c'était la statue de la tristesse, de la tristesse qui habit la vie. Et l'homme sentit qu'il devenait fou s'il ne disait pas son idée.

'Alors il prit cette statue de la tristesse, de la tristesse qui habite la vie; il la brise; il la fondit, et il en fit la statue de la joie, de la joie qui n'habite que dans l'instant.' *Œuvres Complètes,* III, 84.

'Each of my books . . . all that time' / 'Chacune de mes œuvres est en réaction directe *contre* la précédente. Je ne me satisfais complètement dans aucune, et je ne danse jamais *à la fois* que sur un

pied; l'important c'est de bien danser tout de même; mais à chaque
livre, je change de pied, l'un étant fatigué d'avoir dansé; l'autre
de s'être reposé tout ce temps.' Letter from Gide to Jammes,
6 August 1902, in *Francis Jammes et André Gide, Correspondance
1893–1938* (Paris, 1948), 199–200.

99   'I owed . . . my soul' / 'Je ne dus le salut de ma chair qu'à
l'irrémédiable empoisonnement de mon âme.' *Œuvres Complètes*, II, 89.

99–100   Gide remarked . . . to authorize evil / 'toujours tâchant d'in-
sinuer en vous l'autorisation du mal.' Delay, *Jeunesse*, II, 137.

6   DISCOVERING SYMBOLISM

103   among the audience . . . 'sacred books' / W. B. Yeats, *Autobiography*, 213.

His biographer . . . this view / Roger Lhombreaud, *Arthur
Symons* (London, 1963), 95–6.

105   In an essay . . . rather than 'symbolist' / Arthur Symons, 'The
Decadent Movement in Literature', *Harpers Magazine*, LXXXVII
(Nov. 1893), 858–67.

as Max Beerbohm indicates, . . . Yeats would insist . . . 'of his
fathers' / Quoted in Lhombreaud, *Arthur Symons*, 127.

106   He had so meditated . . . 'true symbols' / W. B. Yeats, *Collected
Works in Verse and Prose* (Stratford-upon-Avon, 1908), I, 227.

112   'I myself owe . . . of Corbière' / T. S. Eliot, review of Peter
Quennell, *Baudelaire and the Symbolists,* in *The Criterion* (Jan.
1930), 357.

7   TWO FACES OF EDWARD

113   'on or about . . . character changed' / Virginia Woolf, 'Mr.
Bennett and Mrs. Brown', *Collected Essays,* 4 vols. (London and
New York, 1966–7), I, 320.

114   one of the few essays . . . patronizing note / Lascelles Abercrombie, 'Literature', in *Edwardian England*, ed. F. J. C. Hearn-
shaw (London, 1933), 185–203.

115   'everybody got down . . . I have forgotten' / W. B. Yeats,
Introduction to *The Oxford Book of Modern Verse* (Oxford, 1936),
xi.

118   'terminological disingenuousness' / H. G. Wells, *Experiment
in Autobiography* (New York, 1934), 573–8.

120   'I am . . . about Life' / Quoted by Harry T. Moore in *The
Intelligent Heart* (New York, 1954; London, 1955), 191.

121   ash-buckets . . . or moonlight / Ford Madox Ford, *Collected Poems* (London, 1914), 17.

123   miracle was not 'scientific' / Letter from Shaw to James, 17 January 1909, in *The Complete Plays of Henry James*, ed. Leon Edel (New York and London, 1949), 643.

'squeeze the guts out of it' / Quoted by Ford Madox Ford in *The English Novel* (Philadelphia, 1929), 147.

126   'History is one' / Wells, *Experiment in Autobiography*, 619.

'luminous halo' / Virginia Woolf, 'Modern Fiction', *Collected Essays*, II, 106.

'Your "subject" . . . where they are . . .' / Ford, *The English Novel*, 147.

127   'The thing his novel' . . . really *about* / H. G. Wells, *Boon* (London and New York, 1915), 106, 109; *Experiment in Autobiography*, 527-8.

128   'inside the object . . . the outside' / T. E. Hulme, *Speculations*, ed. Herbert Read (London, 1949), 180-1, 213.

'mere muffled majesty . . . "authorship"' / Preface to *The Golden Bowl*, in *The Art of the Novel*, ed. R. P. Blackmur (New York, 1950), 328.

'In decency . . . a vortex' / Ezra Pound, *Gaudier-Brzeska* (London, 1916), 106.

8   A POSTAL INQUIRY

132-3   'I am in double trouble . . . on the rocks' / Unless otherwise indicated, quotations in this essay are from *Letters of James Joyce*, vols. II and III, ed. Richard Ellmann (London and New York, 1966).

133   'O! the lowness . . . sunk to!' / James Joyce, *Finnegans Wake* (London and New York, 1939), 171.

137   'One story . . . beating about the bush' / *Letters*, II, 199-200.

138   'Some people . . . at present engaged in' / Ibid., 89.

139   'Dear Mother   Your order . . . starving in Paris' / Ibid., 29-30.

140   'My dear Jim if . . . the future' / Ibid., 22.

141   'The shortest way . . . *via* Holyhead' / James Joyce, *A Portrait of the Artist as a Young Man* (reissued London, 1960; New York, 1964), 254 (250).

145   the first draft of *A Portrait* / 'A Portrait of the Artist', in Robert Scholes and Richard M. Kain, *The Workshop of Dedalus* (Evanston, Ill., 1965), 60-8.

145   'disliked anything . . . knockdown row' / *Finnegans Wake*, 174.

146   'assumed dongiovannism' / James Joyce, *Ulysses* (reissued London, 1960; New York, 1961), 251 (196).

150   'My darling . . . unhappy love' / *Letters*, III, 63.

9   'HE DO THE POLICE IN DIFFERENT VOICES'

155–6   His chiselled comment . . . 'illusion of disillusion' / F. O. Matthiessen, *The Achievement of T. S. Eliot*, 3rd ed. (New York, 1958), 106.

156   *The Wastè Land* manuscript / T. S. Eliot, *The Waste Land*: A Facsimile and Transcript of the Original Drafts including the Annotations of Ezra Pound, ed. Valerie Eliot (London and New York, 1971). Unless otherwise indicated passages from *The Waste Land*, and from correspondence about it, quoted in this essay are from this edition.

157   'First we had . . . and walked home' / *The Waste Land*, 5.

158   'The white-armed Fresca . . . female stench' / Ibid., 39.

      'A bright kimono . . . Oxford Street' / Ibid., 33.

      '—Bestows one final . . . and spit' / Ibid., 35.

159   'Full fathom five . . . gold in gold. . . .' / Ibid., 119.

      'the longest poem . . . three pages further' / *The Letters of Ezra Pound*, 1907–1941, ed. D. D. Paige (London and New York, 1950), 169.

161   'I expected . . . kind to her' / Bertrand Russell, *Autobiography: 1914–1944* (vol. II) (London, 1968), 54–5.

      'still perpetually baffling . . . gift of argument' / Ibid., 174.

      as has been said . . . / Robert Sencourt, *T. S. Eliot: A Memoir* (London and New York, 1971), 53.

162   'I am every day . . . for both' / Russell, *Autobiography*, II, 55–6.

162–3   Her journal . . . 'very very nervous' / Unpublished journal of Vivien Eliot in the Bodleian Library, Oxford.

163   'I was fond . . . what they enjoyed' / Russell, *Autobiography*, II, 19.

164   'Cable came . . . *Most terrible*' / Unpublished journal in the Bodleian Library.

166   'To talk over a poem . . . clear and natural' / W. B. Yeats, letter to Lady Gregory of 3 January 1913, quoted in A. N. Jeffares, *W. B. Yeats: Man and Poet* (London and New Haven, Conn., 1949), 167.

'London, the swarming life . . . its formal destiny' /   *The Waste Land,* 31.

167   'Kingfisher weather . . . the sea rolled, asleep' /   Ibid., 63.

167–8   He had warned Miss Moore /   *Letters of Ezra Pound,* 142.

168   'an outline' . . . 'nacre and objets d'art' /   Ibid., 169.

Index

Abercrombie, Lascelles, on Edwardians, 114
Aiken, Conrad, on Eliot, 165
Aldington, Richard, Eliot writes to,
165
ambiguity, as literary method of Gide
and Wilde, 99
anality, in Luther, 9; in Joyce, 149
Arnold, Matthew, admonished by
Wilde, 60; relation to Wilde, 62–3,
64, 68
art and artist, Wilde's theories of, 70–
5, 77–8, 96; Joyce's conception,
134–5, 140–1
asthma, biographical treatment for,
12–13; as artistic motivation, 15

Bainton, Roland, on Luther, 7–9
Balderston, Katharine, on Dr. Johnson's masochism, 2
Balzac, Honoré de, Wilde's borrowing from, 85; silver mines, 145
Barthes, Roland, on independence of
critic, 61
Baudelaire, Charles, Sartre's biography of, 4–5, 6; relation to Poe,
81; Wilde compared to, 82; father
of symbolist movement, 102; and
reader, 129; and Eliot, 166
Beach, Sylvia, mentioned by Joyce,
150
Beardsley, Aubrey, on Herod as
Wilde, 58

Beckett, Samuel, on compensation,
16; compared with Wilde, 41; on
ethics, 87
Beerbohm, Max, on Symons and
Yeats, 105
Bellow, Saul, on surfeit of criticism,
60; miracles, 130
Benn, Gottfried, on religions, 118
Bennett, Arnold, as Edwardian, 114;
on ordinary life, 120
Berenson, Bernard, and Wilde, 94
Bergson, Henri, on consciousness,
65
biography, literary, present difficulties
of, 1–16; Freudian-existential, 4–7;
Marxist, 5, 6; Gothic, 7; Freudian
and post-Freudian, 7–13, 15–16;
chronology in, 15; in fictional
characters, 17–20, 37–8
Blake, William, personal mythology
of, 29; interpreted by Yeats, 106,
108; on mental fight, 107; and
Hayley, 138; and Eliot, 167
Blind, Mathilde, on Ladislaw and
Lewes, 172
Block, Haskell M., on Mallarmé, 173
Blunt, Wilfrid Scawen, effect of
prison on, 75
Bobrowski, Thaddeus, on Conrad's
attempted suicide, 18
Boswell, James, on Johnson's private
life, 2–3; use of gossip, 11; on
Johnson's hypochondria, 13–15

Bouilhet, Louis, compared to Pound, 166
bovarysme, Flaubert's relation to, 25
Brabant, R. H., as model for Casaubon, 20–2
Bradley, F. H., Eliot's dissertation on, 160
Bray, Charles, letter of George Eliot to, 20
Bruant, Aristide, friendship with Wilde, 82
Bryant, Jacob, in Casaubon, 22–3, 24
Bücherwurm, Professor, as anticipation of Casaubon, 20–1
Buddhism, as form of Christianity, 22–4
Budgen, Frank, Joyce's friendship with, 152
Bunyan, John, George Eliot on his limitations, 31
Burne-Jones, Edward, Wilde's notice of, 54
Butler, Samuel, *The Way of All Flesh*, 116
Byron, Lord, relation to Stendhal, 81; *Childe Harold*, 143

Carlyle, Jane, on G. H. Lewes, 30
Carlyle, Thomas, on G. H. Lewes, 30
Carrington, Dora, 4
Casaubon (character in *Middlemarch*), models for, 19–29, 172; and Ladislaw, 29–38
Casaubon, Isaac, Pattison's biography of, 19
casaubonism, defined, 25
Catholicism, Wilde's interest in, 66–7, 80; modernism, 116; Joyce's attitudes, 135–6, 149–50
Chapman, John, on Brabant, 21; publishes Mackay, 23
Chaucer, Geoffrey, 15
Christ, and John the Baptist, 51; as artist (Wilde), 59, 77–8, 95–6; and authority, 75; Wilde's association with, 88; and his mother, 95; Gide and Wilde on, 96–7; Lawrence on, 117–18; Joyce on, 153
Christianity, Brabant on, 26; Bücherwurm on, 22; Ruskin on, 52;

Wilde on, 95–6, 97; Gide on, 96–7; in Edwardian period, 116–20
Chus and Mizraim, *see* Cush and Mizraim
Claudel, Paul, and Gide, 87
Cobbe, Frances Power, on Mackay as Casaubon, 23
compensation, as biographical explanation, 16
Coleridge, Samuel Taylor, *Lyrical Ballads*, 110
Conrad, Joseph, interpenetration of his life and art, 17–18; *Heart of Darkness*, 17–18; biography by Baines, 18; attempted suicide, 18–19; *Lord Jim*, 19; as Edwardian, 114; on marvels, 121; symbols, 123–4, 126; sense of himself as writer, 129
Corbière, Tristan, read by Eliot, 112
Cozzens, James Gould, his neo-Edwardian novel, 122
Crane, Hart, on *The Waste Land*, 155
criminality, as element in art, 70–3, 76–8
cross, as symbol in Yeats, 111
Cross, John Walter, meets George Eliot in Rome, 31–3; as model for Ladislaw, 31–8; interest in Far West, 33, in railroads, 32–3; schooling at Rugby, 34; called nephew, 34; his imagery, 34; his felicitous ignorance, 35; political views, 35; fished out of Grand Canal, 36; his preface to *Impressions of Dante*, 37; biography of George Eliot, 37
Cush and Mizraim (or Chus and Mizraim), Bryant and Casaubon on, 22; Ladislaw on, 28–9, 35

Dali, Salvador, on *Mona Lisa*, 53
Dante, studied by Cross and George Eliot, 34; and Virgil, 42; and Joyce, 151; and T. S. Eliot, 166–7
Daru, Pierre, Ruskin's partial dependence on, 48
Dedalus, meaning of name, 141
Defoe, Daniel, 2
Delay, Jean, on Wilde's parties, 82; on Gide's mother, 95; questionable

theory about Gide's complex, 99, 178; on Wilde's authorization of evil, 99–100

Dickens, Charles, and *The Waste Land*, 156–7

Diderot, Denis, sexualized prose of, 16

Dilke, Sir Charles, on Casaubon and Dorothea, 19–20

Donne, John, revival, 129; curiosity of, 149

Dostoevsky, Fyodor, epilepsy, 12–13

Douglas, Lord Alfred, introduced to Pater, 53; in Blidah with Wilde, 83, 87–8, 89; unmasked by Gide, 90; affair with Wilde, 92

drift, a favourite word of Pater, 65–6

Dryden, John, compared with Edwardians, 115

Edel, Leon, biography of James, 10–12; use of Freudian techniques, 10–11

Edward VII, King, nature of Edwardianism, 113–31; in *Ulysses*, 131

ego, biographical perils of, 4; Wilde on, 89

Eliot, George, effect of her life on *Middlemarch*, 17, 19–37; on models for *Scenes of Clerical Life*, 19, 171, heroes in, 31; as Casaubon, 25–9; *Felix Holt*, 27; love for Lewes, 29–30; Hetty in *Adam Bede*, 31; Tito in *Romola*, 31; reconciliation scene in *The Mill on the Floss*, 36; marries Cross, 34–8

Eliot, Henry Ware (T. S. Eliot's father), death of, 164

Eliot, T. S., on biography, 1; on impersonality, 19; on surfeit of criticism, 60; from narcissus to rose, 94, 111; on Symons, 112, 178; as Edwardian, 114; on God and Christ, 117; *The Waste Land*, 155–68; *Four Quartets*, 157; first marriage, 160–2; 'The Death of Saint Narcissus', 163

Eliot, Mrs. Valerie, edition of *The Waste Land*, 155–68

Eliot, Mrs. Vivien, marriage to Eliot, 160–2, 165

Ellis, Havelock, goes to Paris with Symons, 104

epilepsy, biographical treatment for, 12–13

Erikson, Erik, biography of Luther, 7–9; compared with Sartre, 9; theory of crisis, 8–9

Evans, Isaac, reconciled with George Eliot, 36

Evans, Lawrence, on Wilde-Pater rift, 53

existentialism, in biography, 4–7

Faulkner, William, fictional techniques, 11

fetishism, in Joyce, 149

Fisher King, in *The Waste Land*, 163

Flaubert, Gustave, biography by Sartre, 4, 6–7, 15; and *le bovarysme*, 25; on Salome, 39; on artist, 135

Fleischmann, Martha, Joyce's liaison with, 151–2

Ford, Ford Madox, as Edwardian, 114; on subjects for literature, 121, 126

Forster, E. M., as Edwardian, 114; religious imagery, 119, 120, 131; symbols, 123

Francini Bruni, Alessandro, Joyce writes to, 142

Freud, Sigmund, Jones's biography of, 4; Erikson's revisionism of, 7–9; on anal, oral, and genital, 9; *Psychopathology of Everyday Life*, 10; Edel's capricious use of, 10–11; Painter's post-Freudian biography, 11–13; theory of sublimation, 13; *Interpretation of Dreams*, 101

Frye, Northrop, on independence of critic, 61

Galsworthy, John, as Edwardian, 114; symbols, 123; plays, 126–7

Gandhi, Mahatma, Erikson's biography of, 9; and Joyce, 153

Genet, Jean, Sartre's biography of, 4, 5–6, 15; crime and art, 77–8

Gide, André, on Nietzsche and Wilde, 61; records Wilde's view of prison, 75; authorization of evil, 78; and

Gide, André – *continued*
  Wilde, 81–100, and homosexuals,
  84, 90, 95, 96; and Goethe, 85;
  Les Nourritures terrestres, 86, 88–
  9, 90, 97, 99; *Si le grain ne
  meurt*, 87; *L'Immoraliste*, 90, 98;
  Corydon, 90; *Les Cahiers d'André
  Walter*, 89, 91, 92, 93; *Les Faux-
  Monnayeurs*, 86, 91, 97; *Le Traité du
  Narcisse*, 93; Protestantism, 94–5;
  and Bible, 95–6; *La Porte étroite*,
  98
Goethe, J. W. von, Gide's interest
  in, 85, 89
Gogarty, Oliver St. John, Joyce's
  mythical adversary, 138
Gonne, Maud, Yeats's love for, 103;
  its symbolical aspect, 106–8; com-
  pared with Nora Joyce, 147
Gosse, Edmund, writes on Mallarmé,
  102; *Father and Son*, 116
Gothic biography, 7
Granville-Barker, Harley, God in his
  plays, 117, 118, 119; miracles, 122
Gregory, Lady, collects folklore, 121;
  Yeats's letter to, 166

Haight, Gordon S., publishes new
  letter by George Eliot, 20; on
  Brabant as Casaubon, 21, 25; on
  Bryant, 22; on Mackay, 23; on
  letter to Miss Lewis, 27; on Pattison
  as Casaubon, 172
Hardy, Barbara, on seeds in *Middlemarch*, 26
Hardy, Thomas, mocked by Joyce,
  136–7
Heine, Heinrich, use of Salome (in
  Atta Troll), 39, 40, 41; and Joyce,
  146
Hellenism, espoused by Wilde, 67,
  100
Hennell, Sara, on pedantry, 22–3
Hérédia, José-Maria de, Wilde with,
  81, 95
Herod (character in *Salome*), compounded from three Herods, 40–1;
  relation to Salome and John the
  Baptist, 41–2, 57–9
heroism, Joyce on, 143

Heywood, J. C., version of Salome
  legend, 41
Hiphil and Hophal, Cross's ignorance
  of, 35
Homer, 3
homosexuality, of Simcox, 30; of
  Wilde, 67, 69–71, 75–6, 84; of
  Gide, 84
Hulme, T. E., on intensive manifolds,
  128
Huysmans, J. -K., on Salome, 39; discussed by George Moore, 182;
  influence on Symons, 103, 104;
  theory of symbolism, 109
hypochondria, Boswell on Johnson's,
  13–15

Ibsen, Henrik, Joyce's letter to, 143
id, damage of biographer's over-
  stating, 4; and literary technique,
  99
identity crisis, in Luther, 8, 9
imagists, Edwardian relation to, 128
impotence, nature of Casaubon's
  sexual deficiency, 25–6
impressions, favourite word of Pater,
  64, and of Symons, 64, 108
Isaacs, J., on symbolism, 109

James, Henry, biography by Edel, 10–
  11; on lack of criticism, 60; religious imagery, 119; on life, 120, 121;
  miracles, 122; symbols, 123–4;
  on novelistic theory, 127; on
  drama, 128; on enjoyment, 129;
  and Joyce, 154
James, William, on consciousness,
  65; on religions, 117
Jammes, Francis, Gide's letter to, 98
Jerrold, Douglas, 30
John the Baptist, as painted by Leonardo, 51, 53; in Wilde's *Salome*,
  57–8
johnycrossism, illustrated, 37
Johnson, Dr. Samuel, on biography,
  2; Balderston on, 2; his life by
  Boswell, 2–3, 13–15; hypochondria, 14
Jones, Ernest, biography of Freud, 4

Joyce, Giorgio (George), James Joyce's letters to, 134

Joyce, James, on biography, 1; *Finnegans Wake*, 63, 117, 126, 134, 144, 153; symbolic rose in, 111; as Edwardian, 114; defection from religion, 116; *A Portrait of the Artist as a Young Man*, 116–17, 124–6, 131, 133, 135, 144, 145, 154; *Ulysses*, 117, 131, 138, 142, 144, 147, 151, 152, 153, 158; religious imagery, 118–19, 120; *Dubliners*, 18, 136; on life, 120, 121; on miracles, 122; symbols, 124; *Stephen Hero*, 126, 127, 143; letters of, 132–54; art and religion, 134–6; on Hardy, 136–7; on socialism, 137–8; on *Sinn Féin*, 138–9; on Ireland, 140–2; and friends, 141–2; and Ibsen, 143; and wife, 145–51; *Chamber Music*, 148; *Exiles*, 149; on *The Waste Land*, 155

Joyce, Lucia, James Joyce's letters to, 134

Joyce, May (James Joyce's mother), his letter to, 139–40; her reply, 140

Joyce, Nora Barnacle, elopes with Joyce, 134, 136, 142, 143; relationship with him, 145–51

Joyce, Stanislaus, letters from James Joyce to, 134, 143, 144; relation with brother, 152–3; diary of, 135

Kafka, Franz, as type of modern genius, 15

Keats, John, biographies of, 7; theory of Negative Capability, 99

Key to all Mythologies, speculations on author of, 20–8; key mentioned by George Eliot, 23–4; as love, 37

Kurtz (character in *Heart of Darkness*), and Conrad, 17–19

Ladislaw, Will (character in *Middlemarch*), on Orientalism, 24; on German mythologies, 35; Lewes as model for, 29–30; facial resemblance to George Eliot, 28–9; George Eliot's first character to be

good and good-looking, 31; Cross as model for, 31–8

Laforgue, Jules, on Salome, 39; discussed by Symons, 102; read by Eliot, 112

Larbaud, Valery, praises *Ulysses*, 142

Lassalle, Ferdinand, Wilde's interest in, 137–8

La Touche, Rose, Ruskin's attachment to, 45–6

Law, William, 3

Lawrence, D. H., as Edwardian, 114; on religion, 117; *The Rainbow*, 117–18; on life, 120, 121; miracles, 122; symbols, 124; and Joyce, 154

Leonardo da Vinci, Pater on *Mona Lisa*, 52–3; *John the Baptist*, 51, 53

letters, writing of, 132–54

Lewes, G. H., as model for Ladislaw, 29–30; as model for Casaubon, 29–30, 31

Lewis, Maria, George Eliot's letters to, 27–8

Lhombreaud, Roger, on Symons, 103

Linton, Eliza Lynn, on Brabant as Casaubon, 20–1; on George Eliot's marriage to Cross, 36–7

Louÿs, Pierre, friendship with Wilde, 81, 174; breaks off, 82–3; helps Wilde with *Salome*, 84

love, as Key to all Mythologies, 37; Joyce's unwillingness to say, 146–7

Luther, Martin, Erikson's biography of, 7–9; his limitations considered by George Eliot, 31

MacBride, John, marriage to Maud Gonne, 107–8

Mackay, Robert William, as model for Casaubon, 23–5

MacNeill, Mrs. Josephine, on Eliot, 159

Maeterlinck, Maurice, and language of *Salome*, 40; and Symons, 104, 109

Malamud, Bernard, miracles, 130

Mallarmé, Stéphane, on Salome, 39, 40; *Hérodiade*, 40; on flower absent from all bouquets, 90; on symbols, 91; relation with Wilde, 93; visits

Mallarmé, Stéphane – *continued*
Swinburne, 101; Gosse on, 102; Symons on, 109; lectures in England, 103; translated by Symons, 108
Mallock, W. H., parodies Pater, 53
Marlow (character in *Heart of Darkness*), and Conrad, 17–19
Marx, Karl, in biographical interpretations, 5, 6
Masefield, John, on change in style, 115
masochism, in Joyce, 148–9
Masonry, Wilde's interest in, 66–7
Matthiesson, F. O., on Eliot, 155
Maugham, W. Somerset, passive heroes in, 127
McCarthy, Mary, on Venice, 46
Merrill, Stuart, friendship with Wilde, 82
Millais, John Everett, relation to Ruskin, 43–9, 54
Millevoye, Lucien, and Maud Gonne, 107
Monroe, Harriet, and Eliot, 160
Moore, George, *Confessions of a Young Man*, 102; on symbolism, 105; religious imagery, 120; effect on Joyce, 124
Moore, Marianne, and T. S. Eliot, 167–8
Morrison, Arthur, ordinary life of, 121
Murray, Josephine, Joyce's letters to, 134
Myers, F. W. H., on George Eliot as Casaubon, 25
mythology, not Brabant's interest, 21; Bryant's system of, 22–3; Mackay's key to, 23–4; Ladislaw's views on, 28–9

Nabokov, Vladimir, on art as illicit creation, 71
Napoleon, on valets, 3
Narcissus, Wilde's fable about, 93–4, 96; Gide on, 93, 96; Eliot on, 163
Nerval, Gerard de, discussed by Symons, 102, 109

Nietzsche, Friedrich, compared with Wilde, 61, 100; on death of God, 117
Noh drama, and Yeats, 40
Nordau, Max, on degeneration, 101
novel, George Eliot's contamination by, 27–8; Mrs. Transome's infection by, 27; Wells vs. James on, 127

Oedipus complex, as biographical pattern, 4
Onan, image in *Middlemarch* of, 26–7
Orwell, George, on biography, 1
O'Sullivan, Vincent, on Wilde, 173, 178
Ouroussoff, Princess, sees halo on Wilde, 82

Painter, George D., biography of Proust, 11–13
paranoia, in Joyce, 149
Parnell, Charles Stewart, admired by Joyce, 141
Pater, Walter, as presence for Wilde, 42, 53–9; interest in athletics, 43; view of Salome, 52; on Renaissance, 52–3, 55–6; on *Mona Lisa*, 52–3; on *John the Baptist*, 51, 53; Winckelmann essay, 55; his *Marius the Epicurean* criticized by Wilde, 56; on Wilde's *Intentions*, 62; and Arnold, 63; and Wilde, 62–6; on drift, 65–6; on consciousness, 66–7; reviews *Dorian Gray*, 66; influence on Symons, 104; habit of writing 'Well!', 133
Pattison, Mark, as model for Casaubon, 19–20
Picasso, Pablo, on art, 63
Pinney, Thomas, on George Eliot's view of Mackay, 29
Podhoretz, Norman, on criticism as art, 64
Poe, Edgar Allan, related to Baudelaire, 81
Pope, Alexander, psychology of, 11; and *The Waste Land*, 157–8
Pound, Ezra, marries Dorothy Shakespear, 107; symbolic rose in, 111; on Symons, 112; on the gods, 117;

taste in poetry, 128; and *Mauberley*, 131, 157, 165, 168; friendship with Joyce, 152; on *The Waste Land*, 157–60; *Cantos*, 168

Praz, Mario, on Salome as *femme fatale*, 39; on Wilde's play, 40

Pre-Raphaelites, Wilde, Ruskin, and Pater on, 53–4; iconography of, 102

prison, effect on Blunt, 75; on Wilde, 76–7, 79–80

Pritchett, V. S., autobiography of, 2

Proust, Marcel, Painter's biography of, 11–13; his asthma, 12–13; on Whistler and Ruskin, 39; reproves Gide about Wilde, 81; reproves Wilde, 85; religious imagery, 118

psychohistory, a *caveat* for, 9

Quinn, John, Eliot's letter to, 165; given *Waste Land* MS., 165–6

Régnier, Henri de, dines with Wilde, 82; reports Wilde on marriage, 92

Renaissance, Ruskin's view of, 46–8; Wilde on, 47; Pater on, 52–3

Renan, Ernest, his version of Christ's life, 95

Renard, Jules, on Gide and Wilde, 84

Rhymers' Club, Symons and Yeats at, 105–6

Richards, Grant, Joyce's letters to, 136

Richards, I. A., on psychology of taste, 66

Rilke, Rainer Maria, on initiatory moments, 42

Rimbaud, Arthur, discussed by Symons, 102, 109

Rome, for barren honeymoons, 24; George Eliot's meeting with Cross there, 31–4, 38; Lewes's view of, 31

rose, as symbol in Yeats, 111–12

Ross, Robert, homosexual relation with Wilde, 69–70, 92

Rugby School, Ladislaw and Cross as pupils there, 34

Ruskin, Effie (later Mrs. Millais), her life with Ruskin, 44–7

Ruskin, John, impotence of, 25; as presence for Wilde, 42, 53–9; as roadbuilder, 42–3; goes with

Wilde to *Merchant of Venice*, 44; *The Stones of Venice*, 44–53; *Sesame and Lilies*, 45, 46; on the Renaissance, 46–8; numerological passion, 48–9; view of Salome, 52; and Turner, 54

Ruskin, Margaret (John Ruskin's mother), memorial to, 48

Russell, Bertrand, and Eliot, 160–2

Russell, George (AE), advises Maud Gonne, 107

Sacher-Masoch, Leopold von, Joyce's resemblance to, 148

Salome, as image in art and literature, 39–40; in Wilde, 41–2; Ruskin on, 52; Pater on, 52

Samuels, Ernest, on Berenson, 178

Sartre, Jean-Paul, as biographer, 4–7, 9; on Baudelaire, 4–5; on Genet, 5–6; on Flaubert, 6–7; use of chronology, 15

Savoy, edited by Symons, 104; symbolism in, 107, 108

Schwob, Marcel, friendship with Wilde, 82

Scotsmen, Dr. Johnson on, 3

seed, as image in *Middlemarch*, 26–7

selfhood, biographer's quest for, 1–2; as Edwardian concept, 122

Sencourt, Robert, on Eliot, 161

Shaw, Bernard, religious imagery, 119–20; selfhood, 122; miracles, 122–3

Shakespear, Mrs. Olivia, affair with Yeats, 107

Shakespeare, William, on ages of man, 9; *The Merchant of Venice*, 44; *Othello*, 45; Wilde's theory of sonnets, 70; shyness, 147; and Joyce, 151

Simcox, Edith, George Eliot's rebuff to, 30

Sinn Féin, Joyce on, 138–9

socialism, Wilde on, 57, 70, 74–5, 92, 95, 97, 98, 100; Joyce on, 137–8

Sparrow, John, on Pattison, 19–20

Spencer, Herbert, as model for Casaubon, 20; rejected in favour of Cross, 34

Spencer, Theodore, Eliot's remark to, 156, 159
Spinoza, Baruch, on union of sexual and excretory, 149
Spitzer, Leo, biographical analysis of prose style, 16
Stendhal, compared with Wilde, 62; relation to Byron, 81
Stephens, James, asked by Joyce to finish *Finnegans Wake*, 133
Stowe, Harriet Beecher, inquires about Casaubon and Lewes, 29
Strachey, Lytton, biography of (by Holroyd), 4; as biographer, 15; anti-heroic, 127
Strauss, David Friedrich, meets George Eliot, 21
suicide, Conrad's attempted, 18–19; Wilde on relation to art of, 59, 97
Sullivan, John, Joyce's campaign for, 144–5
Swinburne, Algernon Charles, on Christianity, 95, 117
symbolism, lack of ethic, 97; discovery of term, 101–12; Yeats's understanding of, 106–8; defined, 109–10; in England, 126
Symons, Arthur, *The Symbolist Movement in Literature*, 101–12; life of, 103–4; his aesthetic theories, 105–6; shares rooms with Yeats, 105–6
Synge, J. M., miracles, 122, 123

Thucydides, and Greek tragedy, 45
Tintoretto, Jacopo Robusti, Ruskin on, 56

Valéry, Paul, Gide writes to about Wilde, 82, 85, 86; jokes about Wilde, 86
Venice, Ruskin on, 44–53
Verdenal, Jean, and Eliot, 164
Verlaine, Paul, visits England, 102–3; meets Symons, 104; discussed by Symons, 109; read by Eliot, 112
Villiers de l'Isle-Adam, P.-A., Comte de, his *Axël* and Gide, 93, and Yeats, 103; discussed by Symons, 102, 104, 109
Virgil, translated by Dr. Johnson, 3;

as presence for Dante, 42
Vittoz, Dr. Roger, consulted by Eliot, 165
vorticism, defined, 128

Wainewright, Thomas, effect of criminality on, 70
Waste Land, The, as postwar poem, 131; MS., 155–68. See also Eliot, T. S.
Weaver, Harriet Shaw, Joyce's letters to, 144, 147
Webb, Beatrice, on Herbert Spencer, 20
Wells, H. G., as Edwardian, 114; on God, 118; miracles, 122–3; on history, 126; novels by, 127; and Joyce, 153
Whistler, J. M., sues Ruskin over review, 54
Whitman, Walt, on evil effect of art, 72–3
Wilde, Oscar, on biography, 1; his *Salome*, 39–59, 79, 92, 98, 99; reviews Heywood's *Salome*, 41; two crucial experiences, 42; effect of Pater and Ruskin on, 42–3, 53–9; goes with Ruskin to *Merchant of Venice*, 44; on *Renaissance*, 47, 75, 76; *De Profundis*, 47, 59, 90, 96, 97, 98; rift with Pater over Douglas, 53; 'Helas!', 54–5, 65–9, 75; Ruskin and Pater in *Dorian Gray*, 56–7, 66; 'The Soul of Man under Socialism', 57, 70, 74–5, 92, 95, 97, 98, 100; and Herod in *Salome*, 58–9; *The Importance of Being Earnest*, 59, 79; on criticism, 60–80; *Intentions*, 62, 71–4, 97, 98; on history, 64; homosexuality, 67, 69–71, 75–6, 80, 84, 91, 92, 95, 96, 102; *The Picture of Dorian Gray*, 69–71, 72, 79, 84–5, 92, 99; 'Lord Arthur Savile's Crime', 70; 'The Portrait of Mr. W. H.', 70; *The Ballad of Reading Gaol*, 76–7; and Gide, 81–100; Protestantism, 195; parable of the sculptor, 98; *Lady Windermere's Fan*, 99, 100; on symbolism, 104
Wilson, Edmund, biographical

theory of, 16; on symbolism, 109
woman, in Wilde, 39, 41; and Joyce,
153-4
Woodberry, George, writes of meeting Wilde, 58
Woolf, Virginia, on change in human character, 113, 115; dislike for certain contemporaries, 117; as Edwardian, 114; on miracles, 121; on plot, 126
Wordsworth, William, *Lyrical Ballads*, 110, 155

Yeats, W. B., effect of Wilde's *Salome* on, 40; on Wilde's *Intentions*, 62;
on impressions, 64, 108; on art, 78, 98; on Christianity, 95-6; *The Wind among the Reeds*, 101, 110-12; on *Axël*, 103; shares rooms with Symons, 105-6; and Maud Gonne, 103, 106-8; *Cathleen ni Houlihan*, 107; and symbolism, 101-12; on literary shift in 1900, 115; autobiography, 116; on God, 117; religious imagery, 118-19; on mask, 121; on unity of forms, 126; against externality, 128; on Pound, 166

Zeno, Carlo, Ruskin on death of, 48